In Memory of

George Meredith

I0966207

LIVES & LEGENDS

of the

CHRISTMAS TREE SHIPS

Fred Neuschel

THE UNIVERSITY OF MICHIGAN PRESS ANN ARBOR

To Sue, who launched the project

Copyright © by Fred Neuschel 2007
All rights reserved
Published in the United States of America by
The University of Michigan Press
Manufactured in the United States of America
♾ Printed on acid-free paper

2010   2009   2008   2007   4   3   2   1

A CIP catalog record for this book is available from the British Library.

Library of Congress Cataloging-in-Publication Data

Neuschel, Fred.
    Lives and legends of the Christmas tree ships / Fred Neuschel.
        p.   cm.
    Includes index.
    ISBN-13: 978-0-472-11623-2 (cloth : alk. paper)
    ISBN-10: 0-472-11623-1 (cloth : alk. paper)
    1. Christmas tree industry—Michigan, Lake, Region—History—20th
century.   2. Christmas trees—Transportation—Michigan, Lake—
History—20th century.   3. Michigan, Lake, Region—Commerce—
History—20th century.   4. Intercoastal shipping—Michigan, Lake—
History—20th century.   I. Title.

SB428.34.U6N48   2007
386'.544—dc22   2007019155

Preface

Dream no small dreams for they have no power to move
the hearts of men.

—Johann Wolfgang von Goethe

*I*t is possible to live your whole life in a community bordering one of the Great Lakes and never know what a role commercial sailing craft played in the history of the region. Even for people who lived near the lakes a century ago their maritime heritage was but a dim memory—perhaps only stories that they heard at the knee of their parents or grandparents.

Bruce Catton, the famed historian of the Civil War, was one of those who grew up by Lake Michigan and yet was unaware of the role that sail craft and sailors played in that part of the world. Like many boys of his generation, Catton was captivated by trains, and, late in his life, he wrote a beautiful memoir of his youth entitled *Waiting for the Morning Train*. By then, however, he had discovered the sailors who had quietly slipped from the scene within a decade or two of his birth and whose role had been recorded only in hard to find fragments. He heard about a sailor from Wisconsin whom he described as the "owner, captain, cook and entire crew of a small schooner" and who made his living by sailing over and over again to a rocky shore on the Michigan coast where he gathered, by hand, load upon load of cobblestones to sell in Milwaukee for the paving of streets. This man, Catton was surprised to learn, was but one of many who made such a living on the lake. Equipped with little more than a humble sailing craft, a strong constitution, and an entrepreneurial spirit they assumed a place as hands-on builders of their community.[1]

All around the lakes there are cities, towns, and villages that were birthed and built by mariners. On Lake Michigan there are the renowned cities (Chicago and Milwaukee), the lesser cities (Green Bay, Manitowoc, Michigan City, St. Joseph, Muskegon), and the many towns (Kewaunee, Kenosha, South Haven, Pentwater, et al.). Still others had their day and are gone. Even the outlines of their streets and buildings have been obliterated as the land they stood on has been reclaimed by the forest or buried by the sand. Lincoln, Silver Creek, Alaska, Twin Creeks, Horn's Pier, Singapore are no more, their memory preserved, if at all, by no more than a roadside sign. But even the communities that still flourish have become disconnected from their maritime heritage. The succeeding eras that brought the railroads and highways by which their economic life is now sustained have obscured the earliest times.

Algoma, Wisconsin, is one of those towns where the maritime heritage of the region has faded but has not been entirely forgotten. Fishers, both men and women, keep alive Algoma's relationship to Lake Michigan. A few old fishing shanties still tell of the days when the shellback fishing boats worked the local waters. On the bluff just north of the river stands the house that residents remember as the former home of the keeper of the lighthouse. But the days of long ago, when the town's name was Ahnapee (Anna-PEE) and Mackinaw boats, sloops, schooners, and steamers came and went daily from April to December, are lost to all but the devoted few.[2] Still, it is possible to piece together some of the history of those days, and doing so provides a unique opportunity to see the lives of Great Lakes sailors for what they were in the days of commercial sailing.

In the dreams of many of its earliest Euro American citizens, Ahnapee was destined to become one of the great port cities on the Great Lakes. As they envisioned it, a vast and limitless hinterland stretching to the Mississippi River and beyond would produce a prodigious flow of crops and goods for an ever-expanding and insatiable market east to the Atlantic's shore. The happy residents of Ahnapee would be able to direct the flow of nature's bounty and humanity's ingenuity, and for their efforts they would become prosperous and influential leaders of society. Others would see the dream materializing and come from near and far seeking their own security in the jobs that would be produced. The town would grow, and all would benefit from the fulfillment of the dream. Everyone would be rewarded fairly in proportion to the efforts they made. Harmony would exist in the community, and the twin ideals of democracy and capitalism would be actualized.

In the heart of the community was the harbor at the mouth of the Wolf River, and the dreamers foretold that the gifts of the earth would literally flow to this point, brought downstream to docks and piers where boats would come to carry them away to other markets. Those same boats would bring back the goods that the town's prosperity would allow everyone to own. Still other boats would move in and out of the harbor with catches of fish, adding to the community's wealth. Passenger boats would arrive carrying new seekers with new talents and ambitions to enrich the town. As time went by, piers and breakwaters would be built at the mouth of the river, and boats would come to Ahnapee for refuge from Lake Michigan's storms just as people had come seeking refuge from the political and economic tyrannies of life elsewhere.

Center stage in the dream, of course, were the sailors who worked on the boats that visited the harbor. When there were only the crudest of roads and railroads were yet too big a dream for even the biggest of the dreamers, it was the sailors who provided the lifeline for Ahnapee. The limestone to build the school, the steam engine to operate the sawmill, the dry goods to sell in the mercantile establishment, the circus to amaze and entertain, the street-corner evangelists to seek the souls of the lost, the steam shovel to excavate the harbor, the harvesting machines to extend the farmers' yields, the water pump to fight fires, the encyclopedia salesman to enlighten the mind, and the occasional flimflam artist to populate the jail—all of this and much, much more came by boat, while, in return, the products of the forests and the farms flowed out on the same vessels. The work of the sailors' hands was everywhere in this maritime community.

As is usually the case, the dream did not materialize, at least not fully, and certainly not for everyone. A look at a map provides some immediate evidence of why Ahnapee never became that lakeside metropolis. Its northern latitude guaranteed an intemperate climate. Ahnapee was far removed from the arable plains that were destined to become the nation's breadbasket. The topography of the land offered no obvious path by which to access an expansive hinterland. Even the tree cover included few of the coveted pine, while it held an overabundance of trees of much less monetary value that had to be cleared before farming could take place. Finally, the lakeshore provided nothing close to a natural harbor. There would never be a haven for ships there.

Human nature, too, had its role in spoiling the dream. Competition, greed, prejudice, and blindness to the needs and contributions of others were part of life in Ahnapee just as they were in any other community in the country. Its citizens were highly attuned to the differences that divided people into class, sect, and party. In other words, Ahnapee was neither a harbor of refuge to protect ships from lake storms nor a refuge to which people could flee from the social tempests of the age.

But debunking the dream and seeing the forces at play in the community only helps us to see more clearly the importance of the role that sailors played among their fellow citizens. What follows is the story of Ahnapee's sailors. They belie the image of the sailor as a nomadic ne'er-do-well whose home is wherever the ship last dropped anchor. The lives of these sailors were firmly anchored in the community. They had a personal stake in how tensions were handled and a specific role in changing the balance of power within the community.

The sailors of Ahnapee also had a direct and profound effect on each other. In doing similar work, taking similar risks, dealing with similar issues, and finding similar solutions they formed a fellowship among themselves. There were raucous good times and painfully bad times. The sailors could compete and try to shut each other out, and at other times they could welcome into their circle the newcomer who looked to the water to make a living and keep body and soul together. Frequently, those who gravitated to the water had suffered hardship and deprivation on land, and such was the case with two Ahnapee farm boys named August and Herman Schuenemann. As is so often the case with sailors, the Schuenemann brothers became more famous through their deaths than they did through their lives. But a visit to the Ahnapee of their childhood and young adulthood, and an acquaintance with the other sailors of Ahnapee who formed their fellowship, provides a vibrant and vivid picture of the day-to-day lives of the Great Lakes sailor. Like the sailor from Wisconsin referred to by Bruce Catton, the sailors of Ahnapee ploughed the same furrow through the lake over and over again, bringing the most basic building blocks of society to the places where they were needed.

Bruce Catton clearly believed that these sailors deserve their own eulogy, but he would not allow it to be filled with saccharine sentimentality. He refused to romanticize a life of drudgery even if it was accompanied by fair lake breezes and more than one's fair share of beautiful sunsets. "That Wisconsin sailor who traded in cobblestone," he wrote, "may indeed have been a free spirit who had not yet been crowded out by the truck and the diesel engine, but he must have been leading a dog's life just the same." Catton the historian cautioned his readers against becoming prisoners of the past who see virtues that were not there and conclude that the golden age is somewhere behind them.[3]

So, while the temptation is still there to burnish the past with a rosy glow, the goal here is to answer Catton's call for truth and see the life of the mariner in the maritime community for what it really was in its nitty-gritty, day-to-day actualization.

As it turns out, that life was not pure drudgery, human exploitation, or crippling poverty. Those things are part of the history, but there were also accomplishment and reward and a sense of being part of a community larger and more important than oneself. There was opportunity to lift oneself out of the dead-end life of a farm laborer or mill worker. There were comradery, humor, adventure, challenge, perseverance, loyalty, ambition, and achievement. And, truth be told, there were also unconscionable acts of risk taking, foolish acts of pride and stubbornness, selfish deeds of thievery, and all the other things that human nature seems to pass on from one generation to the next.

As the nineteenth century closed, the sailors' tools and talents became obsolete, and as the opportunities began to fall away, many of them moved on to other pursuits. Some became farmers or fishers. Some found a place in industrial endeavors. A few moved to steam vessels. Others used their monetary, social, and intellectual capital to start new businesses. But not all moved on. Some clung tenaciously to the life of an independent mariner and tried to survive as small fish in the big pond. Theirs was often a less happy fate. To do their work they took risks that seem unimaginable today. Experience had so inured them to danger that it gradually lost its threat and became part of their accepted routine. They showed flawed practical judgment in exposing themselves and others to danger and hardship, and they stooped to behavior that suggests the need for thoughtful examination of their moral judgment. But, together with their more socially mainstream comrades, they all contributed to the picture of the mariner in the maritime communities across the Great Lakes.

Contents

ONE

THE DISAPPEARANCE
OF THE SCHOONER
Rouse Simmons

You all may bless your happy lot, who dwell safe upon the shore,
Free from the tempests and the blasts that 'round us sailors roar.
It's little you know of the hardships, nor do you understand
The stormy nights we do endure off the shores of Michigan.

—Lyrics from the song
"The Shores of Michigan"

*O*n Saturday, the 23rd of November, 1912, an event occurred on Lake Michigan that has left an indelible mark on Great Lakes history. The schooner *Rouse Simmons* was lost off Two Rivers Point approximately halfway between the Upper Peninsula of Michigan, from which it had sailed, and Chicago, its destination. The *Simmons* and its cargo of ten thousand or more Christmas trees disappeared without a trace, leaving a lot of room for a curious and saddened public to fill in the blanks with their own projections. Out of this tragedy arose a popular and enduring legend that has inspired poems, books, songs, paintings, and a musical that has played across the United States and in England. It has even inspired philanthropic acts on a large scale. There have been thousands of shipwrecks on the Great Lakes, but, in our collective memory, this one is different. It, more than any other, has become the stuff of legend.

In Chicago the *Rouse Simmons* was popularly known as the "Christmas Tree Ship."[1] Its arrival, usually around Thanksgiving, in the Chicago River was a cause for celebration. With the opening of the commercial shipping facilities in the new harbor at the mouth of the Calumet River south of the city, Chicagoans were less and less likely to see lake vessels coming in and out of the Chicago River. The obsolescence of commercial sailing craft made it even less likely that one would see a schooner. Forty years before as many as a hundred schooners could arrive at the busy port in a single day. The river was lined with the masts of the schooner fleet and overhung with the smoke and ash from steamers and tugs moving constantly up and down the river, causing innumerable traffic jams as bridges swung open to allow them to pass.[2] Railroads now had surpassed shipping as the mode of transportation for which the city was most renowned, and the stockyards rather than the lumberyards were the storied places of industry. So, to see a schooner come into the Chicago River and tie up, especially at a central location like the Clark Street bridge, was a chance to reminisce about days gone by. Then to see the electric lights strung up and the sign hung out—"Christmas Trees for Sale—My Prices are the Lowest"—completed a scene that wove a rich fabric of sentimentality and celebration, bringing the past and present together with a tradition that was timeless to those who had grown up with the Christmas tree.

The man who brought the Christmas Tree Ship to Chicago was Captain Herman Schuenemann, a first-generation German American with a warm and cheerful disposition and a wonderful gift for marketing. To those who came each year to buy a tree from the captain he was the embodiment of the holiday tradition. His gleaming eyes, round cheeks, broad smile, and bushy mustache could not help but suggest the images of Santa Claus that were found everywhere at that season. His calloused hands—ungloved; seemingly impervious to the cold; and permanently dirty from pine sap, bark, and dirt—gave the impression of a man who relished hard work, laughed at the cold, and thought only of the joy that his trees would bring to the homes of thousands of Chicagoans. He spoke perfect English but with a slightly

Germanic accent, and his booming voice seemed to bring the old world heritage of Europe (from whence most Chicagoans came) together with the new world of opportunity and enterprise in America. The presence of his wife and daughters, who set up shop in the schooner's cabin and made garlands and wreaths from the boughs of the evergreen trees, gave those who visited the Christmas Tree Ship the feeling of being welcomed into the home of the proprietor himself—the closest that Chicagoans could come to meeting the mythical Father Christmas.

The achievement of Captain Herman Schuenemann was that he brought all of these elements together to create an ethos that became as powerful a symbol for Chicagoans as the clocks at the iconic Marshall Fields store on State Street, the water tower on Michigan Avenue, or the Wrigley Building. Whether by careful study and calm calculation or (as was more likely the case) by a natural gift for sensing and responding to the desires of people's hearts, Herman Schuenemann made himself the ultimate seller of Christmas trees. Between wholesale business with local merchants who sold trees from their stores, direct sales from the deck of the *Rouse Simmons* to passersby, and special orders from organizations and individuals that wanted a magnificent tree to dominate a space and focus a celebration, he could sell tens of thousands of trees each year.

Herman Schuenemann gained the stature of an urban icon even though his entrepreneurship never made him rich and never placed him in the ranks of the corporate entrepreneurs of the city. He remained one of the folk, accessible, immediate, and touchable to the average Chicagoan while still larger than life for his heroic deeds. For what could be more heroic than to sail a three-masted schooner the length of Lake Michigan in late November when temperatures dipped below freezing, when winds frequently reached gale force, and where legendary equinoctial storms had claimed the lives of hundreds over the years? Whether by intuition or the cunning of a good marketer, Herman made himself a commodity of sorts as he transformed himself each December into Captain Santa.

By 1912 the Christmas tree was no longer an expression of only northern European Teutonic cultures. No longer was it shunned as a heathen symbol by the inheritors of the congregational and free-church traditions that had once dominated and defined propriety for the society of the Northeast and upper Midwest. Nor was the tree present only in communal gathering places such as the church hall or the lodge, as was frequently the practice in prior generations. The Christmas tree had broken through religious, ethnic, and economic barriers and had become an accepted symbol of the season for all strains of Christianity and an affordable commodity such that homeowners and apartment dwellers by the tens of thousands could have their own trees in their own parlors.[3] The custom of using live candles on the tree could readily be abandoned by urban dwellers who had access to electricity and to small colorful lights made especially for the tree. And mass production gave families ready-made ornaments with which to adorn the tree, while merchandisers hyped sales of everything Christmas by promoting the tradition of gift giving and making sure that the newspapers kept strict count of how many shopping days were left before Christmas.[4]

So also had the Christmas tree become an important tool of the philanthropic. It was de rigueur for the wealthy and politically ambitious of the community to be photographed by a Christmas tree presenting gifts to orphaned children. In factories, Christmas trees were set up and decorated by employees as a morale booster. Institutions that capitalized on the gift giving spirit, such as Chicago's Marshall Fields store, were festooned with garlands, wreaths, and trees of grand proportions.[5]

A year later (1913) Chicago would have its first municipal Christmas tree lit by Mayor Harrison in Grant Park during a festival that included speeches, opera, band music, grand trumpet fanfares, choral works, and costumes to complement the elaborate show. To capture the light and make the event more dazzling, steam engines from the railroad that followed the lakeshore east of Michigan Avenue were stationed in the background behind the illuminated trees and archways so that the smoke from the engines' stacks would reflect and diffuse the light into the sky. An estimated crowd of ten thousand spilled out of the lakeside park and onto Michigan Avenue that year to see the lighting of the tree. The children in that crowd were no less influenced by popular culture than are those a century later. One young boy is quoted as asking his father why the man lighting the tree (the mayor) wasn't fat. For him, Santa was the logical person to light the tree, and Santa was, if anything, fat.[6]

So there should be little doubt that in 1912 there were many Chicagoans who had a subconscious bookmark that would periodically cause them to wonder if the Christmas Tree Ship had yet arrived at its familiar berth in the river by the Clark Street bridge. Parents would be planning the outing to buy the tree just as surely as they would plan to buy the goose and the stuffing for dinner. Fathers with children in hand, in their arms, or on their shoulders would pause on the bridge at Michigan Avenue or Rush Street just in case they might be fortunate enough to be there when Captain Schuenemann's ship arrived.

But that year, 1912, the tradition of Chicago's Christmas Tree Ship came to a sudden and tragic end.

In September Captain Schuenemann had raised his crew and provisioned his vessel. It was not easy finding men to sail the *Simmons*. The economy of the city was able to provide jobs for most laborers who wanted to work. Sailors who had been on the lakes that year had less incentive to accept the risks and rigors of being on the water in November. The captain had to call in a few favors to get the number he needed. One was an old friend and seasoned captain, Charles Nelson, who had sailed with Schuenemann on previous quests for trees. At sixty-nine years of age, Charles Nelson was retired from the lake trade and begged off at first. But, for the sake of friendship, he relented and went along for another season against his better judgment.[7] Another was a teamster who had just become engaged to be married and was itching to earn some extra money. His mother was a friend of the Schuenemann family.[8] Others were residents of the sailors' boardinghouses just west of the river from Chicago's bustling downtown. Some may not have been the healthiest specimens of manhood. (The year before one of the *Rouse Simmons*'s crew died of a heart attack before they reached Sturgeon Bay. His body was left in Sturgeon Bay to be buried in a pauper's grave because the poor man's family did not have the wherewithal—or was it the motivation?—to have his body shipped back to Chicago.) But the captain could not afford to be choosy.[9]

Captain Schuenemann didn't have a lot of cash to flash around to attract the interest of sailors. He only had the promise that *if* they had a successful voyage up the lake, and *if* they came back with a load of Christmas trees, and *if* they accomplished this before the market was glutted with trees from some other adventuresome entrepreneur, there would be enough money to reward everyone handsomely. The merchants of Chicago understood the nature of the business. They had dealt with Captain Schuenemann before, and he had come through on his promises. So when he walked into Rothschild's Wholesale and Retail Merchandise they welcomed his business, and the liquor, hams, slabs of bacon and pork, corned beef, roasts, steaks, lard, blankets, and cots that he bought went on his tab. Noebling's General Hardware extended credit for eight boy's axes, three axes weighing three pounds each, and four ax handles. Captain Mannes J. Bonner, the owner of the controlling interest in the *Rouse Simmons,* also trusted the Chicago Christmas tree merchant. He not only agreed that the schooner could be used for the trip, he did not ask for any security. Neither did he insist that Captain Schuenemann pay him the money that he still owed from the year before for towing the vessel out of and into the Chicago harbor.[10]

In debt, but charged up by the prospect of success in his venture, Captain Schuenemann left Chicago in the *Rouse Simmons* early in October for Thompson's Pier, a small community long since abandoned, a short distance south of Manistique, Michigan. The captain was gambling his financial well-being, if not his life, on the voyage, but it is doubtful that he had a moment of hesitation. These were heady times for him. He had been in the Christmas tree business for years and had seen and survived just about everything that could go wrong: leaky vessels, unhappy crew, bad weather, bad economy, even fatalities. In spite of the hardship he had managed to expand his business by forming the Northern Michigan Evergreen Company and by investing in land near Thompson's Pier. The land was called "cutover" because it had once been owned by a large lumber company that had come in and cut all of the marketable trees, leaving only the unwanted trees and waste behind. This was not pretty land, nor was it fertile. To a farmer it would have provided a nightmarish existence. But for Captain Schuenemann, it provided just what he

needed: young pine trees, the firstfruits of the forest's efforts to reju-
venate itself, which could be harvested for use as Christmas trees. At
$10 an acre, Captain Schuenemann had bought a number of forty-
acre tracts, completing what amounted to a horizontal monopoly by
bringing every operation of the Christmas tree business under his
control, from the cultivating, harvesting, and shipping of trees to
their marketing and sale.[11]

Still, his wealth was on paper, not in his hand. The captain hired
laborers from the Manistique area to cut, bundle, haul, and load trees.
He bought more supplies on credit and even borrowed money from
local merchants to pay for services for which he could not write an
IOU. As each new debt was accumulated, the stakes of his gamble
increased. It seemed like a sure thing, though. All he had to do was get
the trees to Chicago in time to catch the wave of Christmas buying.
He already had the brand name; everyone knew that Schuenemann
meant a good deal. And he had the best location and the perfect venue
for selling his trees: Chicago's Christmas Tree Ship. The only thing
that could go wrong was if someone else saturated the market before
he got there. Timing was the final ingredient for success.[12]

The year before the captain and his crew had reached Chicago in
time to start selling trees at Thanksgiving, and it had worked out
well. That was Captain Schuenemann's plan again for 1912. Leaving
Chicago at the beginning of October and allowing enough time to
make the voyage down the lake and back meant that there were
barely six weeks available to get the work done in the forest. Of
course, it wasn't the heavy logging operation that is usually pictured
when we think of tree cutting. Most trees were for use in homes. But
still, they had to be cut, transported to dockside, compressed and
bound tightly, and loaded on board. The hold of the schooner, 8.4
feet deep and nearly 27.6 feet wide and 123.5 feet long, would be
filled first through the hatches in the deck. Then more trees would
be loaded onto the deck of the boat, covered with wooden scant-
lings, and tied down securely.[13] This deck housing was 10 or 11 feet
high and necessitated raising the booms of the sails and reducing canvas when the schooner was under way. Sail handling would be trick-
ier, and access to the hatchways, bilge pumps, and pin rails (where the
ropes used for adjusting the sails were tied off) would be more

difficult, but it wasn't unusual for lake schooners, especially the lumber carriers like the *Rouse Simmons,* to carry such large deck loads.[14] Later it would be reported that at least a few eyebrows were raised when the size of the load was seen. One estimate placed the number of trees on board when the schooner sailed as being over thirty thousand, when more typically the quantity of trees carried by one of the Schuenemann ships in the later years of the business was estimated at ten thousand.[15] A sailor who had signed on in Chicago quit the crew before they left upper Michigan and later reported that there was no stone ballast in the bottom of the hold to stabilize the ship by acting as a counterweight to the force of the wind on the sails.[16] Others stated categorically that the *Simmons* was in very poor shape to be making the voyage.

Certainly, there was good reason to wonder about the captain's judgment in using the old schooner for such hard duty. He had been visiting that region for years before he began using the *Rouse Simmons.* Some would recall that in 1906 it was another old schooner, the *George L. Wrenn,* that Captain Schuenemann brought north to Manistique. That year the marine editor in Ludington described the *Wrenn* (also spelled Wren) as being "out of commission" most of the year and "wasting her life away in the Chicago river." In Manistique the marine reporter described the schooner as being "a sorry sight" above the waterline, but he supposed that it was tight enough below the waterline to be able to sail the lake. Others in the north country would recall the year that Captain Schuenemann used the aging schooner *Mary Collins* and ended up being driven ashore before he could get his precious cargo of trees to market.[17]

But apparently the captain was not dwelling on past hardships and failures. He had faith in his vessel, and he had faith in his men to bring it safely to Chicago. The plan was to be there before Thanksgiving, and when a northwest wind started to rise on Friday, November 22, the *Rouse Simmons* was loaded and ready. Captain Schuenemann would take advantage of the blow to make a fast trip south.

While only a few have overtly criticized the captain's actions on that fateful day in 1912, none have ever defended his judgment or boasted of his skills as a sailor.

As that weekend approached activities were normal for the season elsewhere on the Great Lakes.

On Lakes Huron and Michigan lumber hookers were picking up
board lumber and cordwood from northern supply points. At the
head of Lake Superior steam freighters were loading ore for steel mills
to the south. On Lake Erie boats of various descriptions were
upbound with their holds full of coal. Soon, they would be passing
grain carriers that were loading in Duluth, Fort William, Chicago,
and Milwaukee and heading downbound to Buffalo, where many
would pass the winter serving as floating storage bins because the
huge grain elevators were already full. The car ferries that connected
railheads in Michigan with those in Wisconsin were operating on
normal schedules. Passenger service still ran regular and frequent
schedules between the major cities and towns of the lakes. In spite of
a snowfall earlier that month, fishermen were pleased to be able to
tend their nets without having to contend with ice. In fact, a general
order had been issued to all lifesaving stations around the lakes to
extend their season beyond the first of December, the customary
closing date, because the relatively mild weather had kept many boats
active in trade and fishing.[18]

The official forecast that the National Weather Service issued that
Friday gave no particular cause for alarm.

Washington, D.C., Nov. 22

The weather forecast is as follows:

For Wisconsin: Local rains or snow Saturday; colder at night;
   variable winds becoming northwest and brisk; Sunday fair.

For Upper Michigan: Local snow or rains Saturday, variable
   winds, becoming northwest and west and brisk; Sunday
   fair.[19]

This would not be the kind of weather that a recreational yachtsman
would relish, but it was hardly cause to stop a merchant sailor.

Some, benefiting from the perfect vision that comes with hindsight, would look back and say they had seen it coming. But none
could have known that on the upper lakes the closed-fisted blow of
the season's first punishing gale was about to be felt.

Map of Wisconsin/Lake Michigan

As Friday night approached, the wind built ominously out of the northwest over the Upper Peninsula of Michigan and Lakes Superior and Michigan. Temperatures dropped slowly from a "balmy" forty degree range. Rain began to fall.

When Saturday morning dawned rain had turned to wet snow. The winds were strengthened to gale force. In Menominee and Sault Ste. Marie a combination of heavy wet snow, ice, and wind had brought down telephone and telegraph wires during the night, cutting off communications and bringing rail traffic to a halt. Up to eight inches of precipitation accumulated on wet ground, which would already have soaked in the first few inches. In the north, the storm moved through the Soo and on to upper Lake Huron. Further south, it broke across Green Bay, hesitated ever so briefly over the Door County Peninsula, and then swept unhampered across Lake Michigan.[20]

Captains around the lakes were forced to make judgment calls. In the fall, when unexpected weather was the norm on the Great Lakes, most operated under a policy of sail when you can and run for shelter when you must. Those who sailed on Friday—and they were numerous—found themselves on Saturday contending with an unexpected tempest and looking for refuge.

As the captain of the steam barge *Markham,* Hans Hermanson, passed through the Straits of Mackinac and on to Lake Michigan he could not have known what a terrible decision he would soon be faced with. His vessel was towing an old schooner, the *Lyman M. Davis,* once the pride of Muskegon but by then converted into a barge. The schooner was loaded with lumber and under the command of Captain Chris Hermanson, Hans's brother. Together, the two vessels would sail into and through the gale-force wind and blinding snowstorm of Saturday the 23rd—a storm that the tug captain would later say was the worst he had experienced in twenty years—so bad, in fact, that, as reported in a newspaper account, "for the first time in his life he put on a life preserver."[21]

On the other side of the lake the steamer *Isaac W. Stephenson* came into the harbor at Sheboygan with its captain frantically looking for help. He had lost his consort, another schooner turned barge, out on the lake. Tempers flared when a local tug captain did not respond fast enough for Captain Strahan's taste, and he felt compelled to take the *Stephenson* back out into the storm to rescue the barge.[22]

At the entrance to the Sturgeon Bay Lake Michigan Ship Canal, there was a chaotic scene as vessels came in looking for shelter from the blast, setting off a domino effect. When the steamer *Louis Pahlow* arrived with a barge in tow its wake caused another vessel to break loose from its moorings and collide with a government derrick scow, setting the scow free to be carried by the current out into Lake Michigan. Several vessels went to get a line on it and bring it back, but they ended up chasing the scow down the coast almost as far as Ahnapee before they were successful.[23]

Lives were imperiled, but none had been lost. Before the day ended, however, the gale of November 23 would prove itself the most deadly storm of 1912.

The first fatalities occurred on the east shore where fishermen had gone to work, undaunted by the leaden skies, advancing low pressure, and slowly falling temperatures. Only when the gale struck did the little fleet of boats off Pentwater, Michigan, hasten to the shelter of the harbor. Each boat in turn had to navigate the narrow opening between the two stone piers that jutted out into the lake. The lifesavers, seeing the danger, had launched their surfboat and were standing ready inside the breakwater to render assistance as needed.

For a while it seemed that the fleet had responded just in time to prevent the pursuing sea from catching the small boats and sweeping them up in its fury. But the *Two Brothers,* the last boat to come in, failed its skipper and crew at the critical moment. The small craft lost its ability to steer as it approached the stone piers. It was at the complete and utter mercy of the soulless lake. People on shore watched, powerless and horrified, as the waves rose behind the small tug, lifting it up and hurling it forward only to bring it crashing down onto the piers. Even the lifesavers could do nothing. Their captain reported later that when his men "beheld her again it was to see her fling herself like a living thing up on top of the pier end, rest there for a moment poised, then lose her balance as a sea struck her, and tumble backward into the lake." In the brief moments during which the boat teetered on the brink, three men were seen on board. The two crew members, August Christianson and Tony Johnson, moved to the stern and dove into the surf. The third, Captain Elhamer, came out to the bow and clung tight as the *Two Brothers,* now broken and doomed, slid backward into the retreating surf.

Then there was nothing.

The lifesavers took heaving lines to the end of the south pier, but when they arrived the lake had obliterated any trace of the *Two Brothers.* The tug, Captain Elhamer, August Christianson, and Tony Johnson were all drawn down by the undertow. The lake had claimed its first victims of the day, and at least for the time being would hold them fast in its grip.[24]

While this was happening on the eastern shore of Lake Michigan, a little schooner, the *Three Sisters,* was setting out from Marinette, Wisconsin, on Green Bay. Captain Klumb had trouble raising a crew that morning. Neil Tillman, a regular crew member, had given up the sailing life for the winter and left for the safer haven of a lumber camp. Ike Wanderberg was supposed to be aboard the Marinette-based boat but went AWOL. He overslept. Captain Klumb and his pickup crew of two had no such good fortune.

The gale found the *Three Sisters* on the bay, along a lee shore, and pinned it down near the mouth of the Red River, on the Wisconsin side of the bay. Captain Klumb put out an anchor and attempted to wait out the storm. But when Sunday morning arrived the bay was still enraged. Either the stalemate had to be broken or the seamen given up to a certain death. The captain dove into the water and tried to swim ashore on his own. With the help of two volunteers, the local pastor, who had encouraged his parishioners to go to the aid of the *Three Sisters* rather than attend church, rescued the captain with a rowboat. A second man was picked up by another local hero whose little boat capsized several times before he succeeded in reaching the schooner. Yet a third sailor was found dead from exposure among the bales of hay near the bow of the *Three Sisters* where he had sought shelter. Unfortunately, the courageous responses of the men on shore were not to be rewarded. Both sailors who made it to land died a short time later.[25]

These were the stories that were being told when, on Monday, November 25, the commerce on Lake Michigan began to return to normal. At Pentwater, Michigan, the lifesavers patrolled the beach in expectation of finding whatever wreckage and bodies Lake Michigan would relinquish from the *Two Brothers*. At Sturgeon Bay the steamer *Louis Pahlow* had undergone some quick repair work and had cleared. A steamer and a tug, *Sylvia,* returned from Ahnapee with the government's derrick scow in tow. The *Isaac W. Stephenson* passed through the canal from Lake Michigan to Green Bay and continued on to Marinette with its consort, *Resumption,* safely in tow. The Sturgeon Bay lifesavers returned to their station after having arrived too late to be of assistance at the wreck of the *Three Sisters*.

Ironically, nobody was talking about the one event of that November weekend that would have the most profound and long-term effect. There were only a few clues to indicate that another, larger tragedy had occurred. Questions must have been fomenting in the minds of the very few who had seen the clues on Saturday, but there were no answers to be had.

One of those left wondering was the captain of the car ferry *Ann Arbor No. 5*. After making his scheduled call in Manitowoc, Wisconsin, that stormy Saturday, he had headed his ship back out into the lake for a crossing to Frankfort, Michigan. But when he found how rough the lake had become, he changed course for a safe haven to the north, the entrance to the Sturgeon Bay Lake Michigan Ship Canal. About two o'clock that afternoon the *Ann Arbor No. 5* was several miles north of Kewaunee, Wisconsin, and five miles offshore steaming into the wind. The lake appeared empty until the captain saw a three-masted schooner obviously having great difficulty. Its mainsail was down. It was flying only a staysail, a jib, and a reefed foresail. Even so it was badly heeled over before the wind. Rightly or wrongly, the master of the *Ann Arbor No. 5* steered a course to yield way to the old schooner but offered no assistance because it was flying no signal of distress.[26]

A short distance to the south and about an hour later, the lifesaver on watch at Kewaunee that Saturday saw a three-masted schooner that did have distress signals flying. It was well offshore and apparently headed south running before the northwest gale. Captain Craite was notified of the sighting. He decided against going to the schooner's aid with the oar-powered surfboat available to him. Subsequently, his efforts to seek the assistance of a gasoline-powered boat in Kewaunee were unsuccessful. What he did do was telephone the next lifesaving station to the south, where there was a gasoline-powered surfboat, and report that a schooner in distress was bound in their direction.[27]

The words of Captain Sogge of the Two Rivers Life Saving Station tell what happened next.

> At 3:10 P.M. The Capt. of the Kewaunee Life Saving Station called me by Telephone stating a Schooner under short sails headding [sic] South and under good heaway [sic] and about 5 miles out from his Station was displaying a flag half mast.
>
> The wind was blowing Strong W.N.W. and fair weather for the Schooner to make good allong [sic] this Shore and I expected the schooner would be near Two Rivers Point about 5 P.M.
>
> At 3:20 P.M. I launched the power Lifeboat and at 6:20 I was about 13 miles North of this Station but nothing to be seen of the schooner. At this time weather got very misty and started snowing heavy.
>
> I considered the schooner had change [sic] her course and steered E. out into the Lake. I turned about and came home, arrived at the station 8 P.M. I called up the Capt. of Kewaunee Station and informed him our results.

Captain Sogge's report is notable for what it does *not* say. The horizon was empty. Visibility was good at least until they reached their furthest point north. They saw no ship in distress. No wreckage. No flotsam. No lifeboat. No survivors. No bodies. Nothing! Still they searched. It began to snow heavily. Visibility declined. Night fell. The men returned from what the captain would later describe with a classic understatement as "not a very pleasant trip" with nothing but unanswered questions.[28]

For a while what had happened on the lake between Kewaunee and Two Rivers, Wisconsin, remained no more than a matter of speculation in the minds of lake mariners. Except for the sighting by the captain of the *Ann Arbor No. 5* and the lookout at Kewaunee, there was no reason to believe that a tragedy had occurred.

But with the arrival of Thanksgiving Day, November 28, the questions began to be asked with an urgency that had been missing until then. Chicagoans, family and friends of the crew of the schooner *Rouse Simmons,* reported that the ship was missing and began to press officials for a response. Calls were made to lifesaving stations around the lake in hope of hearing some word that the schooner was lying in shelter at an out-of-the-way anchorage. Some thought of Bailey's Harbor, Wisconsin, because a number of ships had sought refuge there during the recent gale. Others must inevitably have thought of the sighting at Kewaunee and the unfruitful search of the Two Rivers lifesaving crew. No matter what the theory, one thing still eluded those who sought answers . . . evidence!

There was no wreckage, no cargo washed ashore, no bodies, no survivors, no witnesses of a sinking. The easiest and most likely explanation was that the *Rouse Simmons* had merely been delayed by the storm. For ten days after the gale of November 23 nothing could be said beyond the fact that its whereabouts was unknown.

Then on Tuesday, December 4, almost a week after family members and loved ones of the crew began to worry out loud, there was a sudden and dramatic turn of events. The *Rouse Simmons* became front-page news in Chicago. It was as though the proverbial smoking gun had been found. Only in the case of the venerable old lumber schooner, it was wreckage—the long-sought proof of its fate. No one seemed to recognize that this wreckage magically appeared a week and a half after the last time that the schooner was seen. Or, if someone did question the report, it was lost in the sudden uproar created when the loss of the *Rouse Simmons* made the news.

While all of the Chicago daily newspapers eventually became involved, the *American,* the *Daily News,* and the *Daily Journal* were the first to break the story. "CHRISTMAS SHIP LOST," exploded the banner headline of the home edition of the *American.* "FIND WRECKAGE, FEAR CHRISTMAS BOAT SANK," proclaimed the *Daily News,* and "SANTA CLAUS SHIP AND 13 MEN LOST IN LAKE," read the *Daily Journal.*

With these first tidings began a Great Lakes legend that, since that time, has been treated with sensationalism by some, fictional creativity by others, and historical scrutiny by only a few. What the newspapers wrote has been the single greatest influence on shaping the legend. But paradoxically, through their reporting, the *Rouse Simmons* and the gale of November 23, 1912—to say nothing of the *Two Brothers* and the *Three Sisters* and the men who sailed these boats— have been lost. Between the six daily newspapers that competed for their attention, Chicagoans were fed an amalgam of fact, rumor, hoax, fantasy, and sentimentality. If a question had no answer, the newspaper reporters found an answer; and if they could not find an answer, they made one up.

So began the legend of the Christmas Tree Ship, and, like most legends, it has been so cherished and has become so much an object of sentimentality that it seems almost sacrilegious to raise questions about what happened that day. The answers might sully the legend, tarnish the icon, and deprive us of a story that is so beloved. But the question remains: how was it that between twelve and seventeen men were on Lake Michigan at the most dangerous season of the year in a vessel that was obviously unseaworthy, clearly overloaded, manned by a pickup crew, and commanded by a captain of dubious ability?[29]

The direct causes seem obvious—poor judgment, the heartless whim of nature, the lure of a gamble that could pay big. But this story has deeper roots and much to teach us about life in the industrial heartland of America during the period of its most dynamic growth. A comprehensive answer to the question promises to reveal a life, a people, and a kind of work that have been largely forgotten even though they were essential to the very existence of hundreds of communities around the Great Lakes.

TWO

Lake Michigan
Short-Haul Sailors

[Schooners] Jenny Mullen, Emerline, Isolda Bock, Wm.
Chapman, A. M. Avery, Caledonia, Vermont, and Arun-
dal Is [*sic*] the vessels that is lying here windbound. We
can't do anything because it is too wet. All we can do is go
from one to another and talk, telling storys [*sic*] to each
other and talk about former days.

—Diary of Captain Soren Kristiansen,
Lake Michigan schooner captain, 1891–93

The Schuenemann brothers grew up in Ahnapee, Wisconsin, a
small polyglot community comprised mostly of immigrant families
from Germany, Belgium, Switzerland, Bohemia, Ireland, Scotland,
Canada, England, and the eastern United States. It began as a sawmill
town; developed into the hub of an agricultural community; and
moved haltingly into a more mechanized, industrialized era in which
it seems never to have become comfortable. Today the town lives
under a different name—Algoma—off the beaten path that tourists
take to the popular midwestern resorts further north on the Door
County Peninsula. Known best to outsiders as a haven for sport-

18

fishing, the town still bears a strong resemblance to the completely maritime-dependent town that it once was.[1]

By 1912 the town of Algoma (née Ahnapee) had moved past the days when the harbor was the heart of the community. The coming of the railroad; the building of improved highways; and the disappearance of products that were most suitable for shipping on the small, shallow draft, wooden vessels rendered the harbor much less important. In the river there were remnants of days gone by. One in particular was the sunken hull of a scow-schooner that was built in the town almost thirty years earlier and had been one of its most stalwart servants. Many residents about town remembered the days when sailing vessels were vital to the commerce of towns around the shore of the lake. Some of these townspeople had been sailors themselves and had served as crew on lake vessels. They might have moved on to other pursuits such as fishing, farming, or skilled labor, but the names of the little vessels that had called Algoma home and of the big vessels that sailed on by as they rolled down to Cleveland and Buffalo still had a place in their memories. The *Rouse Simmons* had never dropped anchor at Ahnapee, but there was not a maritime person in town who would not have known its reputation. And, even though the Schuenemann family had long since moved to Chicago, there were plenty of folks who remembered August and Herman and recalled with fondness the days when their town was on the "Christmas Tree Coast."

So it was that in Algoma, and in dozens of towns all up and down the coast of Wisconsin, Michigan, and northern Illinois, an anxious watch was kept by individuals and small groups from the maritime community. Everyone wanted to believe that the *Rouse Simmons* was not that ship that disappeared off Two Rivers Point, and the sighting of any of the few schooners still in service on the lake that winter caused a ripple of hope and anxious anticipation to pass through the community. The mere prospect of such a tragedy, as tragedy always does, drew the community together in shared hope, grief, and loss. Surely, the association with Christmas heightened the sentiments, but for the maritime community the passing of the *Rouse Simmons* had other, even stronger, emotions attached to it. It was another reminder of the loss of days gone by when schooners dominated the lakes and when promise for the residents' own prosperity was bright.[2]

Captain Arthur E. Dow hailed from Manitowoc, Wisconsin, about forty miles south of Ahnapee and just a few miles south of Two Rivers, where the lifesaving crew had gone out to search on the evening of November 23. He knew both of the Schuenemann brothers and their families and felt the loss of the Christmas Tree Ship personally. A captain specializing in short hauls himself, he had worked most of his life on and around small commercial sailing craft. He was visiting Chicago when the news broke of the disappearance of the *Simmons* but was called home suddenly by word of his wife's illness before he had time to pay a visit to the grief-stricken family of Captain Schuenemann. So, from Manitowoc, he wrote a heartfelt note of condolence to Rose Schuenemann, the widow of Herman's brother August. "I am awful sorey [*sic*], I have lost [Barbara's] address so cant rite [*sic*] to her[.] I think that the Simons [*sic*] went down some where north of here[.] if you see hermans [*sic*] wife tell her that if I can do any thing to help her that I am anxious to do so[.] if any thing shows up around here[,] I will let you know."[3] With this note we have a fragmentary but important reminder that behind all the hype, there was a community that knew and supported the Schuenemann family.

Captain Dow was well qualified to feel compassion for the Schuenemanns because he could recall some of his own November voyages. Six years earlier (1906) he had loaded the small schooner *Larabida* with ten thousand trees cut in Michigan and set sail for Chicago. Caught in a late November gale, he and his small crew were lucky to escape with their lives. Their vessel was blown onto the Point Petersen Reef near Naubinway at the foot (north end) of Lake Michigan, and they were forced to abandon it in the ship's boat and make their way to shore in high winds and crashing surf as night fell and the temperature dropped well below the freezing mark. Undoubtedly, they would have perished if there had not been a deserted fisherman's cabin nearby where they were able to find shelter and build a fire by which to warm themselves.[4] Three years later Captain Dow had to leave the side of his gravely ill son to make the same trip to Naubinway to secure a load of Christmas trees. While he was there his son died, and he was called home to the funeral.[5]

Arthur Dow, August Schuenemann, and August's brother Herman were part of a class of independent sailors that might be called "short-haul sailors." By the end of the nineteenth century their livelihood was doomed, but for three-quarters of a century these men had filled a valuable need on the Great Lakes. They were a different breed than the nomadic sailors who would pick up a ship in one port, sail to another, collect their pay, and then seek another "trick" or live unattached until they ran out of money and decided to look for a berth on another vessel. There were plenty of the nomadic types on the lakes who found work on the vessels that carried grain and iron ore from Chicago, Escanaba, Marquette, and the like, to Cleveland, Erie, Buffalo, and so on. Some were saltwater sailors who had been on deepwater vessels to other continents or sailed coastwise up and down the eastern seaboard of the United States. They came to the lakes in large numbers when wages were higher. Others were freshwater sailors who worked on boats from the headwaters of Lakes Superior and Michigan to the foot of Lake Ontario. In the winter, some would lay up, but many sought seasonal work on the oceans or in the Gulf of Mexico or in the pineries of the north. They were transients. Their homes were wherever they hung their hats. Their affiliation with land-based communities was loose, and their family life was either unorthodox or nonexistent.[6]

Short-haul sailors, in contrast, were a distinctly different group. They put down their roots in lakeside communities, raised families, went to church, voted, joined the Masons or the Oddfellows, invested in other local businesses, and had a real stake in the future of their towns. They were not professional sailors who had formal training and licenses to prove it. They would laugh to see anyone show up on their quarterdeck wearing a uniform. They learned their skills on board boats owned by themselves, their families, or their neighbors and became captains not by having a piece of paper (a certificate, a license) but whenever the boat's controlling owner trusted them enough to give them command. They did not sail for the big fleets that were owned by lumbering, mining, or manufacturing companies. A long voyage for them would be several hundred miles, and

Herman Schuenemann (*center*) with W. K. Vanaman (*left*) and Mr. Colberg (*right*), 1909, on board a Christmas tree ship in the Chicago River. (*Chicago Daily News* negatives collection, Chicago History Museum, DN-0006926.)

some worked their whole careers rarely leaving the lake whose shore they inhabited. They were individual entrepreneurs who were in charge of every facet of the operation from maintenance of the boat to making contracts with shippers.

A short-haul sailor could never have hoped to own, or even command, a three-masted schooner like the *Rouse Simmons,* nor would he ever have had a purpose for one of the 125-foot, two-hundred-ton standard-bearers of that day. The vessels of short-haul sailors were small and much less comfortable than the larger commercial sailboats. Often they were built by the sailors themselves (or by their neighbors) on the banks of the local river, using material from the surrounding countryside. As a group these vessels were derisively called the "mosquito fleet," the implication being that they were considered a nuisance to the skippers of large sailing vessels and steamers. (Some might even have said that they should be swatted out of the way as a mosquito would be.) But in the hands of a short-haul sailor these humble boats made life possible in small towns and pier communities all around the shores of the Great Lakes.

In 1891 and 1892 one such short-haul sailor kept a diary of his work as a captain of two small scow-schooners on Lake Michigan. The captain was a Norwegian immigrant, Soren Kristiansen. The vessels that he served as master (as well as part or full owner) were the *Mishicott* and the *Vermont*.[7] Reading about the captain's life on Lake Michigan gives one a great sense of how the short-haul sailors lived. Two things dictated their lives—the weather and the marketplace. When both were working for the sailors, their lives were pleasantly boring, as is plain from Captain Kristiansen's documentation of weeks and months of activity shuttling between Onekama, Michigan, a small town north of Manistee, and Sheboygan, Kenosha, or Milwaukee, Wisconsin, with cargoes of bark for the tanneries. There was time for some rather prosaic, witty, and wise observations about the world in which he lived and worked. Of a sunset: "The sunset was clear and dark red, leaving a hazy bank all around the horizon." Of the occasional visitations from birds: "We have two bird passengers on board. They are cold and hungry and have nothing to pay their fare with." And of the tedium of work: "Now we are glad that we are thru [*sic*] with the bark season because bark and trouble follows like good chums."

When the weather or the marketplace turned against Captain Kristiansen, his life became more "interesting," although not in the way that he would have wanted. After telling how his vessel was punished by a storm offshore of Sheboygan that came near to claiming his vessel, if not his life, he added this sobering postscript: "News came from Port Washington that the scow *Silver Cloud* capsized. . . . She . . . started to leak so bad that they could not keep her with the pumps. The captain then went down in the cabin to see about his wife and child and while he was there the scow capsized and drown [*sic*] the three of them. . . . The other three sailors clung to the rigging and was [*sic*] saved."

The time on the water, however, was not the only time that the captain recorded, and from his notes about life on shore, and especially in Onekama, which he described as looking "like a city in Scotland" (except for the saloons!), it is clear how connected and invested he was in the community, whether it was in helping to save the town's hotel from burning down in a fire, attending a worship service with other Scandinavian immigrants, helping to outfit the vessels of fellow sailors in the spring, or just lounging about the deck of another becalmed boat for the telling of stories or critical discussion of the cut of another boat's jib. So, for all the time that he spent on the water, his life was nonetheless anchored in the community of Onekama, and for all the time that he spent alone with the small crew of his little scow-schooner, his life was integral to the lives of his fellow short-haul sailors.[8]

More than friends, the short-haul sailors were sometimes mentors, sometimes rivals, and always brothers. It was within this fraternity that both August and Herman Schuenemann were nurtured and educated. Some of these sailors came from families whose lives had been embedded in maritime pursuits for generations. Others literally came right off the farm to become sailors if for no other reason than because they needed the work. If these newcomers could attach themselves to a short-haul captain whose vessel primarily traveled in local waters, and if that captain and vessel were fortunate enough to find a consistent source of work, then the sailors did not have to break their ties with their families or their hometowns. Far from becoming rootless, wandering laborers who had no permanent relations with or investment in their communities, these sailors were a vital part of the workforce with a strong motivation to be involved in the social, economic, and political life of their towns. What's more, they were a vital part of each others' lives.

Not all short-haul sailors on Lake Michigan engaged in the Christmas tree trade, but the number that did is surprising. Most of the season, they carried other commodities. Wood, shingles, and stone were perhaps the most common. But with the Christmas tree trade some found a niche market that was monetarily rewarding as well as enhancing their place within the community.

Although there is no systematically kept record of how many Christmas tree ships there were on Lake Michigan, it was surely more than people have henceforth recognized.[9] Through newspaper searches ninety-one separate trips made by vessels carrying Christmas trees have been positively identified between 1876 and 1920, with the peak of activity being in the last decade of the nineteenth century and first decade of the twentieth century. In those twenty years there were at least fifty-five voyages. But in the decade in which the *Rouse Simmons* was used, there were only ten known tree voyages. At least sixty-one different vessels were used by twenty-four different captains, but August and Herman Schuenemann were far and away the most active. During the thirty-year period that they were known for a certainty to have been active in the trade they either made or arranged to be made twenty-six of the ninety-one known Christmas tree voyages on Lake Michigan. In spite of their dominance, however, it is important to realize that, in many ways, they were not unique among their peers but rather were the most well known of a large community of short-haul sailors on the lakes. They accomplished what they did by doing something that was a key to survival of many of the vessel owners and captains—they found a demand that they could meet and exploited it to the fullest.

Just as striking is the statistic that eight of the twenty-four sailors positively identified in the trade lived a significant portion of their careers in Ahnapee (Algoma), Wisconsin. These eight sailors made or arranged to be made at least forty voyages between them (44 percent of the known voyages).[10] So perhaps it would be appropriate to identify Ahnapee as the capital of the maritime Christmas tree trade.

The cities at the south end of Lake Michigan, especially Chicago and Milwaukee, with large numbers of northern European immigrants who knew and valued the traditions of Christmas, were the prize markets for trees, and in the closing decades of the nineteenth century and the first decade of the twentieth century the demand for trees was increasing there. At dockside the trees could be wholesaled to commission merchants who would sell and distribute them to local retailers throughout the city. Neighborhood grocery stores were the obvious locations for selling trees, but coal yards, candy stores, and even department stores got into the business. Churches, hospitals, schools, orphanages, and factories bought large trees for the enjoyment of those who worshipped, visited, lived, or worked inside. Political aspirants and social climbers of urban society seized the opportunity to polish their public images by generous donations of food, gifts, and trees—all the better if a reporter or camera was nearby. The Salvation Army sought to make sure that, at least for that day, the poor of Chicago did not go hungry or neglected. A growing middle class was able to observe Christmas with some of the indulgence that is synonymous with the holiday today. Whereas children in former days had to go to the church or school hall to see a tree decorated and lit for a single night of festivity, more and more families were bringing trees into their homes, where they would grace the parlor for days and became the focal point of home rituals. Electric lights and glass ornaments were replacing candles and chains of dried fruits. Gifts were becoming larger, more elaborate, and more expected.[11]

Large merchandisers opulently decorated their stores with evergreens and capitalized on the season with advertisements spread across multiple columns of both English- and German-language newspapers. Soon after the beginning of the twentieth century, the Marshall Fields store in Chicago began the tradition of putting up a large tree in the tearoom—the tree was so large that the doors of the store had to be removed to bring it in, and block and tackle was needed to raise the tree into place. Holiday shoppers came in mass to the downtown stores and were delighted and amazed with innovations such as the installation of moving stairways between the floors in the Boston Store, which was a competitor of Marshall Fields.[12] Merchants took special pains to appeal to the large German population that lived just north of the Chicago River and west of North Clark Street. In 1912 Marshall Field & Company advertised in *Die Illinois Staats-Zeitung* that they had replicated a German village in miniature on the eighth floor of their magnificent State Street store. The whole display had been imported straight from Germany and was placed in the huge toy department (der Spielwaren-Verkaufsraum).[13] The Boston Store had a different lure for the German shoppers of Chicago. They were selling Christmas trees specially packed in "patented bags" so that they were guaranteed to be fresh when brought home. "You'll wonder why no one had thought of this idea before" (Sie warden sich wundern, weil niemand vorher auf die Idee kam), proclaimed the Boston Store's advertisement. "Nothing is more beautiful than a Christmas tree in a home" (Nichte ist Schöner als ein Weihnactsbaum im Hause). The store was using Christmas trees as loss leaders to get the customers into the store, and they were on sale for half price.[14]

As Christmas trees became more popular, competition developed between the tree captains who supplied the markets. There were, after all, only a finite number of trees that were needed, and they had to arrive at the dock with near perfect timing to meet the seasonal demand. A week too early and they would not be able to hold their freshness until the holiday. But a week too late and the market could easily be glutted by competitors. So tree captains made their own unique contributions to the stories of how lake captains enjoyed the thrill of a race and the incentive of extra profit. They shared the same race to the prize that set in motion earlier scenes of fleets of wind-driven craft racing down the chain of lakes to be first with a cargo of grain or plowing across Lake Michigan to fill the avaricious needs of the lumber dealers.

In 1889 the *Door Country Advocate* marine reporter interviewed Captain William Armstrong, another contemporary of the Schuene-manns, who, like them, lived in Ahnapee, Wisconsin. The reporter wanted to make the point that the Christmas tree trade could be quite lucrative for the captains who dared to sail at that season of the year. Captain Armstrong agreed. "Some of the owners of hookers frequently make more money out of Christmas trees than they do out of their entire season's work, but these instances are not very numerous." Armstrong's point was that for every one who hit it right and made a good profit, even doubling the investment in the voyage, there were multiple captains who barely profited from their labors. It was a gamble. That year Captain Armstrong took thirty-five hundred trees, ranging from four to twenty feet tall, to Chicago on his schooner *J. W. Wright*. He estimated that their value would vary from 25¢ for the four-foot "children's trees" to $10 for the large trees meant to command public spaces.[15]

The captain's method of procuring the trees was to put out word among the farmers of the region that he was buying evergreens and trust that the farmers would bring trees to him on the dock. That year, even more trees came in than the schooner *Wright* could carry. But the tree captains would meet still another problem when they arrived at the city. Farmers from all across the state of Wisconsin had been doing the same thing as the farmers of the lakeshore counties of Door and Kewaunee. The only difference for the inland farmers was that instead of taking their pine, balsam, or fir trees to a pier to sell to the schooner captain, they took them to the country store closest to them. They sold them to the storekeeper for credit against their bill, or, if they were lucky, for credit that could be used to buy Christmas presents for their families. The storekeeper would then have the trees pruned and bound and ship them by train to any one of the numerous towns or cities of the upper Midwest. In the second week of December 1888, it was reported in Milwaukee that seven train cars, each loaded with fifteen hundred to eighteen hundred Christmas trees, had arrived in the city along with one tree schooner. Altogether, the commission merchants downtown expected as many as seventeen to twenty rail cars, containing a total of as many as thirty thousand Christmas trees, to arrive in the city. That was stiff competition for the lake captains. Some years trees were too plentiful—a "drug upon the market"—and those that were not sold had to be burned. The unlucky captain might find his hoped for profit no more tangible than the smoke from burning evergreens.[16]

The first time that a Schuenemann—in this case the older brother, August—engaged in the Christmas tree trade was probably 1876. That year the little village of Ahnapee sent two vessels south with trees on board. August Schuenemann may have been in the crew of the schooner *William H. Hinsdale* (he had been crewing for several seasons for Captain Doak; the *Hinsdale* was one of Johnny Doak's boats and was captained by Albert Sibilsky, a close associate of August Schuenemann). This vessel took thirteen hundred trees to Racine, Wisconsin, where they were sold.[17] The second Ahnapee vessel, the scow-schooner *Lady Ellen,* commanded by Captain John McDonald, endured a worse fortune. Captain McDonald found the market for trees glutted when he arrived, and, to add insult to injury, he had to pay to put his scow-schooner *Lady Ellen* into winter quarters in Chicago because the season made the return to Ahnapee too hazardous.[18] This did not discourage Captain McDonald, however. The next year he was back in Chicago with another load in time for the holiday. In the *Inter Ocean* there was a telling comment about how the vessels of the tree captains were viewed in the big city. The paper described the *Lady Ellen* as an "insignificant looking craft." But the productivity of the little scow-schooner was praiseworthy enough to be mentioned. The small vessel had earned $650 for its owner that year, and "she still had her canvas on."[19]

The pressure started before the trees got to market. As captains found good sources of supply, they had to compete with each other for the farmers' trees. They could not win the competition simply by paying a higher price to the farmers, for the tree captains rarely, if ever, had much capital to spread around. Instead, familiarity and friendliness were their main avenues of appeal. But, sometimes even that wasn't a sure bet. One year, two popular captains showed up at Sturgeon Bay to buy trees at the same time. One was Captain August Schuenemann with the schooner *Seaman,* no stranger to the waters of Green Bay. The other was John Patrick Clark, who had a reputation not only as a sailor but also as a Falstaff-like figure on the docks—a lovable rogue whose lack of honor was overlooked because of his humor and free spirit.

Captain Clark's vessel was the thirty-four-year-old veteran of the lakes *Kate Hinchman,* a schooner that he had saved from moldering away in a marine cemetery, where it had sunk to the bottom in shallow water. Insiders around the docks could not have avoided the recollection that Captain Clark had used the *Kate Hinchman,* once a proud member of the grain fleet, to salvage a load of water-damaged corn from a wreck. Captain Clark was perhaps one of the few who could see the obvious value in his soggy cargo. He would have it turned into "corn juice" (a sobriquet for whiskey). Clark's entrepreneurial vision apparently was aided by his personal taste and prodigious tolerance for whiskey, for the night of the salvage mission there was a party on the deck of the rescued grain boat and a man overboard alarm was sounded in the midst of the revelry. "The alarm subsequently proved to be a false one," was the report. "It was only Captain John Patrick Clark poking the 'corn juice' out of the hawse pipes." And what does it mean to "poke the corn juice out of the hawse pipes"? An idea comes to mind in remembering what a drunken man with a very upset stomach might do for relief while leaning over the rail (hopefully the leeward rail) of his boat![20]

Both Captain Schuenemann and Captain Clark knew that the gift of gab and a warm welcome were essential to convincing the local farmers to sell them their harvest of Christmas trees, but to sweeten the deal, a libation—or, more likely, several—was also offered. This marketing strategy did not escape notice, although it was discreetly hidden behind a bit of old sailor's jargon. In the sailing navy "splicing the main brace" meant having a drink of grog. The marine reporter used the phrase to disguise the tree captains' behavior: "Of course it is needless to say that the 'skip' [skipper] that splices the main brace the oftenest is the best man." Perhaps Captain Clark had too many of those friendly drinks of "corn juice," for, in the end, it was Captain Schuenemann who was first to clear the harbor on his way to Chicago with both the deck and hold of the schooner *Seaman* full of evergreens.[21]

Unfortunately, the tree captains of Lake Michigan left no statements explaining their motives for undertaking such a risky trade. Perhaps it was the chance to reap a windfall profit mixed with the sharp competition between themselves and others. Perhaps it was a propensity embedded in their characters to be adventurers and risk takers. All that remains to speak to their motives is the mute witness of their actions. One of the most bizarre of these was the 1902 voyage of the little schooner *O. Shaw*, commanded by Captain August Strecklow. After loading trees in Bay de Noquette (Little Bay de Noc) at the northern extremity of Green Bay, he sailed south without the benefit of a crew member to help him handle the vessel, which was sixty-seven feet long and with a capacity of forty tons. On his course to Sturgeon Bay, where he would pass through the ship canal from Green Bay to Lake Michigan and then continue his voyage south, the captain in his thirty-two-year-old vessel was struck by a gale. When the winds reached the peak of their ferocity, they found the *O. Shaw* anchored in the shelter of Pensaukee Point. But when the wind shifted direction the point no longer afforded protection, and the vessel began to bear the full brunt of the gale. Rather than risk dragging anchor and being blown ashore the captain decided to make sail in hopes of finding a better refuge at Sturgeon Bay. But, alone, he did not have the strength to bring in the anchor. Near the stroke of midnight, his entrapment suddenly ended when, by the force of wind and wave, his anchor chain parted and the schooner was blown back out into Green Bay. Captain Strecklow was up all night and managed by dint of his own perseverance to steer the *Shaw* into Sturgeon Bay shortly after first light. There he paused in his journey to request that two anchors be sent from Chicago for his vessel and to seek a crew to help him take the *O. Shaw* home on the last leg of the trip. Presumably the anchors arrived, but no one ever stepped forward to serve as crew, and eventually Captain Strecklow continued his journey sailing the *Shaw* single-handedly.[22]

To the astute twenty-first-century observer there is something very familiar about these stories of risk taking, braggadocio, and scheming on the part of the short-haul captains. They evoke reminiscences of the testosterone laden world of the modern locker room, race track, sports bar, and fraternity house. Like their modern counterparts, these sailors had their ways of saying one thing while meaning something else entirely. Derisive humor was in actuality a form of recognition. Humiliation often stood in where congratulation would be expected. In the competitive male world friendships can be very strong and yet never be explicitly mentioned. Praise is more often implied than stated outright. Among the short-haul sailors baiting, hazing, teasing, and mocking were carried out in full public view, while at the same time their behaviors were disguised from innocent ears by the use of jargon ("splicing the main brace") and picturesque code ("blowing the corn juice out the hawse pipe"). In these stories is found the strange manifestation of a fraternal bond that comes in the form of an insult that is really a backhanded compliment.

One way to join the fun and defang those critics who might have a more biting critique was for the sailor to put down his own accomplishments before someone else had the chance to do so. That's what Captain Arthur Dow did after news spread about how his schooner, the *Augustus,* struck the piers as it was entering the Sturgeon Bay

Lake Michigan Ship Canal. The newspaper reporter actually found Captain Dow's performance virtuosic in that instance. His vessel had lost its rudder and thus could not be steered normally. So the captain used the sails of the vessel to steer it. (Sheeting in the foresails while allowing the aftsails to luff would cause the boat to turn in the direction away from the wind. Sheeting in the aftsails and luffing the foresails would turn it in the opposite direction.) While this may sound like a matter of simple obedience to the laws of nature, it's not that easy to do, and the reporter pointed that out to his readers. The captain, he said, performed "very skillfully." But when he asked Captain Dow to account for how he saved his crippled vessel, his answer was flippant and self-effacing. It was done "by luck and thunder," said Captain Dow.[23] When sailors found humor in the foibles, mistakes, and misfortunes of themselves or their comrades, they abandoned the conventions of polite society. They engaged in a behavior and used a lingo that held them together as a community in the same way that groups in our time have their peculiar initiation rituals, inside jokes, and stories with special meanings.

When the humor was imposed, rather than invited, it could have more of an edge and could certainly be more embarrassing. The sailor who was the target of the jabs could be protected by withholding his name, but certainly those within the maritime community knew exactly whose leg was being pulled. Here is how one such story came out in the local newspaper in 1879: "It is said that a certain young man not far from this city, who boasts of considerable bravery, hired out to the captain of the *Evening Star* as a sailor, but when the heavy storm came up just before she left port he was seen carefully concealed behind a pile of posts waiting for the vessel to leave. Of course he isn't a sailor boy but he tells of his daring feats just the same."[24] There is an element of "put up or shut up" in this story, but it could also well be that this young man was being teased rather than shunned and that he was welcome aboard the *Evening Star* the next time it sailed as long as he knew that he had not yet attained the rank of the other men who walked the deck.

The mockery was not saved only for the sailors; sometimes the boat was the object of derision. That was the case when a little schooner from the small coastal community of Bailey's Harbor, Wisconsin, came into the harbor at Ahnapee (about forty miles south). The cargo it took away—beer, butter, and eggs—was consistent with its diminutive size and its humble mission in life. It was noted by the folks of Ahnapee that since the vessel's last visit its name had been changed. It used to be *Queen of the West;* the new name was *Rippling Wave.* There must have been a smile on the newspaper editor's face as he set the type giving his opinion of the name change—"very appropriate."[25]

The giving and receiving of public displays of comic disrespect was actually very adaptive in marine circles. To be able to publicly ridicule someone without risking rejection by him, or to be able to be ridiculed without suffering permanent ostracism, made sailors significantly safer in an inherently dangerous kind of work. The use of humor made it safe to show your foibles and even announce your mistakes. The only price to be paid was some verbal derision, and there was always the possibility that soon the shoe would be on the other foot and the derided would have a chance to cast derision on someone else. Inevitably all of the captains would take their turn as derided and derider. Operating on a shoestring, sailing a decrepit old vessel, and being able to afford little more than a minimal unskilled crew of sailors meant that all would sooner or later suffer the mishap or make the mistake that was at least publicly humiliating if not life threatening. The whims of the weather and the nature of the work made groundings, capsizings, and even sinkings common. The key to survival was to be able to go public with your predicament and appeal to others for help. When a sailor got into trouble it was usually another sailor who pulled him out of the drink physically or metaphorically. If the price to pay was being made the subject of some inside jokes, it was well worth it, and the fun would come when your rescuer needed rescuing himself some day.

THREE

THE SAILORS' SCHOOL
OF HARD KNOCKS

All life is learning.
—Author unknown

A stellar example of the kind of teasing that a short-haul sailor had to live with comes with the story of Captain Johnny Doak and his scow-schooner the *Ella Doak*. Maligned in Milwaukee, he was lauded in Ahnapee.[1]

Each fall in the early 1870s unflattering stories about the *Ella Doak* and Captain Johnny Doak made their way up and down the docks around Lake Michigan. The scuttlebutt was always how Captain Doak and the *Ella* had managed to end up on the beach again. A catalog of the vessel's calamities is truly impressive. Near the end of 1871 the little scow-schooner left the harbor at Racine, Wisconsin, in such a leaky condition that it had to put back into port immediately and be pumped out by the local fire company's steam engine. In the fall of 1872 calamities came in a set of three: first the scow-schooner struck a bar near Port Washington, Wisconsin, while heavily laden with a cargo of brick; shortly afterward it dragged anchor and went ashore at its home port of Ahnapee where it was loading wood and railroad ties; and two days later (now fully loaded) it struck the Hitchcock and Mashek Pier at nearby Kewaunee in a strong sou'easter. In the last of these incidents the *Ella Doak* had its mizzen sail carried away and came to rest in some shallows one hundred feet offshore, where it pounded the bottom badly until rescued by a tug. In 1873 the vessel was involved in a serious collision in the Chicago River and, one month later, was again fast on the beach, this time at South Manitou Island in Lake Michigan.[2]

The year 1874 allowed for no exceptions. The *Ella Doak* was driven by a storm toward Sheboygan, Wisconsin, where it approached the harbor entrance laden with a cargo of posts and pursued by wind and waves. The scow missed the opening and ended up so badly battered by the pier that it filled with water in twenty minutes and had to be towed to a mud bank where it could rest temporarily on the bottom.[3]

Finally, 1875 saw the fatal blow to the hardworking and well-worn little scow. Its mission was to load stone lifted from the bottom of Hedgehog Harbor just inside Death's Door on Green Bay, Wisconsin. The vessel was to carry its cargo to Ludington, Michigan, where waterfront improvements were under way. After an August day of loading stone in close to the shore (it was called "hooking" because the "hook," or anchor, was used to hook the vessel in shallow water close to shore where stone was easily accessible), Captain Orange Conger moored the *Ella* out in the harbor. During the night a storm rose out of the west, and, in spite of its anchor being out on the rocky bottom, his scow-schooner was once again on the beach by morning. In his home port of Ahnapee, Wisconsin, acceptance of the finality of the vessel's fate was juxtaposed with eternal optimism. There was, after all, a reason to feel optimistic even in such dire straits, for this was the craft that had been pronounced lost so many times before only to rise and sail again. "Her outfit is being removed and her hull will be abandoned," said the *Ahnapee Record* newspaper. But with the next dip of the pen the reporter opined, "It would not surprise anyone at all to see Captain John sail into our harbor with the [*Ella*] *Doak* in less than a week."[4]

Because Doak had such a reputation for suffering calamities it is no wonder that the docks were buzzing with talk about the captain and the scow-schooner from Ahnapee. No doubt with a wink and a smile, sailors dubbed the *Ella Doak* "Queen of the Beach"—a name that dogged the vessel for the rest of its days and beyond. It was, of course, a coronation of humiliation. In Milwaukee, where the dubious title had been bestowed, there was a biting edge in the sarcasm heaped upon Captain Doak's boat. "Keep it up," wrote the *Milwaukee News* after one of the 1873 mishaps. "That craft is good for a century yet."[5]

The people of Ahnapee, however, rose to the defense of Captain Doak and his scow. Rather than focus on the number of times the vessel had ended up on the beach, they trumpeted the number of times it rose again and pronounced it the "Everlasting Ella." And, while others might tell stories about mishaps, the people of Ahnapee could rightfully point out that there were at least as many times that Captain Doak had brought the indefatigable *Ella* through perilous situations *without* a scrape or bruise. When the scow arrived in Ahnapee in the midst of a raging November storm, the editor of the *Ahnapee Record* was rhapsodic as he described the vessel threading its way through the narrow entrance between the piers. "The danger . . . will be appreciated when it is known that the width of the channel is only fifty feet, and that the sea running directly in, was breaking over the government piers. Remarks are often heard reflecting upon the prudence of the commander of the *Doak*. That he 'takes the chances' now and then is doubtless true, but those who censure him, do not consider the many alternatives involved in every situation of peril. It may be that if there were more seamen possessed of Capt. Doak's steadiness of nerve, self-reliance and knowledge of the calling, disasters would be of less frequency. Like the brandy Grant used to drink which Lincoln wanted for the rest of his generals, Capt. Doak's 'recklessness' would vastly improve many skippers."[6]

Johnny Doak was hard on his vessel, but he was no less hard on himself. While most Great Lakes sailors sought winter quarters for at least four months of the year, Captain Doak and his vessels kept sailing. The hardships of winter on the lake were great. Vessels fell captive to the ice. They could be locked in a field of frozen white for days at a time. Navigational aids were taken in. Lifesaving crews disbanded.

Air temperatures ranged from the forties to subzero. Winds out of the north, northeast, and northwest could blow with gale force while the ice made the few harbors of refuge that existed harder, if not impossible, to enter. Sails and rigging, heavy with rain or wet snow one day, could be frozen stiff the next, making it a monumental task to take in, set, or even trim sail. Decks, ladders, ratlines, rails, and bulwarks could be treacherously slick. Heavy layers of clothing might protect against the wind but made it hard to move about with agility. On one occasion Captain Doak's vessel sprang a leak, and he and his crew spent long hours submerged to their waists on their waterlogged vessel with the air temperature below freezing. At another time a fire had to be built on deck to thaw out the windlass and chain so that the anchor could be brought on board.[7]

In December 1871 the *Racine Weekly Journal* observed, "The *Ella Doak* is the only vessel that never furls her wings, . . . all seasons are alike to her." That winter, the fiercest that Captain Doak ever faced, was also his finest hour. Two months earlier the upper Midwest experienced the greatest conflagration ever recorded in North America. It was in every horrible aspect of the word a "firestorm," and it struck not in one locality but in many from Minnesota to Michigan. The combination of drought, wind, human folly, and fire destroyed the heart of the great city of Chicago, devastated dozens of smaller towns, laid waste thousands of acres of forest and farmland, and brought the lives of hundreds of individuals to an unimaginably horrifying end—horrifying for those who died and, often, horrifying for those who survived to find their loved ones' ashes. Nowhere was the loss of life greater than in northeastern Wisconsin, and Peshtigo, a lumber mill and manufacturing town, will always be remembered as the place where the most concentrated human suffering took place. More than twice as many lives were lost in that one small town as in all of Chicago, and many of the most graphic and heartrending images of the death and devastation come from Peshtigo survivors.[8]

As the fire and wind were ravaging Oconto County on the west side of Green Bay, the same holocaust was being replicated in northern Kewaunee County and southern Door County on the east side of the bay. George W. Wing, the man who would soon become the editor of the first newspaper in Ahnapee, was living in Kewaunee, ten miles to the south along the shore of Lake Michigan. The day after the worst of the firestorm, Wing drove his carriage north from Kewaunee to Ahnapee. "There was not a bridge or corduroy [log-surfaced road] left after going over the Leindecker Hill; not a fence left standing," he later wrote. "Discouraged men and women and children sat in groups upon their household furniture piled in the roads; cattle huddled near them; barns were burned, and as we progressed further north, many houses were in ruins; roads were impassable from blackened fallen timber, and we drove through fields where the ashes were from one foot to a foot and a half deep. Not a green thing anywhere, just one succession of blackened stubs for miles." Later, Wing and his companion drove deeper into the burned over region and deeper into the horror. "The roads leading into the Belgian settlement were strewn with dead cattle, carcasses of bear and deer; fragments of vehicles burned to the irons; ditches and cleared fields strewn with smaller game and wild birds, blackened ruin everywhere. We met men with blackened, discouraged faces; women with stunned, despairing eyes; homes, household effects, school houses, churches, everything gone!"[9]

For those who survived the fire the trial had just begun. The winter of 1871–72 was one of the harshest ever to be recorded in northern Wisconsin. Early in December thermometers on upper Lake Michigan recorded temperatures of twenty degrees below zero. In between the spells of bitter cold, warm winds brought air temperatures of forty degrees above zero. Rain, sleet, and snow were intermixed in an infinite variety of patterns. This was what families bereft of shelter, clothing, food, and livelihood had to face for months on end. Their spirits traumatized by a fire of apocalyptic proportions; their bodies ravished by cold, hunger, and want; their minds obsessed with how life could go on in a land where the earth had been scorched, they suffered to the limit of human endurance.

Partly by the efforts of their citizens, but mostly by the whimsy of the wind, the lakeside communities of Clay Banks, Ahnapee, and Kewaunee were spared. At Ahnapee, Captain Doak's home port, the fire burned right up to the back door and threatened to take the sawmill but then, miraculously, stopped in its tracks.[10] Their good fortune made these towns places of refuge for many from the burnt district and also made them distribution points for the relief that soon came pouring into the region from across the nation and across the sea. Unlike in Chicago, Green Bay, or Peshtigo, however, no railroads could reach these lakeshore communities. Their links with the outside world were the harbors and piers and the vessels that plied Lake Michigan. On the lakeshore anxious people came to await the arrival of goods on which their comfort, if not their very survival, depended. There a small fleet of intrepid sailors came throughout the months of winter bringing life-giving gifts. Among that fleet was Captain Johnny Doak with the scow-schooner *Ella Doak*.

Racine was the port from which Captain Doak sailed with his vessel that "never furled [its] wings." Barely more than a week after running against the harbor pier and being forced to call upon the local firemen and their steam driven pump to help save his craft, Captain Doak had made quick repairs and was off again with a cargo of provisions for Clay Banks. A local observer noted that the departure of the scow-schooner *Ella Doak* on that cold December day was most unusual. "On getting outside the piers she immediately became unmanageable, taking a course of her own, heading for the beach, and run [*sic*] along the shore one or two miles, when she suddenly shot out into the lake, and so sailed out of sight. The lake is so full of ice as to prevent vessels from making much headway."[11]

In all likelihood, it was the ice that caused such erratic behavior. The *Ella Doak* came through but not without a struggle. When the vessel arrived back at Racine on January 6, after ten days out on the lake, it could not make the harbor. The mainsheet had parted, there was an offshore wind, and the schooner became "enveloped in a sea of floating ice." After several days within shouting distance of land, the *Doak* was hopelessly blocked from its intended goal and had to turn and hurry to Milwaukee, where it found safe harbor until conditions improved at Racine.[12]

December and January were the most treacherous months on the lake. Several boats had been damaged, and at least one had gone missing. The Chicago schooner *Crossthwaite* was locked in the ice on Lake Huron for a month, and the men on board were forced to take axes to its bulwarks to provide wood for the cabin stove. On Georgian Bay, several lumber schooners were abandoned in the ice, and their crews traveled by dogsled and foot, staying in Native American villages at night until they reached a railroad that took them to Toronto and a connecting line home to Chicago. On Lake Michigan, the schooner *Exchange* won the battle with the ice, but a crew member was so badly frozen that he was in danger of having both feet amputated.[13]

This kind of hardship would make even the stoutest sailor begin to doubt his calling. Mutiny was not necessary on the Great Lakes. A port was never far away, and frequent contact with land made it possible for sailors to simply bide their time and walk away from their vessel. On at least one occasion that winter Captain Doak, who employed men whom he knew personally, was in very real danger of losing his crew altogether. It was on that cruel voyage to Clay Banks. "Stopping at Manitowoc . . . Captain Doak found his crew unwilling to again assume the hardship of a trip in midwinter, but after much argument, finaly [sic] persuaded them to again embark." Captain Doak's powers of persuasion must have been prodigious. The *Ella Doak* had stopped at Manitowoc because it had sprung still another leak and was in need of repair. And when the scow left port to continue further north, further into danger, it did so without a yawl boat swinging at the davits or a second anchor on board![14]

In spite of the hardships, doubt, and conflict, the *Doak,* with its captain and crew of three, made two other voyages out of Racine that January and several more before the spring. Conditions made it impossible to follow a schedule. One round trip to Clay Banks and back was accomplished in an amazingly short four days. The next trip, however, was four days old before the scow-schooner was even out of sight of Racine. On January 23 the supply laden vessel was blown back by a strong easterly wind only to be iced in.[15]

While Captain Doak left behind no words of his own to describe his heroics, another lake captain did. William Callaway, a British seaman who came to the Great Lakes in 1857, was master of the schooner *Toledo* that winter, and his vessel was chartered by the Milwaukee Relief Committee to carry supplies to the fire victims. In his personal memoir he recounts the return from his second voyage to Ahnapee with supplies. Within sight of warmth and refuge back home in Milwaukee, the *Toledo* went aground outside the piers

An example of a schooner being towed by a rowboat in the absence of wind. The schooner is the *Belle W. Culbert*. (Courtesy of the Wisconsin Maritime Museum, Manitowoc, Wisconsin.)

because its centerboard was frozen in the box and could not be raised. Captain Callaway and his men jettisoned a portion of their cargo of wood and then used saws to hand cut a channel from the mouth of the harbor to Wolf & Davidson's Shipyard, where the schooner was repaired. After this ordeal, the captain looked after his own comfort. "I got home as quickly as possible," he remembered. "When I took off my coat and pants they were frozen so hard they stood up alone." Nonetheless, Captain Callaway, like Captain Doak, did not stay sheltered in port any longer than necessary. As soon as the *Toledo* was repaired, he loaded it again with supplies for Ahnapee. It took three weeks and the help of two of the Grand Haven steamers acting as ice-breakers before he could reach the lake again.[16]

The days of waiting were days of desperation for the needy people of Kewaunee and Door Counties, and it seems that there was a matching desperation on the part of the captains who sought to bring help. "I . . . arrived about a mile off the end of the pier [at Ahnapee] at daylight one Sunday morning, when the wind died down," recalled Captain Callaway. "I had the boat lowered, and towed the vessel into the pier [by rowing]. There was a large crowd of people on the pier, and I shall always look back with pleasure to seeing those joyful faces, and remember the way they received us, with shouts and cheers. As soon as we got alongside the pier we began unloading. There was a string of teams a mile in length, each awaiting their turn to load what the relief committee allowed them."[17]

To fire survivors, the mundane cargo of the relief ships was as valuable as gold, though it was no more than baled hay, seed, farm tools, or wagons In the burned over district farm animals had been deprived by the fire of any browse, and what had been mowed and stored away had gone up in smoke as barns and sheds were consumed. Humans and beasts clung to life together, sometimes with several families and their farm animals all sharing the same rude house. Diseases like typhoid spread more easily under such primitive conditions, and there were no medications nor any doctors to minister to the suffering. By midwinter, there were reports that several families had been forced to slaughter their farm animals because the animals' death from starvation was imminent. The farmer forced to such an act of desperation must have agonized, knowing that he was sacrificing his future for the sake of easing the present suffering but a short time. Without horses, cows, or oxen, the people of Kewaunee and Door Counties would not be able to operate their farms the next spring. There would be no future if they had no livestock. There would be no future unless relief arrived.[18]

Fourteen years after the fire Captain Johnny Doak was laid to rest in Woodlawn Cemetery in Allouez, Wisconsin, a few miles from his parents' home in DePere. Several decades later, his remains were disinterred and moved to another plot in the same cemetery. The reason for the move is obvious when it is noticed that his father and mother are buried just a few feet away. But then the eye is drawn to another monument, an obelisk, which is much larger than the tombstones that mark his parents' graves and bears the family name Williamson in large block letters. On that obelisk are the names of that family and the dates of their deaths: John Williamson, age 32, died October 14, 1871; Catherine Williamson, age 25, died October 14, 1871; John Williamson, age 58, died October 16, 1871; James Williamson, age 32, died October 16, 1871; Frederick Williamson, age 16, died October 16, 1871; Maggie O'Neil, age 19, died October 16, 1871; and Maggie Williamson, age 19, died October 16, 1871. All died within two days of each other. All death dates were within a week of the catastrophic firestorm. And all died at Williamsonville, Wisconsin, a small sawmill town in southern Door County that was reduced to ashes by explosive fire and tornadic wind. It only remains to be discovered that Johnny's younger sister was Catherine Doak, whose name after marriage was Catherine Williamson, to realize just how personal the tragedy of the firestorm was to Johnny. The decision to sail that season, come what may, might well have been made as Johnny went home in October 1871 to his mother's house, where seven wooden caskets were laid out in the cramped parlor in preparation for burial.[19]

This overview of the careers of Johnny Doak, William Callaway, and other winter sailors brings forth a dynamic picture of the community of mariners within which the lake captains of the Schuenemanns' generation lived and worked. Although some shipmasters in this community had training on oceangoing vessels, as did Captain Callaway, men like Johnny Doak became ship captains without any formal qualifications and without extensive experience. They did not learn their sailing skills in school. They did not read books or even serve apprenticeships. They accumulated no certificates of achievement, no symbols of rank or expertise, and no titles of honor. They wore no uniforms, belonged to no associations, and formed no unions. They learned by working. Their teachers were those whom they wanted to emulate.

Johnny came by his maritime career through his family. His father, John Sr., was a sailor before him and may have sailed the oceans before he moved to the Great Lakes. He immigrated to Canada from Ireland in his young adulthood and worked in the lumber camps and on lumber hookers on the upper Saint Lawrence River and the Bay of Quinte on the north shore of Lake Ontario. After marrying an Irish Canadian woman from Montreal he moved to Napanee, Ontario, when that area was being heavily logged. Finally, in the economic boom time of 1856, John Sr. moved his family to DePere, Wisconsin, where he worked as a shipwright on the Fox River and passed his skills on to his four sons. One of them, Alexander, was the builder of the three-masted schooner *Kate Doak* that was launched at DePere in 1868. Eventually all of the Doak boys—Robert, John Jr., Alexander, and George—worked as lake mariners, and all but Alexander died at an early age.[20]

The Doaks were not unique. Captains born and raised on the Great Lakes learned their skills by being sailors first. Many of them had extensive experience and plentiful opportunities to test their knowledge and skills before ever being promoted to command a vessel.[21] Ultimately, it was up to the owner of the vessel to decide who would be in command. Experience, skill, reliability, and sobriety were highly prized by owners, as would be expected.[22] But there were also many instances when promotion did not reflect formal qualifications or objective appraisals of skill level.

Some made the leap to captain by virtue of family and personal connections; others became the master of a sailing vessel simply by the possession of capital. Just how easy it was to be recognized as "captain" is illustrated by an episode in the life of Isaac ("Ike") Stephenson. Ike eventually became a very wealthy lumber baron, investor, and politician, but he started out working for a prominent New Englander, referred to simply as "Mr. Sinclair" in Stephenson's autobiography, who had invested heavily in logging on the Escanaba River. Early in his years in the logging industry Ike worked in the pinery and frequently was a passenger on the schooners that brought the lumber from the mill in Escanaba to the market in Milwaukee. His interest in sailing led him to serve before the mast for one voyage, but life in the forecastle was not for him. Ike had higher ambitions for himself. He continued to travel back and forth on the schooners and was curious enough to observe and learn how they were navigated. Finally, after he had saved some capital of his own, he began to invest in vessels. In 1850 he served as mate on the first of his investments, the schooner *Gallinipper,* under a captain who worked for the logging company. The next season Ike was half owner of the schooner *Cleopatra.* He bought out and replaced the captain of the vessel and during that season made nine trips between Milwaukee and Escanaba. On the first trip Ike met his boss, Mr. Sinclair, in Escanaba. Sinclair was curious about how Stephenson had traveled from Milwaukee, and, after learning that he had arrived on the *Cleopatra* and owned a controlling interest in the schooner, Sinclair asked Ike who the captain was. Stephenson's answer was simple: "They call me captain when I am aboard." In other words, the captain was the one who controlled the purse strings, but this should not be taken as a guarantee that he was an expert mariner.[23]

Ownership was the deciding factor across the lakes as long as the government was loath to regulate. Among the short-haul captains the owner (or part owner) was either the captain of the vessel or decided who the captain would be, and the captain, in turn, chose his own crew. In a small maritime-dependent community like Ahnapee, Wisconsin, this immediately gave captains of the lake vessels a great deal of status. Not only did their vessels perform the essential tasks of bringing the necessities of life and taking away the products of the farms, forests, and mills, they also provided work for young men who might not have an opportunity to make a living elsewhere in the community. Those men who needed work and gravitated to the mouth of the Ahnapee River where the fishing boats and commercial vessels docked were adopted by captains such as Johnny Doak not on the basis of education and training already received but because of personal compatibility and willingness to work. Subjective qualities such as loyalty, comradeship, and work ethic, rather than objective skills, got the landsman his first berth on a vessel, while his quickness to acquire skills and adaptability to hard physical work kept him on board.[24]

Unfortunately, this ad hoc manner of placing men in command of vessels meant that those in charge were not always well qualified. An example from among the sailors of Ahnapee is so stark as to be comical. Billy Dingman, a resident of Ahnapee who was something of a jack of all trades, was given the job of taking a load of bricks to Sturgeon Bay (where there was a building boom going on in connection with the building of the Sturgeon Bay Lake Michigan Ship Canal). He was to use the scow-schooner *Little Johnny* owned locally. Billy had some previous experience crewing on vessels but had never been the master of a vessel. Nonetheless, he confidently loaded the scow with eighty-four hundred bricks and headed out into the lake with a strong southeast wind kicking up breakers along the coast. Experience quickly taught Billy that he was in trouble, and he tried to return to the harbor, but with waves repeatedly broaching his vessel he was forced to bring it to anchor and to seek dry land with his crew in the small ship's boat. As fellow citizens watched, the *Little Johnny* was gradually overcome by the waves. Its cargo sank like the proverbial ton of bricks, and it ended up on the rocks. Word around town, however, was that several citizens knowledgeable about boat handling were sure that the scow and its cargo could have been saved if the vessel only had been handled properly. Billy went on to other pursuits, but understandably he was never chosen for command of any other vessels at Ahnapee.[25]

Still to be considered is that sailing on the Great Lakes was seasonal both because of the weather cycles and because of economic cycles. Sailors had to have other skills that they could use to supplement their incomes. In the winter some worked in the pineries. Others worked in factories or in day labor jobs. The enterprising captains in Ahnapee and other towns like it had their own land-based businesses to fill the gaps when their vessels were not in demand. Some went to harvesting trees. Some engaged in shipbuilding and ship repair. Others learned skills like sign painting or developed small business enterprises such as taverns, restaurants, or specialty stores. One of Johnny Doak's brothers, a well-known sailor in the region, hired himself out as a chimney painter. Another of the Doak boys worked at the trade of moving houses, where working with block and tackle and heaving lines would be a carryover from sailing. Perhaps one of the reasons that the scow-schooner *Ella Doak* "never furled [its] wings" in the winter was that Johnny lacked either the skills or (as is more likely) the desire to find a land-based job.

As imperfect as this informal system for developing sailing skills was, there was nonetheless a system. Among the short-haul sailors of

Ahnapee skill development was through mentoring. It is clear that Johnny Doak was a mentor for a number of young men, among whom were August and Herman Schuenemann.

The earliest date found for one of Ahnapee's Schuenemann brothers to be engaged as a sailor is 1873. That year the older of the two—August—was a member of Johnny Doak's crew on the scow-schooner *Ella Doak.* Other crew members on the *Ella* were Ahnapee sailors Orange Conger, Billy Dingman, and Albert Sibilsky. When Captain Doak bought the old and hard-used schooner *William H. Hinsdale,* he took with him three of the crew of the *Ella Doak*—August Schuenemann, Orange Conger, and Albert Sibilsky. Eventually, Captain Doak sold the *Hinsdale* to his crew, and they continued sailing together after Johnny went on to another vessel. Sometime later August Schuenemann moved on to the scow-schooner *Sea Star* and was made master of the vessel by its owner. Among the crew of Ahnapee men was, once again, Albert Sibilsky. Similarly, Billy Dingman and Orange Conger worked together repeatedly. In addition to serving together on the *Ella Doak,* they later sailed together on the scow-schooner *Little Johnny,* the sloop *Robbie,* and the schooner *Bonetat.* Such parallel appearances of names among the crews of boats is strongly suggestive that personal relationships and working relationships had developed among these men. Skills were passed down from the more experienced to the less experienced. Friendships begun on land deepened as the men learned to trust and respect each others' ability to work together on the water.

This system of mentoring was not unique to Johnny Doak's boats, and Johnny was most certainly not the only captain in Ahnapee to make sailors out of local young men who were looking for work. Indeed, the town of Ahnapee was founded by sailors. The first Euro Americans who settled there did not come by blazing a trail through the wilderness, and they did not arrive with their worldly possessions loaded on an oxcart or wagon. They arrived by boat and started their settlement clinging to the shoreline of Lake Michigan and the streambed of the Ahnapee River. The first sawmill was built by Abraham Hall, who had formerly been the master of the schooner *Rochester.* The first store owner, and the man who built the first pier out into the lake, David Youngs, had been master of the schooner

47

Lady Ann and the schooner *Amelia* and had owned an interest in the *Lady Ann, Union,* and *Julianna,* all of which had a role in helping to establish the fledgling town in the mid-1850s. Two other sailors were associated with some of the same vessels and became prominent citizens in town: Captain Hank Harkins, who was not only a sailor and fisherman but also a shipwright who built several vessels on the banks of the Ahnapee River; and Captain Charles L. Fellows, who built one of the town's first hotels and later built a sawmill at Silver Creek a few miles to the north along the lakeshore. These men (Hall, Youngs, Harkins, Fellows) and others who were important to the town's founding had something else in common, too: they all came to Ahnapee by way of Racine, Wisconsin, a town that owed its existence to mariners from the lower Great Lakes. In a true sense, it could be said that Racine and its early settlers "parented" Ahnapee, just as Ahnapee would one day "parent" other, still smaller, communities along the lakeshore. So progress spread by water links all along the lakeshores, passed on in an ad hoc fashion from person to person and place to place.[26]

FOUR

AHNAPEE, WISCONSIN—
A MARITIME COMMUNITY

Most often the town was established several years before
the settlement of the agricultural hinterland, and the agent
of this expansion was not the simple, dedicated farmer,
but a combination of wily eastern speculators and enterprising frontier businessmen.

—John Haeger, *Men and Money*

*A*s important as it was to have older and more experienced sailors
who passed on the skills and provided the opportunities for learning,
the community also had a vital role in shaping the careers of short-
haul sailors like the Schuenemann brothers. It provided the need that
the sailors were uniquely qualified to fill.

The community of Ahnapee, like so many others around the
shores of the Great Lakes, was largely dictated by geography. In simplest terms, the geographical context was that the community was the
outlet of a meandering river surrounded by dense forest land of
mixed broadleaf and conifer trees interspersed with cedar swamps and
set in a climate that presented a broad spectrum of weather conditions. That this meandering river emptied into Lake Michigan, which
provided a bounty of natural resources as well as a direct water link

to a huge section of the continent in various stages of habitation and development, is, of course, another vital and obvious factor defining the community. On the one hand, the forests and swamps inhibited settlement coming from inland, while the water provided an easy means of egress and regress for the earliest inhabitants who established the first toeholds on permanency. For years after its founding, the community lacked anything more than the most rudimentary roads inland, and those roads that did exist were often impassable for large parts of the year due to snow melt, rain, and poor drainage. On the other hand, the very forests that inhibited settlement also provided a resource that was marketable in far flung places, and the Great Lakes made those marketplaces accessible. For decades after its founding, Ahnapee was shipping forest products south where the prairie states needed them, and, even as the forest was pushed back and agriculture began to take hold on the economy of the region, it only meant that cargo vessels that once carried nothing but forest products then began to carry a variety of products ranging from grains and fruits to lumber and woodenware.

The nexus where the demands of the larger society met the resources of that particular region around Ahnapee was "the mouth." Where the river emptied into the lake was where the engine of exchange created a community and created the essential need for sailors. This was the stage on which much of the drama of the town occurred, and, of course, mariners were some of the main characters.

Ahnapee's first historian, George Wing, provided a vivid picture of just how maritime dependent the town was in its early days. In a reminiscence written about fifty years after the first settlers arrived from Racine, Wing wrote, "All roads led to . . . 'the mouth.' . . . Here was the center of all commercial life and activity. At the top of the hill there stood a frame building known as Youngs' store. It was also the post-office, as well as the emporium of trade, where salt pork, corn meal and other delicacies of the season were exchanged for ties, posts, bark and wood [cut from the land up river where pioneers were carving farms out of forest land]. . . . It was at 'the mouth' that the scows landed their freight from . . . up river ports; that fish boats wandering up and down the shores tied up for the night or in baffling winds; that white winged vessels came from over the blue waters from somewhere; that the weekly steamboat landed; here that the fishermen brought in their daily 'catches' of whitefish, and the men of the town toiled unloading [river] scows and loading [lake] vessels." The "up river ports" that Wing mentions were, of course, not ports in the usual sense of the word at all. They were simply places where families who were clearing land for farming brought whatever they could take from the land that was of economic value—cordwood, cedar posts, railroad ties, telegraph poles, shingle bolts, and shaved shingles. As Wing recalled, "Fifty years ago this river was a busy, teeming highway of traffic and navigation with regular ports of hail and docking along its shores. There were Hilton's Dock, Schmiling's Landing, Munn's Dock, Goettinger's Dock, Eveland's Dock and finally Forestville [nine miles upstream], where the weary scowmen tied up for the night, or stopped to take on a freight of wood, ties and posts."[1]

Wing could have gone on, and, in fact he did, at length, but in a much more prosaic fashion. As year succeeded year, a stronger, more diverse, and more vital community of people gathered around that "mouth." At the end of the century there were still those who could recall Native American wigwams erected on the beach to the south of the river mouth. They could recall also the characteristic "dogleg" bend that the river took when it ran up against the sandbar that was formed at the mouth of the river by the wave action of the lake; the day when crossing the river meant walking out on the sandbar and rolling up your pant legs to the knees so that you could wade across in your bare feet. But soon enough the bar was dredged to at least allow the passage of the fishermen's shallow draft boats and the river scows used as lighters to carry cargo back and forth to lake boats that anchored offshore. The scows could be poled in shallow water and carried a single sail that would be set when the wind was cooperative. They proliferated as more people produced more resources to be shipped. And by 1867 (it would have been sooner if the Civil War had not diverted the economy and life of the region) a small steamboat was built to tow those scows up and down the river to pick up and drop off cargo at the various "ports."[2]

Then came the pier, which allowed lake boats to unload directly onto terra firma. And the pier soon became the piers as the amount of shipping in and out of the settlement increased. Steamboats tied Ahnapee to larger communities to the south—Chicago, Kenosha, Racine, Milwaukee, Sheboygan, and Manitowoc. Immigrants who came to these older towns first quickly learned that there was undeveloped, and therefore cheaper, land to be had at the pier communities like Ahnapee, and so they came, sometimes in droves. While the residents of Racine, Wisconsin, who had been the first to establish permanent dwellings at Ahnapee had arrived in the sailing vessels and fishing boats by which they made their livings, the immigrants came by steamer. Among them were Frederick and Louise Schuenemann and their firstborn child, August.

Johann Friederich Ludwig Scheunemann was already twenty-eight years old in 1850 when he married Louise Caroline Friedericke Bietz (age twenty-four) at Lychen, Germany. If opportunity, at least the kind of opportunity that Johann Friederich thought himself capable of seizing, was there for him in Germany, he had not found it. His marriage to Louise must have been formed at least in part on their mutual determination to strike out in a new direction and find their fortune in North America, for no sooner had they married than they left for New York City. The trip across the ocean exhausted their meager resources, and so they had to live in New York State for several years before they could continue their journey west to Wisconsin, where land was cheap enough to be affordable and where they would be able to meld quickly into the transplanted German culture that was already there. Manitowoc was the Schuenemanns' first home in the west, but they did not live there more than a couple of years. It was a well-established town with rudimentary industries and developed farmland close at hand by the time they arrived. To fit the family budget they needed to seek out cheaper land, and as fate would have it, the land along the Ahnapee River was just being settled. Major Joseph McCormick, a man who had made a living by moving from region to region as the frontier of America moved west, buying land low and selling it high (or at least higher), was promoting the river valley because he had purchased land at the head of navigation on the Ahnapee River and he had a personal stake in pushing up real estate values. The major had convinced other newcomers in Manitowoc to get back on a steamboat and move to Ahnapee; it's possible that he might have been the moving force in the lives of the Schuenemanns as well.[3]

It was 1856, the year that David Youngs built the first pier at Ahnapee and the first year that a steam vessel made regular stops at the pioneer community, when Frederick and Louise left Manitowoc with their three-year-old son, August, and landed at the mouth of the Ahnapee River with their precious savings ready to be risked on some Ahnapee Valley forest land. They may have felt a little like dignitaries as they came ashore, for in those days, people turned out for the steamboat. As soon as it was spotted out in the lake making its ponderous way to the pier a cannon was fired in town to draw all the residents to the lakefront. In spite of the fact that the founders were New England Yankees and Brits who had come by way of Racine, the Schuenemanns would have had no trouble finding some German speakers in the crowd, not to mention on the boat. What greeted them was a very small village of a few homes and businesses crudely built with logs and slabs (the unwanted cuts from the outside of the logs that were sawed in the local sawmill). Roads were no more than wide beaten paths studded with tree stumps and overgrown with sorrel wherever traffic was not heavy. They led away from the pier with a bold promise of leading to rich land beyond but quickly petered out to footpaths or turned into soggy corduroy roads that ended in dismal swampy places. No church had yet been built. No school. No fire hall. No town hall. No warehouses or industry. Pigs roamed the streets along with goats, dogs, and cattle. Sawdust and other detritus from Hall's mill upstream floated in spongy mats on the languid waters of the river. Fishermen's nets and boats could be seen beside the river, and the pungent odor of offal from the fish shanties laced the offshore breeze that greeted the Schuenemanns as they arrived. Yet Ahnapee, when the Schuenemanns arrived at "the mouth," was unbounded potential, untapped opportunity, pure promise.

For the Schuenemanns, however, the potential was never realized, the opportunities were denied, and the promises were unfulfilled. By plan Frederick and Louise should have pioneered a farm to hand on to their children, who, in growing up on the land, would have learned all the skills necessary to provide for themselves and their families in an agrarian society. It started out that way. The couple, then in their middle thirties, bought land and began to homestead. They put nine years of sweat and blood into their investment before their dream started to unravel.

It is hard to imagine what life must have been like for those who were starting a farm in the midst of a virgin wilderness. There had been some logging done in advance of the immigrants' arrival, but not a great deal, and most would-be farmers faced heavily wooded and irregularly drained land. Poor drainage created the swamps, which were often populated by dense thickets of cedar trees. Clearing the land was backbreaking, mind-numbing work, alleviated only by the hope that one day the family might possess a productive homestead like those they saw to the south in settlements that were one and two decades old.

An idea of how labor intensive life was is provided by the diary of another Ahnapee Valley farmer, William Fagg. Fagg had immigrated with his family from Holland as a child and lived initially in Milwaukee until he was old enough to strike out on his own. He spent several years as a lumberjack on the Wisconsin River and its tributary, the Yellow River, and as a sailor and fisherman on Lake Michigan before he chose to settle down. He was still single when he bought his land but quickly met and married a young girl from another immigrant family. His diary tells us that he was an affable and well-educated young man. He made friends with people who had helped found the community and were ambitious in promoting it. These qualities, along with civic-mindedness, contributed to his being elected town clerk. But elected office did not save him from any of the labor that came with homesteading.[4]

The passages from Fagg's diary are often terse, as one would expect of a diary of a man who spent sunup to sundown in hard physical labor, but nonetheless they are very descriptive of a settler's life. There was plenty of work, but there was also lots of socializing among the residents. Here, in less than one hundred words, is a month in William Fagg's life in 1858, his first summer on the homestead.

1. to Cory's on a visit.
2. chop [wood].

3. to Ahnepee [this was an early spelling of the name].

4. chop. rain.

5. raising at Miller's.

6. and 7. very hot.

8. invited help to log.

9. and 10. logged for Nelson.

11. [went] to Wolf with Peters in boat.

12. hath logging bee. . . . plenty men. danced at night. some booze. all went right.

13. and 14. burned brush and logs.

15. S[unday]. heavy rain. it poured.

16. and 17. burned.

18. to Ahnepee.

19. Jos. Remington help me chop.

20. logged for Nelson.

21. to Wolf.

23. 24. 25. chopped. warm.

26. to raising at Stoneman. dance. whisky. fights between Nelson & Sloan. regular dog fight. Sloan pretty well pounded.

27. [ ] over to Peters. rain.

28. to mouth.

29. Sunday. rain.

30. and 31. burned brush.

The raisings, logging bees, dances, drinking and even the brawls all suggest a close and interconnected community. But note that the verbs that are used most are *chop, log,* and *burn.* As one season led to the next the work of clearing diminished, and Fagg turned his attention to hunting, butchering, making ties, shaving shingles, and a dozen other tasks. The one constant month after month was work, while the measures of progress were the recording of the first planting of potatoes or corn, digging a root cellar, raising a barn, and putting on a roof. Little by little, a farm was being created out of the forest.

Frederick and Louise Schuenemann did not leave a written account of their lives on the farm, but they lived within a couple of miles of William Fagg. Perhaps their social ties were different. Perhaps they did not have the language and social skills that allowed Fagg to become a leader in the township. But we can extrapolate with confidence that the fabric of their lives was similar. They, too, would have spent long days chopping, logging, and burning. They, too, would have made ties and shingles, hunted and fished to help keep body and soul together. And in all likelihood they would have begun to enjoy some of the same successes as they cleared enough land for potatoes and corn and, later, rye. They, too, would have joined in the social gatherings that combined work and entertainment in binges that led to exhaustion. But all this was to be cruelly and suddenly interrupted by a war that started thousands of miles away but engulfed the whole country and changed the lives of everyone in it. It was the Civil War, more than anything else, that explains why the first two sons of Frederick and Louise Schuenemann took up the sailor's life.

It wasn't Frederick Schuenemann's war. He had not immigrated to any particular state. "Northerner" and "Southerner" were labels that would not make any sense to him. He left Germany to come to America, any part of America that suited him, all of America. Slavery was abhorrent to him. He had seen too much of servitude and exploitation in the old country, but this problem was not of his making, and it was not up to him to undo it. Even though he had heard that Lincoln was a friend of the Germans, he considered himself a Democrat, as were the vast majority of the residents of Kewaunee County, Wisconsin. Still, when he was called, he went. In the fall of 1864 Kewaunee County was in its third draft, and this time Frederick Schuenemann's name was pulled from the hat. Some dodged, others deserted, and many who could afford it bought substitutes. But duty was in Frederick's nature as surely as blood coursed through his veins. When the time came he marched off to Green Bay and thence to Camp Randall in Madison, to spend a cold, wet, and miserable winter living in a tent.[5]

Finally, he was shipped to the front. But Frederick wasn't a part of

any of the man-eating battles that are so famous, nor was he consigned to the gruesome details, such as digging open graves in which
bodies would be stacked like so much cordwood. Vicksburg was
securely in the grasp of the Northern army by the time his unit started
south. The Mississippi and Ohio Rivers were open highways for the
Union navy to transport its goods and men. The heavy fighting was
happening in the East. He was lucky not to have been sent to Get-
tysburg or marched into the hellish Battle of the Wilderness. Instead,
Private Frederick Schuenemann was part of the great army of occupation. His unit, Company E of the Eleventh Wisconsin Infantry
(known as the "Farmers Guard"), had participated in the battle to
take Mobile, Alabama, the month before Frederick joined them.
From then until the end of the war they served guard duty on the
ground they had captured.[6]

Even without a battle, there were plenty of dark moments. Everywhere a soldier went in the last year of the war there were the injured
and maimed going home, missing legs, arms, hands—missing desire,
spirit, soul. Even in captured territory, there were still acts of violence
against the occupying forces, and no Union soldier could ever feel
totally safe. Pickets were shot from time to time by snipers. Cruelty
flowed both ways. Thieves, even desperately hungry thieves whose
only crime was to steal a loaf of bread or a pie left out to cool, were
sometimes shot at point-blank range by power-drunk soldiers just
because they could. Occupiers were sometimes capable of commit-
ting crimes of lust and bloodlust—upon white or black, slave or free,
it did not matter—that would make a hunter of fugitive slaves or an
overseer seem almost humane. And the Union soldiers were no more
merciful when they found a deserter in their ranks. The army's rules
said they must be punished, but in fact they were too often tortured.

But nightfall always brought a warm meal, a fire to sit by, stories
to tell, and music. There was always a roof, or at least a tent, to sleep
under. And there were other men from Wisconsin in Frederick
Schuenemann's detachment. Some of them were German immigrants like himself. Quiet talk around the evening fire might just as
likely have been in German as in English. The men talked about the
lives they had left behind in Europe, but more than that, they talked
about the land that they had come to. Not the *nation*. The *land*. How

many acres they had cleared; how they had drained the lowlands and swamps. What kind of soil was best for wheat; whether they had committed too many acres to flax. Even at a thousand miles distance, and in a country where the soil and the climate reminded them little of their northern farms, they talked their way through the seasons— preparing, planting, tending, harvesting, storing—observing by word and thought every ritual and task of the life that they were missing, living for the day they would return to the land, *their* land, always ready to match the stride of the seasons, to resume the life of the farmer.

The physical wound that the war left upon Frederick Schuene- mann did not come from a bullet or bayonet but from a disease. He spent a cold and rainy winter at Camp Randall, in Madison, Wiscon- sin, living in a tent city full of raw recruits, learning the manual of arms in English and German. There he contracted the bacterial infec- tion erysipelas, a disease that would neither kill nor deform but would make the remainder of his life miserable. This disease caused painful, burning facial eruptions along with fever, vomiting, and severe headache. At times, the burning spread to his eyes, making it painful for him even to open them to the light of day. Frederick's condition was bad enough to take him out of the line of battle but not so bad that he was sent home. The army needed every warm- blooded body it could find. So, Private Frederick Schuenemann, sometimes seeing clearly, sometimes blinded by his war disease, but always in physical distress, served out his enlistment in the Deep South, beside the muddy and tepid waters of the Mississippi River. And when he came home, he brought his disease with him.

The war effectively robbed Frederick Schuenemann of his dream of having his own farm. When he returned to the Ahnapee River valley, he had to confront the severity of his impairment. It would not allow him to do the hard physical labor of the farm. His two sons, August, age twelve, and Herman, less than one year old when Fred- erick arrived back home, could not pick up the slack. Ultimately, the Schuenemanns were forced to sell the land and move into the town of Ahnapee. This was the crucial turning point in the life of the fam- ily that turned August and Herman toward making a living as lake sailors.[7]

In town the Schuenemanns lived in the Third Ward on the north side of the river, a neighborhood where German was spoken more frequently than English. At least at times, Frederick was able to work as a skilled laborer, but there were more times when his illness kept him from living the full life that he might have had. Life could be crushing with multiple problems stacking up against the family. In 1875 Ahnapee was suffering along with the rest of the nation through an economic malaise. In addition, the winter was particularly harsh that year in northern Wisconsin, and poorer members of the community were left without the ability to heat their homes and fill their stomachs. That year the Schuenemann family appeared on the roll of the county's poor.[8] Frederick's health was in decline at the same time, and in the midst of the winter's cold, he suffered a stroke, and his infection flared to the point where he was totally blind and had to be admitted to the Soldiers' Home in Milwaukee for a protracted stay. It was four months before he could return home, and even then his eyesight was only partially restored.[9] That was the year that Frederick applied for a government pension as a Civil War veteran. It was a fight. Pensions were not awarded lightly, and multiple witnesses had to testify that he was unable to support his family due to his illness. But finally Frederick won. For the rest of his life, he would receive a pension.[10]

Herman was only a babe in arms when his father returned from the war. He was but nine during that crushing winter of 1875. His older brother, August, however, was twenty-two that year and had already found work on the small lake boats that called Ahnapee home. Captain Johnny Doak had taken him under his wing.[11]

As the Schuenemanns looked down from the front yard of the little house where they lived in the Third Ward, the town of Ahnapee spread out before them. The river ran by sluggishly at the foot of the hill, where a bridge crossed to the main business district on the south bank. Fish shanties and drying racks were on one side of the river. On the other side were factories—a brewery, brickyard, granary, sawmill. The mouth of the river with its pier, shipyard, fish shanties, storehouses, and docks opened out to the limitless lake, reaching to the horizon from which the sun rose heralding a daily new beginning. It was easy for a young man who grew up with hardship and poverty to imagine a better life beyond that horizon, especially after listening to the stories of the sailors who seemed to come and go so freely in their white-winged or smoke-spouting vessels. The 1870s and '80s, when the Schuenemann boys were moving from boyhood to adulthood, were the golden decades in the commercial maritime life of the village, and the men who worked on the boats were perfect objects for a boy's idolatry.

Most of the men who worked along the river were part of the early settlement group that had come from Racine and points south, and a good number of them had further distinguished themselves by heroic service in the army or navy during the Civil War. William I. Henry had come as a fisherman and stayed to be a shipwright on the river. During the war he saw some of the bitterest fighting and was rewarded with the rank of major. Henry Harkins was a sailor first and then built many of the river scows that plied the Ahnapee River. He had served on the fleet of Union gunboats that wrested the Mississippi away from the Confederacy. Charles Ross, a ruddy Scotsman, was the town's chief tug captain for years and performed his duties with one arm, having lost the other at the battle of Stone River. John McDonald, another amputee from war wounds (he lost an arm), was the first owner of the scow-schooners *Lady Ellen* and *Whiskey Pete*. These men, and others like them, seized early opportunities wherever they found them and were equipped with the skills that made them successful pioneers in a maritime village. They positioned themselves between the farm and the market and thus became a vital link in the region's economy. They built the river vessels that collected the forest and farm products coming off the land. They built the piers that allowed the produce to be transferred from the river scows to the lake boats that visited the town. They arranged for the forwarding of goods from Ahnapee to the larger market cities to the south. And they took the helm of boats in Ahnapee's small fleet.[12]

Coming home from the war with pluck and drive instilled by the harrowing experience of surviving battle and hardship, they began building almost right away. In the winter of 1866–67 three vessels were being planned for construction on the Ahnapee River. Two were commercial sailing crafts intended for the lake trade. The third was a steamer to be used on the river.[13]

Captain Henry Harkins, shown here wearing his naval uniform, was an early settler, sailor, and shipbuilder in Ahnapee, Wisconsin. (Photo from the private collection of Janet G. Pearson.)

A friendly competition developed between the builders of the two commercial sailing crafts. Both wanted the honor of launching the first vessel constructed on the Ahnapee River, and so the race was on to see which boat would be ready for launching on July 4 to coincide with the one celebration that brought the entire community together. The local favorite was a small sloop of fifty tons capacity being built under the supervision of Captain Henry Harkins of Ahnapee. It was a scow of humble line and small stature, and its name was to be *Irene*. When the scow slipped into the river on July 4 1867, it was a historic day for the little town and a proud moment for the local builder, sailor, fisherman, and war hero Hank Harkins.[14] The only thing that marred the celebration of the achievement was the fact that the rival, and larger, boat, a two-masted scow-schooner christened the *Ahnapee of Chicago,* was completed and launched on the first of the month. The *Ahnapee* had been financed from outside the community, was owned by a Chicago investor, and was built by a shipwright who was "imported" to Ahnapee from Sheboygan. Nonetheless, it was built to serve as a link between Ahnapee and the booming city of Chicago to the south, and few in the Ahnapee Valley could miss the significance of its launch for their economic future. The night before the launching two hundred people from up and down the valley gathered to dance to fiddle music on the vessel's deck and to drink to their future as farmers who would now certainly have a market for their goods in the city where the schooner was owned.[15]

The steam-scow, however, while the lowliest of the three vessels built that winter, was the most vital to the future of the region. Its building was so little celebrated that we don't even know if the vessel was given a name. But its role, and that of its successors on the river, was to be the link between the families that labored in the valley and the world beyond. The vessel's builders were Abisha Perry and William Nelson, and little is known about it other than that it was a small scow with a housing built over its steam engine and a paddle wheel for propulsion at the stern. Yet, humble as it was, the Perry and Nelson steam tug was the vessel that would propel Ahnapee into the future. Before the steam tug local farmers either had to sail their scow loads of forest and farm products downstream with the help of a crude square sail mounted on a removable mast or use a long pole to push the scow down the river in the time honored tradition of rivermen from the East Coast to the Mississippi. The meandering river with its many shallows and bends made the trip arduous to say the least, and the difficulties multiplied with the trip home against the stream. With the Perry and Nelson steam tug, however, farmers and foresters could stay on their land and invest their time in developing it further while the tug crew picked up their scow load of produce and took it to market in Ahnapee.[16]

A specialization of labor was developing in the valley and town.

Farmers stuck more and more to farming as fields were cleared and marketable crops came to fruition. Boatmen took on the particular duties of transporting goods to market. And, in town, merchants and forwarding agents did the work of getting the goods shipped out to the larger markets beyond. This specialization was a sure sign that the economy of the area was growing and diversifying. Those who started out as subsistence farmers were becoming agrarian business-men, and they were growing crops in sufficient quantities to begin to export them to urban communities around the lakes. Capital earned from marketable crops provided the means to buy machinery, which, in turn, increased the productivity of the farmers still more.[17]

Comparing William Fagg's diary of August 1869 with the passage from the summer of 1858 shows a dramatic change in the farmer's life.

August 6 and 7th. cutting wheat.

8th. plowed & hawled [*sic*] in wheat.

9th. to town.

10. cut wheat.

11th. finished wheat & plowed. rain. S. night.

S. 12. cool, cloudy.

Sunday 19th. sowed my winter wheat 4 bush & finished harvesting this week. to Ahnepee Friday. bought new stove,
etc. splendid growing weather.

20. sunny. cold. plowed, logged, burned & dug potatoes this
week.

Chop, log, and *burn* have almost disappeared from Fagg's vocabulary. They were replaced with the words *cut, plow, haul, sow,* and *harvest.* The lumbering that dominated 1858 had given way to the raising of cash crops, and with money in his pocket, William Fagg was able to bring home to his family a modern convenience—a new stove.

The productivity of farmers increased as each year passed. Even the devastating firestorm of 1871 was viewed in hindsight by some as a blessing. It was credited with helping the farmers by clearing the land of timber and turning their attention away from such pursuits as shin-gle making and toward planting. In 1875 the farmers of the region surrounding Ahnapee had a banner year. So much wheat was harvested that the old school building was turned into a warehouse and the Masonic Hall was used as a storage shed by the company in Manitowoc that was buying and exporting the crop. There were days in the fall when eighteen hundred to two thousand bushels of wheat were coming into town in a day.[18] The Manitowoc schooner *Glen Cuyler* took repeated cargoes of bagged wheat, and as the fall rush peaked the schooners *Espindola* and *Industry* also took cargoes.[19] At least two warehouses were built that year for storing agricultural crops awaiting shipment by boat.[20] Even while other regions of the country were experiencing an economic slump, the wheatlands of Wisconsin were prospering. "The farmers have sown their broad acres, and are now in the midst of a bountiful harvest. . . . with a little personal bravery, with a stout hand and a clear conscience, there is not one man in a hundred but that can support his family, keep out of debt, and have a little left at the end of the year," announced the local newspaper. "There is abundance in the land, and all that is required for each to live well is to exercise prudence and common industry."[21]

As the farmers prospered, so too did the rivermen and lake sailors. In fact, people in Ahnapee began to have grand visions of what might become of their village. Other miracles of growth had occurred along the same lakeshore; why not a new miracle at Ahnapee? In the true spirit of boosterism the sky was the limit, but the hype was intended more to sell land and attract settlers and investors than as a sincere prediction of the future.

As the economy grew, however, a new kind of businessman arrived. These individuals came with their fortunes already made and were seeking a place where they could put their capital to work. Their resources were of the magnitude that earlier settlers could only have dreamed of. Their goal was to position themselves so that the town would serve as a moneymaking machine for them. Their opponents called them the "clique" and did everything they could to keep them from using their wealth to corner the town's economy. In the ensuing struggle the community was sorely tested. Some of the most critical battles in the war against this entrepreneurial clique took place at the mouth of the river. Hence, the sailors of Ahnapee played a crucial role in the outcome. Some even became populist heroes.

THE CLIQUE
TAKES CONTROL

An aristocracy of mere wealth is vulgar everywhere. In a
republic, it is vulgar in the extreme. This is the only kind
of vulgarity I saw in the United States.

—Harriet Martineau, *Society in America*

The aggregation of large amounts of capital in few hands
is the first condition for the fulfillment of the most important tasks of civilization which now confront us.

—William Graham Sumner

*L*ike it or not, the farmers and sailors and small businessmen of
Ahnapee had to sit up and take notice of the entrepreneurs. The first
wave of settlers brought enough resources with them to buy some
land and to open businesses like stores and a sawmill, but they were
not wealthy enough to dominate any one area of business. They
competed with each other on a fairly equal basis, and out of that
competition came a small but diverse business community with some
members who were native born and others who had immigrated
from Belgium, Switzerland, Germany, and Canada.

There has already been occasion to mention some of the Racine residents who came early to Ahnapee and helped to lay out the town, build the first pier, start the first businesses, fell the first trees, and break the first ground. It has been noted, too, that they were themselves short-haul sailors—men like David Youngs, Hank Harkins, Charles L. Fellows, Abram Eveland. There were other notable movers and shakers as well in the first flush of settlement before the Civil War, when there were still tree stumps in the middle of the streets and nomadic Native Americans camping on the beach and residents took turns walking to Manitowoc to get the mail. These pioneers arrived with little to their names and built their lives on the most meager of foundations.[1] Samuel and Matthew Perry, two brothers from County Antrim in Ireland who came by way of Toronto, got off the legendary side-wheel steamer *Lady Elgin* in Manitowoc in the mid-1850s and, by chance, met the land promoter Joseph McCormick. Major McCormick spoke to them about the fertile and cheap land further north in the Ahnapee River valley. The Perry brothers were intrigued, and they ended up, along with two more Perry brothers, buying land in the valley. Some of that land almost certainly came from acreage that McCormick had bought as an investment.[2]

Unlike eastern speculators, who bought land through agents but remained absentee landlords, Joseph McCormick had always moved to where the frontier was and was directly involved in the communities that he helped to found. Born ten years after the American Revolution on the banks of the Susquehanna River, and raised in upper New York State, McCormick was a child of the frontier. His father was born in County Antrim, Ireland, and had come to North America as a British soldier. During the Revolutionary War, however, he switched sides to join the American army. Later, he owned an inn at Painted Post, New York, that a French traveler of noble descent described as serving "rusty bacon and coffee" for dinner and providing a bed on which "the sheets had already served . . . for some time," making him "extremely reluctant" to sleep there even when fully dressed.[3]

Joseph's childhood playmates were the rough and ready woodland children, and his first calling was as a raftsman on the Susquehanna River. As the line of settlement moved west, over the Alleghany watershed and down the Ohio River, Joseph went with it, buying land cheap and reselling it to newcomers. Because he knew the ways of business and politics and had befriended people who had risked all to find a new home, he became a leader in the communities that he helped to found. (Both in Indiana and in Wisconsin his local popularity lifted him up to serve in the state legislature. A chapter of his life that cannot be confirmed and may be apocryphal pertains to his role in Texas. He is said to have helped draft the first constitution.)[4] By the time he settled in Wisconsin his advanced age was a real asset. It gave him a special aura as an American who had known people from the founding generation of the democracy. At the same time, the ways of County Antrim were still ingrained in him. The lilt in his speech and the gregariousness of his personality made him an attractive figure to immigrants who, literally, had just gotten off the boat.[5]

With encouragement from McCormick the Perry brothers became important leaders in the community of Ahnapee and the surrounding countryside. They first pioneered homesteads on property in Forestville bought from Major McCormick. But eventually they developed a family business strategy. Samuel moved to the town of Ahnapee, where he opened a store, became a popular leader, and was eventually elected mayor. Matthew, Richard, and John occupied land near Forestville, the furthest point upstream that the Ahnapee River was navigable, and the site of an early mill. They were popular among their neighbors, always ready to help out in a "logging bee" or barn raising, and when Matthew, who played the fife, was around there was music for a dance that lasted through the night.

The brothers' work of cutting trees off the land and floating the harvest down to the village of Ahnapee gave Sam the material he needed to become a commission merchant buying forest products and reselling them as exports from the valley, while importing and selling manufactured goods in his store. Sam earned a permanent place in the business community of Ahnapee, and his name can be found among the leaders who made virtually all the important decisions for the town. His mercantile business became the largest in Ahnapee, and he both contracted with local sailors and invested in vessels of his own to carry the wood products he bought from local farmers. His success may have been part of the reason why he married Major McCormick's granddaughter.

Meanwhile, Matthew and Richard both served in the Civil War and became local heroes for their roles in the Battles of Shiloh, Corinth, and Lookout Mountain. A touching scene from the oral history of the region describes a contingent of troops leaving the pier at Ahnapee, headed for the battlefront. Among them are fifer Matthew Perry and drummer Richard Perry, standing on the deck of the steamer and playing "The Girl I Left Behind Me" as the boat pulled away from the pier. As a part of Company E of the Fourteenth Wisconsin Infantry the Perry brothers were in a celebrated group of Ahnapee citizens that included other local heroes like Major William I. Henry, William Nelson, and William Fagg. For decades after the war, whenever the members of the Grand Old Army would reunite Matthew and Richard would be prominent among them with their fife and drum at the ready.[6]

Men like the Perrys, McCormicks, Youngs, and so on, were vital to the community and formed the core of businessmen who had the wherewithal to create the basic structures that allowed a local economy to develop. Still, they were not at the top of the heap economically. Above them was that very small group of very wealthy men called the "clique" who arrived later. Because they could outspend the core business group, these new arrivals came to dominate the town. While the businessmen of the Perry-McCormick-Youngs type had fluctuating fortunes, the very wealthy had the resources to ride out hard times and take advantage of them by buying up the assets of those whose wealth was depleted. The clique presented two faces to the community. On the one hand, their capital fueled enterprises that provided opportunity for others. On the other hand, their capital also allowed them to have a stranglehold on many of the ambitions of the community. They may have been respected, catered to, even feared by some, but they were not liked. Their cooperation was often necessary to make things work, but it was sought begrudgingly. To challenge their power was to risk ruin. Not to challenge their power was to be subservient.

In 1884 one of those businessmen of the Perry-McCormick-Youngs type wrote a letter to a member of the clique. The poor spelling should not be taken as evidence that the author was uneducated or low achieving. This man had, in fact, been one of the handful whose economic investment, business acumen, and sense of civic duty had set Ahnapee on its course in the first few years of its existence. His name was Matthias Simon, and he had come from Germany. His family's home was the fifth permanent dwelling in Ahnapee and was located on the north side of the river near the bluff, where there was a good view of the lake. At first he engaged in subsistence living by fishing and farming, but as people came to settle in the area and the potential to trade with the outside developed, Matthias made the transition to businessman. He associated himself with several other German immigrants who had the capital and ambition to match his own, and, like the Perrys, they began to wholesale the products of the forest going out of town and retail the manufactured goods that were imported. Like the Perry brothers, Matthias was rewarded with the public's trust. He held the position of postmaster and later became involved in politics, holding offices in the township, county, and state.[7]

For reasons that are not known, Matthias Simon's prosperity did not last, and his influence in the community waned. He spent the last years of his life living at the county poor farm, much to the chagrin of friends and family who knew him when he was what Ahnapee's first historian (George Wing) called "the aristocrat of the pioneer community." At the age of eighty-eight he died destitute and on the dole. The 1884 letter to the member of the clique chronicles a moment in his sad decline into poverty and the clique's ascendance to economic dominance. "Deer Sir, as a Frind I have to ask you for a little aid as Mr. Ellis dit not keep his word with me and dit not git me a plaese in Madison[.] so I am hard up and I would like for you to let me have an order on Fax and Co. or on your own store here in Ahnapee for abouth 15 dollars[.] I will give it back to you agin as soon as I will git work to ern someting[.] I tried [illegible] got anyting to put on my feeth and no provision of any acount. let me here from you soon and help me. your Respectfully[,] M. Simon." Fortunately, most of the early pioneers did not fall on such hard times, but once the clique got together, there were very few projects requiring a major economic investment that were not funded at least in part by its members.[8]

The power and influence that came from being the pioneers of the community was bound to give way to the power of money. Early settlers and immigrants alike were at the mercy of the clique because they threatened to monopolize the marketplace with their wealth. At the core of the clique were two easterners, Charles Griswold Boalt and Edward Decker. They were very different in temperament and background, but when it came to doing business, they spoke the same language.

Charles Griswold Boalt invested himself in Ahnapee, quite literally, but Ahnapee never became his "home" with the sentiments that are usually implied by that word. He was a Connecticut Yankee when he arrived in Wisconsin and remained a Connecticut Yankee until his death. Although he had never actually lived in New England, he was as much of a blue-blooded New Englander as anyone from the New England region could be. Charles's father had moved to Huron County, Ohio, with his family when he was only fifteen years old, and set himself on an ambitious path that took him to a place of great prominence and wealth. At an early age he left the family farm to study and practice law. Whether he did it for love or money, it surely did not hurt his prospects to marry the daughter of a former governor of Connecticut and go into banking. In 1850, he became the president of one of the nation's first successful railroad companies. The railroad, which followed the southern shoreline of Lake Erie, eventually became a vital link in the connection between New York City and Chicago. So, even though he grew up in frontier Ohio, Charles's father was, by marriage, politics, business relations, and money, an integral part of the eastern establishment. Through his veins coursed the blood of the original stock of the nation's founding generation. By his life in the West he zealously carried forward the mission of transforming the wilderness into the garden of civilization. As such he lived the lifestyle of a wealthy mogul and enjoyed his role as the patriarch of a large and influential family.[9]

The Boalt children, under the tutelage of their father, followed the precedent he set of getting an education, marrying well, connecting politically, going into business, and making lots of money. Several of Charles Griswold Boalt's siblings became wealthy entrepreneurs themselves, and at least one of them gained a national reputation as a lawyer and jurist.[10] The common path that the Boalt children followed was to find a place on the expanding geographic and economic frontier of the nation to invest their money and to parlay what wealth they had to an even greater wealth.

Charles's first ventures as a young man in the West took him to Illinois, where the Illinois Central Railroad was being built, and then to Wisconsin, where a rich bed of iron ore was being mined and refined. His early career was obviously guided by the financial interests of his father. As a major investor in the iron mines in Wisconsin, the Boalt patriarch was president of the company, while Charles himself served as secretary. But eventually it was time for Charles to make his own independent forays into the world of business and politics. Five years after he came to Wisconsin to run his father's iron mining business, and two years after he married Agnes Gillet, the daughter of another New England aristocratic family, young Charles Griswold Boalt staked his personal claim in the future of Ahnapee. The U.S. Census of 1860 gives his age as twenty-five and the combined value of his personal and real estate as an amazing $175,000. Before he had even begun his entrepreneurial ventures in Ahnapee he was already far and away the wealthiest man in the town. But Boalt lived "in" Ahnapee for much of the next thirty years without ever being "of" Ahnapee. He was separated from the townspeople by his wealth as well as by his continuing close ties with Ohio. (Once they had children, Agnes took the youngsters and moved back to their home state, and Charles frequently visited them there.) For Boalt, the blue blood, the scion of those Yankees who first lit the lamp of liberty that was destined to shine across the whole continent, Ahnapee was the mission field, the colony in which he established his estate, while Chicago was the city, the engine of commerce, where he went to conduct business. But Ohio always remained his home, and it is there that his remains rest with those of his siblings in the shadow of the massive marble obelisk that marks his father's grave.[11]

Boalt's strategy for securing his place in Ahnapee was consistent and relentless. He would control the mouth of the river and as much of the waterfront as he could take title to. Once he had this geography in his grasp, he would be in a position to profit from all of the trade that came in or out of the town. Everyone—farmer, manufacturer, merchant—would have to pay him a percentage of what they shipped because every vessel would have to dock on his property and every item of cargo would have to pass over his land. One of his first acquisitions, financed by his substantial capital, was a controlling interest in the commercial pier that had been built at the mouth by David Youngs. In addition, he bought about half of the plat of the town, most especially the lakeshore property surrounding the mouth of the river and stretching to the south.[12]

Joining Boalt in his business strategy was Edward Decker, another New Englander who, before the Civil War, had alienated himself from the majority of the citizens of the county by his use of political office to line his own pockets. Decker was one of the coarser specimens of New England culture, not a blue blood who prospered by advantage of his place in society but instead a business shark who prospered by means of his ability to grab and hold onto more than his fair share of the nation's latent resources. The catalog of scandalous activity in which Decker was involved is truly impressive. As the first county clerk he was accused of rigging an election, of levying "most unconscionable" taxes on absentee landowners, of using the tax laws to defraud the Potawatomie (among other Native Americans) of their privately held land, and of using the interest earned on county funds for his private purposes. In what was most certainly a triumph of grassroots democracy, Decker was eventually voted out of the county clerk's office and was never able to get a political toehold in the county after that. But he had already used his position to gain a stranglehold on large sections of the county's marketable resources. Still his self-serving, controlling, and penurious ways of using the money he had virtually stolen from the common purse continued to make him a favorite target of all but those who went to him for a loan. One articulate laborer who came west to Wisconsin from Decker's hometown in Maine wrote home about Decker: "He is meaner and snugger than old Nate Decker ever was. He is worth about 800,000 dollars [but] he skins every thing and every body that he gets hold of."[13]

Boalt and Decker never questioned their right as patricians to dominate the economy of the region. While Boalt was focused on maintaining tight control over the maritime access to the region, Decker tried to restore his political standing, became a banker, and was forever busy with one scheme or another to bring a railroad to the port towns of Kewaunee and Ahnapee. On the personal side of life he was widowed four times and was married five times and drew attention to himself by choosing ever more wealthy women as his brides. (The family of his second wife even accused him of poisoning her so that he could take possession of all her property while marrying a widow of even greater means from Manitowoc.) Decker also raised two sons, David and Edward Jr. His namesake tried to follow his father into politics and failed. A couple of months later he bested his father in his self-serving ways by arranging to disappear from a steamer that was crossing Lake Michigan. While people speculated on whether it had been an accident or a suicide, Edward Jr. was on his way to California with a satchel full of money from one of the family's banks.[14]

Local residents did not miss the fact that Boalt and Decker, with the help of some other locals, had formed a clique that was seeking to have a ruling interest in virtually every aspect of the region's economy. Early on, farmers and merchants, among whom Samuel Perry and Matthias Simon were prominent, recognized that Boalt and Decker were profiting at their expense. The angry opponents of the clique were determined not to make themselves reliant on the clique. Not coincidentally, the majority of these opponents were immigrants from Germany and other European countries. But breaking Boalt and Decker's stranglehold on the town's commerce meant finding a different way to ship goods in and out of Ahnapee.

The response of local farmers and merchants to the clique was to promote various projects for harbor improvement that would allow them to circumvent the clique-owned docking area. The first such effort occurred in 1866 when sixty farmers and merchants formed a joint stock company to build a second pier that was meant to compete with the clique's pier. (Two of the three directors of the pier company were close personal associates of Matthias Simon.) Even though Charles G. Boalt attempted to block it with legal action (he had been elected a county court judge), the Ahnepee Farmers' Pier Company achieved its goal in 1868, and for a while Ahnapee boasted two piers—the original pier at the mouth of the river, which was owned by Boalt and his associates, and another pier several hundred yards to the south.[15] The future looked bright for the farmers after the court gave them authority to build, and progress on construction of the pier went quickly.[16] The first vessel to take on a cargo at the new pier was captained by Hank Harkins, the naval hero, the builder of the *Irene,* and one of the early founders who had moved to Ahnapee from Racine. Still, the clique managed in the end to nullify competition from the Farmers' Pier through a brilliant stroke of chicanery and deception. Boalt hired an agent who surreptitiously bought up the majority of the pier company's stock, using money borrowed from Edward Decker. When the next stockholders' meeting was convened, the clique simply voted their own candidates into office as directors of the company. Thereafter, the Farmers' (or South) Pier was no threat. Eventually, it fell into disuse and was finally abandoned after being damaged by ice in the spring of 1876.[17]

About the same time that Boalt was fighting to assert and maintain his hold on the maritime commerce, he hired local shipbuilder William I. Henry Sr. to build the largest vessel that was ever constructed in Ahnapee. It would be christened the *Bessie Boalt,* after Charles Griswold Boalt's first daughter, Elizabeth. The schooner was a showpiece for Boalt. It represented the link by which he could turn the raw material of northeastern Wisconsin into raw capital by transporting it to the urban markets of Milwaukee and Chicago. He had the schooner built directly on the shore of the lake rather than along the river, probably because its size would not have permitted it to be launched into the river's shallow waters as had the smaller scow type hulls (the *Ahnepee of Chicago* and *Irene*) built previously. The vessel was 103 feet in length, 26 feet at its widest point, measured 8.6 feet from the deck to the bottom of the keel, and had two masts rigged for fore-and-aft sails. It was later reported that the schooner cost $32,000 to build, but it seems almost certain that the cost was inflated, as the same year that it was built commercial boatyards on Lake Michigan were building larger, three-masted schooners of excellent quality for half that much money. It was also passed down in the town's history that the *Bessie Boalt* was the only vessel in Ahnapee to follow such formal maritime practices as keeping strict watches rung in by the ship's bell. Indeed, there are a number of details about the *Bessie Boalt* that clearly suggest that it was meant to be a boat that showed its pedigree—a better class of boat—a blue blood like its owner. It was said that the boat's first captain wore an official uniform with a brass-buttoned coat—definitely not the common standard of dress among Ahnapee sailors, whose work clothes were no different than those of the farmer or the teamster. The captain also had an inside connection that helped him get the job. He was married to Charles Griswold Boalt's sister, Cornelia.[18]

While living on a different social level, Boalt was not completely isolated from the citizenry of Ahnapee. Indeed, he reached out to local talent through his diverse business interests. Two individuals who stand out in addition to William I. Henry, the shipwright, are De Wayne Stebbins and John McDonald. Interestingly, all three of these men had served valiantly in the Civil War and were heroes in town. Henry and Stebbins came home in one piece, but McDonald (as has been mentioned already) lost an arm to a battle wound. (Boalt himself did not serve. He bought a substitute to serve for him and later made a trip to visit the troops and show his moral support for their efforts.) The men Boalt hired, with their natural prominence and respectability, put a presentable public face on his business dealings in the town. The Boalt and Youngs Pier became the Boalt and Stebbins Pier after David Youngs was bought out. Across the river was John McDonald's commercial fishing operation. While Boalt was away from Ahnapee (in Chicago mostly) cultivating the markets for the products that passed over his pier, these men carried on the local business dealings.

It is noteworthy, too, that Boalt's business partners were native English speakers, especially when his nativist attitudes toward immigrants are known. On the one hand, Boalt welcomed immigration because it provided the pool of human labor needed to make the economy of the new West work. But, on the other hand, he clearly felt that the immigrant class in Ahnapee was lacking in respect for the opportunities that their new country offered them and, by extension, for the opportunities that entrepreneurs such as himself had created through their investment of capital. He even went so far as to chastise the non-English-speaking citizens of Ahnapee publicly by turning the word *Germans* into a rubric of dishonor. Boalt, the xenophobe and capitalist, chose a Fourth of July speech to the whole town of Ahnapee to speak out. He boldly called his immigrant neighbors' loyalty and commitment to a democratic society into question, arguing that any "German" who questioned the right of capitalists (such as himself) to dictate the terms of labor to the workingman was subverting the principles upon which the country was founded. Such residents were ingrates who did not recognize the opportunities that their new country offered. They were self-indulgent, seeking the easy road to economic success rather than working hard to gain their wealth by their own toil and sweat. Even more insidious, they were communists and religious fanatics who sought to undermine progress by opposing the economic ambitions of true Americans and patricians such as himself.

Of course, tension between native born and immigrant Americans was a pervasive fact of life in America. "The average American citizen in those days . . . was inclined to look down on the man of foreign birth as not quite as good. . . . To use a common phrase, a 'Dutchman' is all right, but Americans are just a bit superior as men go."[19] In Wisconsin there were some clear battle lines drawn with legislation that pertained to using English only in public schools and debates over consuming alcohol, especially on the Christian Sabbath. Labor unrest was also associated with foreign instigators. But successful politicians were learning to be more conciliatory toward the German population if they wished to be elected.[20] Boalt, however, was not only not conciliatory, he was pointedly antagonistic. He believed he was battling against an active plan among Ahnapee's "Germans" to subvert the proper order as laid down by the founders of the nation and followed by native born Americans such as himself.[21]

Imagine the parade that Independence Day down Steele Street past the business establishments of Melchior, Kohlbach, Reinhardt, and Perry. The German brass band played martial music as it walked in formation down the street. Young boys with German, Slavic, and French accents shouldered play guns made out of sticks, giving their imitation of what their soldier-heroes must have looked like as the Yanks marched through Atlanta and Richmond. The immigrant priest of Saint Mary's Roman Catholic Church walked with dignity, wearing all the fine vestments that were due his office, blessing the crowds in his thick accent and leading a guild of devotees who carried the magnificently colored statue of the Virgin Mary. The young

FOURTH OF JULY INDUSTRIAL PARADE.
AHNAPEE, WISCONSIN, JULY, 1886.

The Fourth of July parade at Ahnapee in 1886, six years after Charles G. Boalt's antagonizing speech to the citizenry. (State Historical Society of Wisconsin, WHi(X3)38443.)

girls and boys of the catechism class from the German Lutheran church, dressed in bleached white, stiffly starched shirts and dresses, were shepherded by their pastor. Members of the volunteer fire department pulled their steam pump down the street eagerly anticipating that they would be drinking German beer at Weilep's or Barstar's Tavern at the end of the day. Aspiring mechanics and sportsters with names like Hamachek and Pavlecek showed off the newest invention—the bicycle. Politicians and civic officials who came from the German ward north of the river, laborers in the furniture factory who had left the farm to live in cramped tenement housing, and women with babes in arms and calloused hands stood by the bunting draped reviewing stand and waved small American flags.

No one in this conglomeration of humanity shared Charles Griswold Boalt's life experience as a native born American raised in the home of a wealthy industrialist with a fragile and artistic mother and a nanny to lay out his clothes in the morning, check his lessons in the afternoon, and draw his bath at night. But it was to this congregation that Judge Boalt delivered his scolding words about the ingratitude of the immigrant class and their lack of appreciation for the American way that he exemplified.

SAILORS IN THE
BATTLE FOR THE HARBOR

Hope springs eternal in the human breast.
—Alexander Pope

*C*harles Griswold Boalt's speech was, of course, an expression of his personal beliefs and his personal interests. "In our desire to acquire property we must respect the rights of others [already] in the possession of their property," he told Ahnapee's "Germans." The property rights that were being challenged were *his* property rights. "In the desire to acquire influence we must avoid destroying the reputation of others by slander." The reputation that was being slandered was *his* reputation. And, in a maritime-dependent town, it is not surprising that the particular property rights and principles that were being challenged had to do with the harbor. For Boalt his rights as a landowner clearly gave him the power to dictate what happened on the waterfront, but growing opposition in the town was fed by a rising sentiment that the harbor should provide an equal opportunity for all citizens to transact business. Boalt saw no conflict between what was good for him as an individual entrepreneur and what was good for the community. But in this conviction he stood with the minority of Ahnapeans.

The more that farmers, merchants, and owners of small manufacturing businesses prospered, the more pressing became the issue of who dictated access to Ahnapee's waterfront. The decade of the 1870s was the time for this battle to reach a feverish peak. At the same time that farmers began producing cash crops far in excess of what they could sell locally or even regionally, merchants were able to bring into town the kinds of manufactured goods that farmers could now afford to buy. Everything from mechanized farm tools to the modern phenomenon of pretailored clothing became marketable. In addition, the kinds of agriculture being practiced were expanding, and so farmers of the area were buying such imported stock as fruit trees, sheep, and livestock. Meanwhile, brickmaking, furniture making, tanning, and lumber and grist milling were some of the industries that sought markets beyond the region's borders. All of these commodities moved by boat.

The defeat of the farmers who had formed the cooperative pier company in the late 1860s demonstrated the power of entrepreneurs like Boalt and Decker to maintain economic control over the community. But the Farmers' Pier Company was only the first in a series of attempts of the citizenry to reclaim the harbor as a community asset. The next groundswell of public opinion demanding a harbor with free access came in 1870, two years after the clique took over the Farmers' Pier. This time the appeal was even more broadly based, and it resulted in the citizens of the township voting to support a $20,000 bond issue in order to raise money for the river to be opened to commercial traffic.[1] With a dredged channel, so it was thought, lake vessels could navigate upstream beyond the land owned by the clique, thus breaking the clique's stranglehold. William Fagg, the farmer and town official whose diary was dipped into previously, recorded his enthusiasm for a community harbor: "election April 6th [1870]. Great excitement. Harbor or no Harbor. Harbor unanimously carried."[2] In fact, the vote was a resounding 262 in favor with only 23 voting against. The people had spoken. It could not be denied. An open harbor was clearly a popular cause.[3]

But it was one thing to approve a bond issue. It was yet another to sell the bonds and collect the money. The project languished. The people who wanted the harbor were not the people who had the large sums of capital to invest.[4] Ahnapeans learned that they needed another source of money, and they, like citizens all over the Great Lakes region, began to look to the federal government. Competition for harbor improvement funds was fierce in the age when pork-barrel politics was invented. Every sizable lakeshore community had some rationale for asserting that their need was greater or more worthy than that of other towns. For Ahnapeans, the rationale was that Lake Michigan needed harbors of refuge to protect shipping from the frequent life-threatening storms that struck the lake at all seasons. Ahnapee, they argued, was in an ideal position to offer protection for those vessels that were passing up and down the lake between the populous cities of Chicago and Milwaukee and the more protected waters of the straits connecting Lakes Michigan, Huron, and Superior. Ahnapee's community boosters took up the challenge of beating the drum for the harbor of refuge designation.

Even before the bonds approved in April 1870 could be issued, the government came through with a public works project that would build a harbor of refuge at Ahnapee by deepening the Ahnapee River and building protective piers at the mouth. In that bright moment of hope, it must have seemed that the prayers of the clique's opponents had been answered. But instead the survey made by the Army Corps of Engineers in preparation for the project uncovered a problem that would ultimately prove fatal to the building of a harbor. A short distance upstream from the mouth of the river, the surveyors found a massive shelf of limestone underlying the river bottom. At that point the depth of the river was barely five feet, and as one traveled upstream from there, the overall depths did not improve. It was at once apparent that digging a channel deep enough for lake vessels to sail upstream would not only mean dredging but also blasting and digging inch by inch and foot by foot through solid limestone. All of a sudden the government developed a strong ambivalence about the project. Alternatives, such as building a protected harbor out in the lake by constructing offshore breakwaters, began to seem more feasible.[5] In the end, the corps reduced its commitment to that of building two piers out into the lake, one on either side of the mouth. The piers would at least make the river immediately adjacent to the mouth available to shipping by eliminating the sandbar that kept lake vessels of commercial size from entering the river—or so it was thought.[6]

Not only was the commitment of the U.S. Army Corps of Engineers to make harbor improvements at Ahnapee less than had been hoped for, the progress was also excruciatingly slow. The resources of the engineers were spread thinly all up and down the coast. The flow of appropriation money was often delayed. Some funds that were promised never materialized, and a new round of public meetings would be held in an effort to raise funds locally.[7] Nonetheless, any progress on the harbor was a victory over the clique and was a cause for general celebration in the town.

A new ray of hope broke through the clouds in 1874 when (late in the year) the harbor commissioners were able to cajole or coerce the federal authorities into bringing in a steam dredge from Two Rivers, Wisconsin. Surely this rattling, clanking, smoke-spewing leviathan would be the end of the sandbar. As the day approached for the work to begin on deepening the channel between the government piers, preparations were made for a day of jubilation. Word was sent in advance announcing when the dredge was due in Ahnapee. A sentinel was posted on the bluff near the lakeshore to watch for the arrival of the salvific steam dredge. When the dredge was spotted making its ponderous journey down the coast word was spread from house to house, and the townspeople turned out in mass. The Ahnapee Brass Band (comprised of German musicians, it should be noted) had been enlisted ahead of time to provide entertainment for the crowd and a hero's welcome for the dredge and its crew. Ahnapeans young and old stood enthralled beside the river to watch the long arm with the bucket on the end take its first huge scoop of sand and silt. Flags were unfurled in a show of patriotism and a celebration of democracy that proved a counterpoint to Judge Boalt's Fourth of July speech. The band struck up the "Battle Hymn of the Republic," evoking the Civil War sentiments of a hard won victory, with the theological overtones of a divine epiphany ("Mine eyes have seen the glory of the coming of the Lord") and the apocalyptic image of the redemption of the righteous ("Glory, glory, hallelujah, his truth is marching on!").[8]

If hard work, enthusiasm, and desire had been enough to solve the problem of the sandbar, the battle would have been over in 1874. But the perennial frustration was that even with the government piers protecting a channel into the mouth of the river, the sandbar kept forming, and even when the dredge came to remove the impediment, it kept re-forming.

Still, the popular movement for an improved harbor would not be denied. In 1875 a new tool was added to the armamentarium being marshaled against the harbor problems. The new tool was a drilling platform that allowed multiple holes to be drilled into the limestone ledge that blocked commercial craft from proceeding upriver. Dynamite was then placed in the holes, and the resulting explosion broke up the rock so that the dredge could scoop a channel to the docks owned by non–clique members. Meanwhile, the extending of the government piers further out into the lake continued.[9]

In the same year a third movement was begun with the goal of raising money locally for harbor improvement. This time the plan was to build a pier in the middle of the river and parallel to its flow, in an area known as "the bayou." The populist appeal of this new pier is evident from the name it was given—the Citizens' Pier. Once it was in place, vessels could load and unload at the new pier without having either to venture up the shallow channel of the river or use the clique's docking facilities.[10]

Once again the clique countered the populist initiative. This time they appealed to the law. D. W. McLeod, writing on behalf of De Wayne Stebbins, spelled out the strategy for blocking the clique's rivals in a letter to Edward Decker. He asked the rhetorical question: "Is it not trespass to the owners of the soil adjacent [to the river] for a vessel to load from scows while anchored in the bayou, or in the middle of the river[?]" Why, he continued, "cannot the owners of the soil shut up the bayou by booming so as to prevent the use of it by the public?"[11] Stebbins was sure that because the clique owned the banks of the river they also owned access to the river and could legally do whatever they pleased with the waterfront. Again, Stebbins to Decker: "I have been talking with [attorney] Foster today about the harbor matter and he says there is not a question about our owning everything, and that we have a perfect right to sink a crib across the mouth if we saw fit. . . . He says the river not being a meandered stream covers the whole ground and the legislature has no right to declare highways without condemnation of land. He also says the harbor tax [levied to raise money for building the Citizens' Pier] is illegal on the same ground; no right to raise tax to improve private property."[12]

In fact, however, Stebbins and attorney Foster were wrong. The state of Wisconsin would not uphold their right to block the mouth of the river, nor would it frustrate the citizens' ambition to build a pier in the middle of the stream. The Ahnapee River was declared to be both a navigable and a meandered stream, and the state law followed the precedent set in 1797 by the Northwest Ordinance in regulating such waterways. While those who owned the banks also owned the soil under the river, by law the river itself was deemed a public highway, and any right of landowners to obstruct navigation was denied. A project mandated by the public, however, could legally obstruct or alter the use of the navigable channel, and, of course, the Citizens' Pier had that public mandate.[13] At last there was a real hope of having an inner harbor that would free the merchants, farmers, and mariners from dependence on the clique.

The Citizens' Pier project came in the mid-1870s—a crucial time in the town's history. On the one hand, an economic depression had the country in its grip, while, on the other hand, the tide of the prosperity from wheat farming was rising in Wisconsin. If Ahnapee would ever have a chance at the brass ring, it was in the mid-1870s. After two decades of backbreaking work clearing the land; raising homes and barns; and living off the proceeds from selling shingles, posts, and logs, farmers finally had a crop that would put money in their pockets. These were days when the streets were crowded with wagonload upon wagonload of wheat and the harbor was crowded with vessels from other ports that had arrived specifically to take the wheat to where it could be graded, stored, and sold.

But, alas, the new project was ill conceived from the start, and the situation in the harbor actually went from bad to worse once the Citizens' Pier was built. It had no beneficial effect on the sandbar. In addition, it narrowed the channel between the government piers, restricting further the movement of vessels in and out of the river. Ships collided. Tempers flared. Fingers were pointed in blame. And,

The scow-schooner *Lady Ellen* caught in the ice in the winter. (Photo from University of Wisconsin–Green Bay.)

in the midst of these calamities, the federal government delivered the *coup de quietus* to Ahnapee's dream of becoming a maritime center. It announced that the plans to build an outer harbor of refuge, consisting of breakwalls behind which lake boats could shelter from the storms, had been abandoned once and for all. Instead, the funds for a harbor of refuge would be applied to the building of the Sturgeon Bay Lake Michigan Ship Canal, which had the backing of corporate giants in Chicago.[14]

Still, "hope springs eternal." If Ahnapee could not be a harbor of refuge, there were other destinies to which it could aspire, if only . . . if only it had the harbor. As the decade drew to a close, the nation was reviving from the brutal depression. The editor of the *Ahnapee Record* spoke for many residents when he wrote that "to insure a good harbor our citizens must take the matter in hand and raise funds to complete the drilling, blasting and dredging above the limits of the government plans." The editor predicted that with a larger harbor Ahnapee would be chosen as the terminus of a rail line transporting trainloads of grain from Minnesota and the Dakota Territory to be loaded on vessels for shipment to the East.[15] In 1879, a fourth wave of popular sentiment propelled yet another attempt to raise money for harbor improvement—this time by subscription. Despite the dire predictions about the impediment of the limestone ledge, the locally raised money—combined with sporadic appropriations still coming from the federal government—was to be used to more aggressively drill, blast, and dredge the channel in the river.[16]

Predictably, Ahnapee's ruling clique once again went on the offensive. They had tolerated blasting and dredging near the mouth of the river, below the Second Street bridge, because they owned most of the adjacent land, but now they resisted any attempt to extend the channel further upstream. In a letter to the mayor and city council, that appeared in the *Ahnapee Record,* Charles G. Boalt and De Wayne Stebbins feigned puzzlement as to why local merchants and farmers would feel the need to defend themselves against extortionate dockage fees: "We have been informed that many citizens believe that in case the improvement of the harbor should cease, or should be confined to that area of the river lying below the bridge, we would take advantage of the situation and charge higher dockage than is now charged. And we have been informed that this impression has induced many citizens to contribute to the fund for blasting and removing the rock above the bridge. We hereby respectfully inform you that we are ready to enter into an agreement with the city authorities to establish the rates of dockage at a reasonable price for a length of time satisfactory to all concerned." But the appeal of the clique fell on deaf ears. The citizenry were not interested in doing business with the Boalt and Stebbins Pier. It was not a matter of avoiding further cost increases; rather, it was a matter of not paying docking fees to Boalt and Stebbins at all.[17]

On the face of it, the battle over access to the harbor at Ahnapee might appear to be only about gaining economic advantage, but in reality it was also about class, privilege, and power. When Charles Griswold Boalt gave his Fourth of July speech castigating the "Germans" for infringing on his property rights and sullying his reputation he was defending his stewardship of the river mouth and lakeshore property to a segment of the population that he perceived as being in a different and subservient class. He portrayed himself and his business partners as benefactors whose hard work and investment had built the nation and created the opportunities that the immigrant members of the community had come to America seeking. Word had reached Judge Boalt that some "Germans" in Ahnapee were critical of their new homeland. They did not feel that the blessings of freedom fell equally upon them as they did upon the native born. So cynical were their views that they called the celebration of American freedom and democracy a "Yankee humbug!" The very idea! Boalt exploded with indignation and paternalism: "Shame on such 'Germans'! . . . They don't represent *our* intelligent fellow German citizens, who have come to this country to be Americans . . . and who are just as thankful for this 'Yankee Humbug' as the Yankees themselves" [emphasis added].

Boalt wanted to believe that the anti-Yankee "croakers" who spoke out against the clique were a small number of radical naysayers, but in fact the croaker leaders were men of moderate views imbued with many of the same ambitions and values as the clique members. They were not an underclass. They were men on the make who actually shared the same goal of business success that Boalt, Stebbins, and Decker had. Their only offense was to claim the right to the same opportunities that others possessed. They did not want to disrupt the world of the clique; they wanted a fair chance to participate in it. They were a strong and vocal contingent within the community, and they would not be cowed by Boalt's reproach. If anything, Boalt's speech made them stronger.

The next summer the croaker leaders were ready to take on the clique. They were not going to open themselves to a public tongue-lashing again. They took the offensive by making public their belief that the Fourth of July celebration was "a humbug controlled by the damn Yankees" and a "money making scheme operated by a certain clique who took it upon themselves to perform the work, not allowing outsiders to assist." In response, an anonymous clique member wrote an open letter addressed to the "dear beloved croakers." "We regret your actions because we believe you are ruining yourselves and the business of this city. Outsiders hearing of your ways . . . would seek a more congenial clime and thus it is you [who] are an eye-sore to the people and a detriment to the community."[18] The two camps were clearly divided, and there was no crossing over.

The croaker leaders can be identified by determining who led the opposition to the harbor front monopoly. Seventeen leaders can be identified, and, of those seventeen, thirteen were immigrants (nine from Germanic states and one each from Ireland, Bohemia, Wales, and Switzerland). One of the principals among them was Samuel Perry, who was the newly elected mayor of Ahnapee at the time that the Fourth of July controversy was raging. Perry's opposition to the clique is easily explained. He owned a dock on the south shore of the Ahnapee River at the end of Third Street and owned a lake vessel that frequented Ahnapee. From there he shipped products brought downriver and received the merchandise to stock his store shelves with the goods that his customers wanted.[19]

It was in this climate of class consciousness and ethnic conflict that August and Herman Schuenemann grew up. Simply by virtue of the fact that their parents were born in Germany and lived in the Third Ward, the Schuenemann brothers were grouped among the supposed ingrates, naysayers, and critics who challenged and "slandered" the clique. As members of the fraternity of sailors, however, they had a reason to join the croakers even without being from immigrant parents. Boalt, after all, was wrong in categorizing all his opponents as "Germans." There were plenty of non-Germans who were critical of the clique, and among these critics were not only farmers and merchants but also the men who had the most direct investment in waterfront activities—the vessel owners, captains, and sailors—and they found their own ways to knock the legs out from under the monopoly.

By 1880 the commerce of the Ahnapee River valley was robust enough to support thirteen local sailors and several small commercial craft that called Ahnapee home. The builders, owners, and crews of these boats joined the constituency of residents interested in breaking the clique's stranglehold on the waterfront. Their importance is reflected in the significance ascribed to an event that occurred in the summer of 1873 when the first vessel of commercial size entered the Ahnapee River to moor at a dock not owned by the clique. The occasion was marked in the newspaper: "This week we have the pleasant task of announcing *the first entrance in our harbor of a sail craft* [emphasis added]. The credit of which is given to Captain John Doak, of the scow-schooner *Ella Doak*. . . . The *Doak* now lies moored near the brewery dock, where she is receiving a new coat of paint and light repairs."[20] The *Ella Doak* was settling in. (Other firsts that the *Ella Doak* racked up that summer included being the first vessel to collide with another while coming into the harbor and the first vessel to winter over in the harbor.)[21] The schooner was making Ahnapee its home, and the owner-captain was not of a mind to pay tribute to the clique for the use of a waterway that belonged to all.

To the people of Ahnapee, the arrival of the *Ella Doak* represented an extremely important milestone on the road to free access to dock space. It was such a significant event, in fact, that it was passed on in the form of a local legend that was only written down a generation later. According to the legend, the *Ella Doak* made its appearance not in July but on Christmas Day 1873, during a fierce snowstorm. Supposedly, the vessel's captain, Johnny Doak, was determined to enter the river so that he and his crew could enjoy Christmas dinner with their families. Unlike ordinary sailors, Johnny was undaunted by the blinding snow, the crashing waves, or Ahnapee's well-known sandbar. To the cheers of an adoring crowd, he sailed his craft miraculously between the piers and over the bar to a safe harbor. "It was a miracle of Christ, worked on this natal day in the good year 1873, and He alone knew how it happened," wrote the recorder of the tale years later. The hyperbole continues. "The *Ella* was buried for a minute under seas and then rose upon the top of a mighty wave, rode like a race horse upon its crest and was thrown bodily, like a chip of bark, over the bar into the quiet river, and there she lay, nose against the bank." The script described was worthy of Hollywood. " 'Take in fore tops'l,' 'lower away jib,' 'get out your breast lines,' shouted Captain John, and when this was done and the *Ella* in snug quarters, the Robin Hood of Lake Michigan executed a Scotch reel on the quarter deck, threw a kiss to his wife Jennie standing upon the river bank, and came ashore to receive the congratulations of his townsmen and eat his Christmas dinner."[22]

The image of Robin Hood is not a random bit of poetic license. Captain Doak was being portrayed quite intentionally as a hero of the common man, a champion of the downtrodden, and the bringer of retribution to the rich oppressors. He, like the romantic bandit of Sherwood Forest, "stole from the rich and gave to the poor." In bringing his schooner into the river, he had defeated the monopolists at their own game. He had shown that there was a way to have free trade in Ahnapee and to avoid paying the "tax" levied by the clique.

In his merry band there were four other local sailors: Alex Doak (Johnny's brother), Orange Conger, August Schuenemann, and Albert Sibilsky. The recorder of the legend elevated the crew as well as the captain to legendary figures. He described them as "a quartet of Jacks known the lakes over, and all of them disciples of the sea who had learned its hard lessons under Captain Johnny." They were not known the lakes over, but they were disciples of Captain Johnny, and they surely did learn their lessons the hard way.

The Schuenemann brothers, August and Herman, were born at just the right time to be caught up in the harbor war in Ahnapee. August was twenty the year that Captain Doak and his merry band sailed into the Ahnapee River. The opportunity to play the role of a happy rogue who rights wrongs by defying the powerful is intoxicating fare for young men. In the years following August remained with Captain Doak and by the age of twenty-four made a small investment as the part owner of an old and decrepit schooner, the *William H. Hinsdale,* which Captain Doak had rescued from abandonment and decay on the Milwaukee River. From there his maritime career progressed, and in his wake followed his brother Herman—younger and perhaps even more impressionable.

But the lessons that the Schuenemann brothers learned in Ahnapee were not just about sail handling, ship maintenance, and the business of being a short-haul sailor. They also learned about the political and social forces that they would meet over and over again in life—forces of prejudice and greed from which a safe harbor can never be found. There would always be cliques wherever they went, but the Schuenemann brothers learned firsthand that they did not have to be dominated by them. They learned to find their independence on the water, where the only risks were the risks to life and limb that they seemed to treat with such nonchalance.

The sailors of Ahnapee may not have had the assets that some of the leaders of the croakers had, but they did have the same vested interests. For them an open harbor held the promise of greater per-sonal gain. For the next quarter century Ahnapee became home port for a group of these short-haul sailors who helped create a new pros-perity and shape the political and social culture of the town. The clique did not go away, and the croakers did not stop croaking. The tension persisted well into the twentieth century, but in the long run the accomplishments of the farmers, merchants, and sailors were those that allowed the community to survive and, at least for a while, thrive.

SEVEN

AHNAPEE'S
GOLDEN DECADE

The sound of axe, hammer and tools of iron is becoming
familiar to the Ahnapee ear. Buildings are in course of
erection on every hand. At no previous time in the history
of this place have the signs of prosperity been so numerous, nor the prospects for the future so encouraging.

—*Ahnapee Record,* April 29, 1875

$\mathcal{T}$he decade of the 1870s had begun ominously in northeastern
Wisconsin. The great firestorm of October 1871 with its tornadic
winds driving tongues of fire to create the kind of heat that is familiar only in blast furnaces was followed by one of the coldest winters
that anyone in the region could recall. With homes and barns burned,
crops and fodder destroyed, witnesses traumatized, and whole families reduced to ashen remains, the surviving remnant huddled
together, human and animal often sharing the same shelter, their
souls numbed by grief as their bodies were numbed by cold.

Ahnapee was spared by the fire. But that is not to say that the loss
and devastation were not felt. Everyone had friends and neighbors, if
not family, who had fallen victim to the fire. Everyone had read the
gruesome headlines announcing the fire that stole Captain Doak's sis-

ter and six members of her family: "Williamsonville Burned—Fifty-seven Men, Women and Children Roasted Alive!" The town of Ahnapee became a depot for relief supplies, and a local relief committee was formed to bring aid to the northern part of Kewaunee County. There could not have been a person in Ahnapee through that winter who was not painfully aware of how much the town depended on the local region to generate the activity that kept the townspeople at work. Without the woodland, where would the poles, shingles, slabs, posts, and lumber come from that passed through the hands of local businessmen and transporters on the way to market? Without the farmers, where would be the demand for seed and tools and labor? Where would be the harvest that needed to be sorted, weighed, and shipped? Where would be the income that would bring customers to the local purveyor of dry goods, milliner, harness maker, blacksmith, or tavern owner?

The unprecedented devastation and utter despair of the fall and winter months made the coming of spring all the more miraculous. The apparent wasteland stretching to the north, south, and west of Ahnapee turned out not to be a wasteland after all. Some would even say in hindsight that the fire had been a boon to the farmers because it burned off vegetation that made it harder to plant the cultivated crops that produced revenue. The realization was dawning that an economy based on woodland products would eventually be a thing of the past for Ahnapee and the surrounding region.[1] The area never had the great stands of pine that made other regions legendary. Through the 1870s sawmills lost productivity and closed down. Sawyers and mill owners looked elsewhere—to the north and west mostly—for work. And farmers were becoming less dependent on earning cash from cottage industries like shingle making because they had enough land cleared that they could begin to raise a surplus to take to market. By the end of the decade lumber dealerships were opening to sell lumber that was being *imported* from Michigan to meet the building needs of the community.

Meanwhile cash crops like wheat became the object of the forward thinking as the center for the production of grain production gradually shifted westward across the continent. Local farmers came together to begin a county fair meant to promote and enhance agriculture in the region. Agents of a variety of harvesting machines can-vassed the area to find farmers who would sponsor their machines and hold a competition pitting one reaper against another. The reports of the results used the same kind of hyperbole and spin that is often thought to be a modern phenomenon. Newspapers carried sto-ries of how many bushels of grain were harvested in proportion to how many bushels of grain were planted. Roads were improved to encourage farmers from further away to bring their grain to Ahnapee, rather than to Green Bay or Kewaunee. Businessmen in the forward-ing business built new warehouses near the river where agricultural products could be stored, and even then the opening of school had to be delayed one year because the old school building had to be pressed into service to hold the wave of grain that came into town and the new school building was not yet finished. Meanwhile farmers were diversifying, experimenting with other income producing possibili-ties like sheep, cattle (both dairy cows and cattle raised for meat), and fruit trees. In fact, agricultural activity in northeastern Wisconsin in the 1870s was vigorous enough to produce an economic bubble that helped to mask the effects of the depression that struck other parts of the country in the middle of the decade.[2]

When the harvest was in, the streets of Ahnapee were alive with traffic long before sunrise. Farmers had loaded their wagons the night before and been content with no more than a couple of hours of sleep before harnessing their horses for the long haul into town. Townsfolk would awake to the sound of horses' hooves plodding down the dirt streets and drivers calling greetings to each other and encouragement to their teams. At the river crossing there would be a traffic jam as wagons got backed up waiting to cross the stream by ferry. And then, as the farmers arrived at the waterfront, dealers would approach the wagons. Their job was to steer the farmers to the warehouses of their employers. But they also showed great interest in getting a look at the farmers' harvests. Grain that was dirty or wet might better be passed up or sent to a competitor's warehouse, while the farmer who took care to bring in a clean crop found himself with several suitors, who would promise the highest return if he would favor their particular establishment. And once the farmer had made his deal and sold his crop, he was no less popular, for there were store owners, equipment salesmen, tavern keepers, and purveyors of a variety of pleasures and luxuries who happily sought his company for the sake of relieving him of some of his hard earned cash.

There must have been something electric about these seasonal rushes. Everything came together. The winds in the spring and fall (when the rushes occurred) were strong and made for fast running times for the sailing ships. The air was cool by the lake, giving comfort to the men who hefted bags of grain or shoved about ties and posts and bales of shingles. But the bottom line was simply that the more quickly the produce of the land could be shipped, the more quickly and completely coffers and purses would be filled. Farmers could buy their seed. Larders could be replenished. The millinery shop would sell more bonnets than otherwise expected. The saloons would be booming. These were flush times, all the sweeter because it hadn't always been so. The editor of the *Ahnapee Record* was rhapsodic. He called Ahnapee "the liveliest place in this part of the state." No city or village north of Milwaukee could surpass the town, he said. And for the future? His prediction was unequivocal: "Great prosperity and success" will be Ahnapee's "crown."[3]

This decade of agricultural progress most certainly had effects on the life and work of mariners, but, ironically, the boats that called Ahnapee their home port did not carry the grain. When, in 1875, the first vessel carried away a load of grain from the pier at the mouth of the river it was the schooner *Glen Cuyler* of Manitowoc that took the cargo. The choice of vessels was the buyer's, and in this case the buyer was Conway Brothers of the larger city to the south. The implications for Ahnapee were multiple. To those who could see the situation dispassionately it must have been crystal clear that the town's place in the economy of the region was secondary to that of cities the size of Manitowoc, which in turn were secondary to the urban hubs of Milwaukee and Chicago. The volume of product, although a great stimulus to a little community like Ahnapee that had never before produced a harvest large enough to export in quantity, was still not nearly the volume that was needed to support the wholesale operations of the cities to the south. And then, of course, there was the problem of the harbor. Shallow, silted and sanded in at the mouth, narrowed by the construction of piers, obstructed by the curse of a limestone ledge, and fought over by parties with conflicting interests, the harbor at Ahnapee would not admit the traffic of the larger ports. Just as Manitowoc, Sheboygan, Milwaukee, Racine, and the like, had served as the primary points of debarkation for the immigrants who arrived from the East and later moved to Ahnapee, so now they were the needed intermediaries to carry Ahnapee's farm products to their ultimate market. This need for transshipment would in turn lower the price paid to the farmer, but "nary a one" was complaining.

Indeed, there was cause for general rejoicing. "Every era has a beginning," wrote George Wing in the *Ahnapee Record* in September 1875. Wing could date the advent of that new era to the very day— it was the Friday, he wrote, "when the schooner *Glen Cuyler* cleared this port with a cargo of wheat for the Conway Bros. It was the first cargo of grain ever shipped from the port, and the present season is the first in which any considerable surplus of grain has been raised in the region tributary to this market." The importance of this event was not only the achievement of this benchmark of progress but also the fact that it arrived so soon after the devastation of the fire that had seemed to portend the end of life for the region: "Its realization has come upon us almost with the suddenness of thought. Instead of empty streets and stores and the prevailing dullness of the past, our thoroughfares are now thronged with teams, and business is brisk." There was confidence that one hundred to one hundred and fifty thousand bushels of grain would pass through the warehouses and over the piers of Boalt and Stebbins and their competitors, the Fax brothers and Roberts and Fellows. Near the end of the year the prediction of the harvest was raised to two hundred and fifty or even three hundred thousand bushels. The fond, though vain, hope of everyone in town was that this change would be permanent and progressive. The "fire-stricken land" was "blooming like a rose."[4]

During all this time the sailors of Ahnapee—the Doaks, Schuenemanns, McDonalds, and others—were busy plying their trade. But Ahnapee's homegrown fleet of vessels was not up to the task of the grain trade. Grain needed holds that were dry and clean, not the qualities that were associated with the simple scows that were built on the river and certainly not the qualities of the well-used vessels like the

William H. Hinsdale or *Colonel Glover* that adventurers like Johnny Doak bought for a song. But there was no lack of work for the sailors of Ahnapee and their boats. There were still tows coming down the river with posts, rails, poles, and shingles. Fishermen were bringing in catches that needed to be shipped to the cities. The work of harbor building at Ahnapee and elsewhere created jobs for the sailors in town hauling timbers to build cribs, rock to fill the cribs, and slabs of limestone for building piers and lighthouses. Smack in the middle of the decade of the 1870s two more vessels appeared in town, both scow-schooners and both locally built, owned, and operated. One bore the kind of name that would come from a chivalrous sailor, *Lady Ellen;* the other evoked a less genteel side of human nature with the name *Whiskey Pete.* Together this maritime odd couple helped to make their owner, Captain John McDonald, one of Ahnapee's more successful businessmen-sailors. His enterprises evolved from commercial fishing to playing an important role as a contractor in the building of the Sturgeon Bay Lake Michigan Ship Canal.

Today the scow-schooner *Lady Ellen* still has much to teach about the kind of boats that called Ahnapee home. Its remains, which have languished on the bottom of the Ahnapee River for over a century, have recently been studied, and, although there is very little left of the ship, the trained eye immediately recognizes in it a type of vessel that has been little known and little celebrated on the lakes but was, in its day, a ubiquitous maritime workhorse. Its construction was nothing like that of the plank-on-frame or carvel built vessels that are usually pictured when Great Lakes shipbuilding is described. The schooner lacked the gracefully curved lines consistent with our mental picture of what a sailing ship should look like. There is no need for terms like *tumble-home, dead-rise,* or *curve of the bilge* to describe the shape of the hull. Instead, the vessel was a simple, shallow, slab-sided box, built from the bottom up to assume a shape that one wag (with some justification, to be sure) called "an outsized cement mason's mud box . . . [with] a few masts, deckhouse and rudder."[5] The bottom was planked from side to side (as opposed to the usual end to end), holding together strong timbers that ran longitudinally from fore to aft. At the turn of the bilge the sides, planked lengthwise, met the cross-planked bottom at a crisp right angle. Instead of the side

97

planks being fastened to frames, the planks were secured to each other edge to edge by boring holes through their entire width and then driving strong iron bolts down through the thick sides of the planks. When the sides were built up to the deck, one could see no interior frames or braces supporting them from the bilge logs up to the deck beams, but inside those wooden walls there was an inner skeleton of long iron bolts that functioned in much the same way as rebar does in modern slabs of cement. What the *Lady Ellen* and *Whiskey Pete* may have lacked in beauty, they made up for with the strength and shallow draft needed to enter the shoal waters around the Door County Peninsula, under which lay a bed of stone, the kind of stone that was very much in demand at a variety of points around Lake Michigan for construction projects.[6]

Five hundred miles to the east, on the north shore of Lake Ontario, vessels that could easily be mistaken for the *Lady Ellen* and *Whiskey Pete* were used for very similar purposes. From that region comes a picture of the work that was passed down by the men who undertook it. This picture describes a maritime trade in the first half of the nineteenth century that coincides, right down to the details, with the work of the sailors of Ahnapee only a few decades later. "There was a coastwise and international trade on Lake Ontario for small coasters carrying grain, farm produce, lumber, cordwood, ashes, salted fish and other items," wrote sailor-historian Lorne Joyce. "[But] when this trade languished the schooners became traffickers in stone, a more arduous venture." The vessels that were favored for this trade were the same plain-Jane scow-schooners. The vessels were broad in the beam and sharp in the turn of the bilge, and "their stability allowed half the stone cargo to be carried on deck" while their "low freeboard and [shallow] holds . . . made for easier tossing aboard the stone." Joyce, who grew up on that coast and knew the last generation of vessels and sailors personally, describes how these vessels ventured into shallow waters to gather "builders" for stone walls, "pavers" for sidewalks, "cobblers" for pavement, and "hardheads" for filling the timber cribs that made up breakwaters and piers. Sometimes working from a smaller barge that could be floated in closer to shore than the mother ship, sometimes working directly from the deck of their scow-schooner, and sometimes standing in the water, the sailors used "long handled rakes with two tines set at right angles" to fish for the stone and dislodge it from the bottom. Once the stone was free, block and tackle could be used to haul it aboard.[7]

This window into the activity of Ahnapee's sailors in the decade of the 1870s provides a tantalizing glimpse of the probable development of the maritime careers of the Schuenemann brothers. Speculation is confirmed by documentation from the end of the decade that older brother August was not only still sailing on the little hookers that called Ahnapee home but had risen to have responsibility for command. At one point Captain Johnny Doak retained ownership of the *Ella Doak* after he purchased the schooners *William H. Hinsdale* and *Colonel Glover,* and so he was operating a small fleet of vessels just as Captain John McDonald was with the *Lady Ellen* and the *Whiskey Pete.* All of these vessels were occupied at various places around Lake Michigan in stone hooking and harbor construction. This flurry of maritime life was noted in the Ahnapee newspaper with a bit of humorous hyperbole from the editor when he wrote that since Captain Doak had bought another vessel the government would have to open a customs house at Ahnapee![8]

In order to keep multiple vessels in operation Captain Doak and Captain McDonald had to hire other masters as well as crew members, and it seems that they almost invariably preferred to hire hometown men. Unfortunately, no systematic and reliable documentation of their hiring has survived. We must rely almost solely on newspaper reports that mention the comings and goings of local sailors, and these reports are spotty at best. So we do not have any positive mentions of August Schuenemann crewing on an Ahnapee boat from 1873 (when he was reported to have been working with Captain Doak on the *Ella Doak*) until almost the end of the decade. But what we do have are enrollment certificates that show that not only did August Schuenemann have an ongoing business relationship with Captain Doak, he also had a financial interest in Captain Doak's fleet. In 1875 alone there were four enrollments issued for the schooner *William H. Hinsdale.* They were dated May 5, May 26, November 1, and November 16, and all were issued at the port of Milwaukee. In each case, the reason given for reenrolling the vessel was a change in

A fleet of snub-nosed scow-schooners drying their sails at Kenosha, Wisconsin. The photographer was Samuel W. Truesdell, well known in Kenosha just after the Civil War. (Photo from the private collection of Brendon Baillod.)

ownership. On the first certificate John Doak is the only owner as well as the master; on the second certificate the owner is Albert Sibilsky while Captain Doak retains the role of master; on the third certificate the ownership is shared by Albert Sibilsky with a two-thirds share and August Schunemann [*sic*] with a one-third share; and the last enrollment in that year gives Albert Sibilsky as the sole owner once again with Captain J. R. Doak as the master. So what is all this changing of owners about? Apparently Captain Doak did not have enough capital of his own to operate all three vessels. Instead, he sold an interest in the vessel (either in whole or part) in order to gain needed capital. Shareholders would have been financially rewarded by taking a percentage of the profits that the vessel made during the period that they held their share. Presumably, an owner of half of the shares would receive half of the income after the expenses of the boat (including wages) had been paid.

An investment in a vessel like the *Hinsdale* did not require a large amount of capital. When Albert Sibilsky bought the whole share of the *Hinsdale* in May of that year he paid $800.[9] Assuming that the value of the vessel was the same, or perhaps a little less due to wear and tear, August Schuenemann's one-third share in the *Hinsdale* in November would have been as little as $250. Still, this was a lot of money for Ahnapee sailors. The question is, what could they expect to earn in return for their investment? The answer, unfortunately, is elusive. It is known that the *Hinsdale* was being used that season to carry stone from the western shore of Lake Michigan to Ludington, where it was purchased for use in construction, and that a boat earned $7.50 for each cord it carried. What we don't know is how many cords of stone the *Hinsdale* could carry. Nor do we know how many such voyages it made or what costs had to come out of the profit before the owner of the vessel could claim his share. A hint, however, might be derived from C. H. J. Snider, who had personal knowledge of the stone hookers that worked on Lake Ontario. He recorded that one such hooker, much smaller and shallower of draft than the *Hinsdale,* could carry thirty tons of stone on deck (the hold was being used for ballast only).[10] Another witness to the trade spoke of a "six toise" scow-schooner, a toise being 216 cubic feet and weighing approximately ten tons.[11]

It is also known that the *Hinsdale* carried other kinds of cargo that summer and fall—bark, wood, and lumber—and had at least one contract with another Ahnapee businessman, Charles L. Fellows. Finally, we know that the elderly *Hinsdale* was in very poor repair and needed constant attention to keep it working through the year. One of the occasions for maintenance followed the episode when its rudder became unshipped and Captain Doak had to bring it into port using only the sails to steer (an event similar to Captain Dow's experience with the *Augustus,* which was discussed earlier). Another was the occasion when the vessel became waterlogged out on the lake in December and the crew had to pump for forty-eight hours straight while they struggled to bring it into Sheboygan.[12] If one were to speculate that such hardships and risks would scare away an investor, he would have to think again. In 1877 August Schuenemann still had an active interest in the *Hinsdale* and invested *another* $450 to take a 50 percent share.[13]

We can only imagine what hair-raising experiences August Schuenemann had while working for Captain Doak, but we can be sure that he was gaining skills as well as the respect of the local maritime community. Charles L. Fellows, once a lake captain himself, took notice of August. As mentioned previously, Fellows was among the original cadre of settlers from Racine that had established the town of Ahnapee under its original name of Wolf River. He was from a maritime family that had moved to the Midwest from Vermont. As the town grew, he prospered and became one of the businessmen who, by competing with Boalt and the other clique members, overtly opposed their schemes to monopolize the harbor. During the grain boom in the mid-1970s Fellows joined with merchant George Roberts to build a warehouse just upriver from the Boalt and Stebbins Pier and warehouse, and their buyers competed for the attention of the farmers, especially those who conscientiously brought in sound, clean, dry grain. Fellows and Roberts became the agents for the Conway Brothers of Manitowoc, who had shipped the first commercial wheat cargo out of Ahnapee in 1875.[14] The local newspaper reported that it was one of Johnny Doak's boats, the *Hinsdale* again, that brought the lumber to town for the Roberts and Fellows warehouse.[15] This may have been one occasion when Charles L. Fellows became acquainted with August Schuenemann's work as a sailor. By the end of the decade, August was working for Fellows, and he had become Captain Schuenemann of the scow-schooner *Sea Star*.

The entrepreneurs of Ahnapee were looking beyond their own town for business opportunities, and their access to boats, as well as their position on the lake, gave them lots of chances. Just as Captain John McDonald got involved in the building of the Sturgeon Bay Lake Michigan Ship Canal and Captain Johnny Doak contracted to haul materials for work on the other side of Lake Michigan, so others invested in projects both near and far. Charles Fellows seized his chance at Foscoro, a small community that had been established around a sawmill and pier by Messrs. Foster, Coe, and Rowe—hence the name, Fos-co-ro. The building of the mill, six miles north of Ahnapee near the mouth of Stoney Creek, occurred the same year as the Great Fire of Chicago, creating the perfect conditions for making money by converting the raw materials of the land into building materials. And so what was described as once being a place of such beauty that it could very well be the "home of fairies" suddenly became a place of commerce where men saw only the opportunity to make a fortune by stripping the land. The mill was built along the banks of the stream and connected by a makeshift railway with a bridge pier that extended one thousand feet out into the lake. Wood cut at the mill could be moved by horse-drawn carts along this railway to schooners that tied up to the dock and could within a day's time be in Milwaukee or Chicago. One opinionated visitor to Foscoro decried the rapacious cutting of the cedar trees to be shipped to Chicago ("that place devoid of all beauty or sense of poetry"). To this commentator the long pier made the town appear as though "some beautiful girl, with a mouth to excite an irresistible desire for a kiss, should all at once put out a tongue like an ant-eater."[16] Another visitor agreed that "the loveliness of the place had all departed" and reported that the only "fairies" to be found there "were the kind that live on blood and sing around your ears to pay for it."[17] While some grieved the loss of the trees and lamented the ugly scars that men made upon the land, others saw such despoliation as the price of progress.

To keep the lumber moving from mill to market, Charles Fellows employed several schooners, among which was the scow-schooner *Sea Star*. It had been built in 1855 in the small rural community of Irving, New York, where Cattaraugus Creek finds its way into Lake Erie. After the *Sea Star* outlived the purpose that it was built for on Lake Erie, the vessel was "sold west," where the kind of work that it was best suited for was still being done. In 1878 the Fellows family bought the vessel, and in 1879 Charles Fellows fired the whole crew and gave the vessel's command to August Schuenemann, age twenty-six, and three other Ahnapee residents: Dan Henry, James McDonald, and James Defaut. For the next several years, Captain August Schuenemann would serve on and off as the master of the *Sea Star*. The command was shared with another man who had a familiar name. He was Captain Charles Nelson. (The 1880 U.S. Census for Ahnapee lists a sailor, Charles Nelson, whose birth country and age suggest that he was the same Captain Nelson who later accompanied Herman Schuenemann on the *Rouse Simmons*.) Another member of the sailing fraternity who joined August on the *Sea Star* was his old friend Albert Sibilsky, a veteran of the *Ella Doak* and *William H. Hinsdale.*

So as the 1870s ended and the new decade began times were good in Ahnapee for the sailors. The winter of 1878–79 was a warm one; several vessels had kept running throughout the season, and the supply of farm produce for export at Ahnapee was good. In the middle of March the ice would normally just be starting to break up, and vessel men would be coming down to the river's banks for the first time to begin the work of refitting, painting, and repairing their boats. But by March 1879 the schooner *Belle Laurie* had already taken a half dozen shipments of wheat and peas for Edward Decker and had returned with general freight and merchandise. On March 15 the schooner *Lucy Graham* was the first to load with wood products (it took two thousand railroad ties), and by the end of the month a trickle of sailing vessels looking for cargoes had become a steady stream.

Once the shipping season began in earnest, wheat shipments were quickly surpassed by other activity. Only a couple of departures per month took grain, and always on one of a handful of vessels thought tight and clean enough for the perishable cargo. The schooners *Belle Laurie, Espindola,* and *Condor* took up to twenty-nine hundred bushels in a load. But lumber hookers veritably swarmed into Ahnapee, peaking in late April when ten vessels arrived on the same day. They joined several others who were already there to make sixteen vessels docked at one time, giving Ahnapee a brief illusion of possessing the "picket fence" look that the Chicago harbor boasted when the fleet was in and the bare poles of the schooners lined the river two and three deep. While most of these were small to moderate sized sailing craft, there were a few heavyweights among them. The three-masted scow-schooner *Moses Gage* (big for its ilk at 128 feet in length and 26 feet at the beam, with a capacity of 225 tons) was as large as the *Rouse Simmons* and other boats of the lumber fleet that regularly shuttled between Chicago and major mill towns. (The schooner *Rouse Simmons* was 123 feet, 205 gross tons.) When the *Gage* docked at the bridge pier on that day late in April, it turned a few heads, no doubt. The vessel cleared after nearly two days in port with seven thousand(!) railroad ties for the firm of L. J. Conway &

Son. More typical, however, was the scow-schooner *Success* (it made eleven recorded visits to Ahnapee in 1879 as opposed to only one visit by the *Moses Gage*). With a carrying capacity of 161 tons it could take away five thousand railroad ties at a time.[18]

There would have been plenty to do even if all the arrivals and departures went off without a hitch. But to add to the challenge, the sandbar, the one that the government piers framing the river's mouth and the Citizens' Pier in the middle of the channel had been built to do away with, had built up once again. When the scow-schooner *Hercules* arrived partially loaded with cordwood and drawing seven feet of water it couldn't get over the bar. Those standing by, as well as the crew, pitched in to hurriedly rid it of its deck load by casting it overboard so that the vessel could gain the protection of the inner harbor. A week later heavy seas threatened several vessels moored to the bridge pier. One of them, the schooner *Conquest,* locally owned, had on half a deck load of posts, and attempts to haul it inside manually by another force of volunteers were unsuccessful until its cargo, too, was unceremoniously off-loaded into the lake.[19]

There were plans, of course, for more harbor work to be done in months ahead, but local businessmen could not wait for the government dredge if they hoped to get their wood and grain to market while the demand and the prices were high. So the Manitowoc business mogul L. J. Conway offered the service of one of his tugs. The results weren't dramatic, but in a week's time, if a vessel captain knew to hug the south pier as he made his entrance, he would find eight feet of water under his bow. That wasn't a lot of water by most standards, but Ahnapee sailors weren't accustomed to much slack anyway.[20]

Freight and passengers came and went, too, mostly on the Goodrich Transportation Line, which ran three steamboats weekly to Ahnapee once the season opened. The elegant side-wheelers *Sheboygan* and *Chicago,* crowned by their octagonal pilothouses with domed roofs and sporting tall flagstaffs out in front of their stacks, switched off on the weekly Chicago to Ahnapee route. At the same time the propellers *Oconto* and *Menominee* both ran between Chicago and Green Bay, one downbound while the other was upbound, and both stopped at Ahnapee on the same day as they passed by each other. They would touch and go, off-loading at the end of the pier owned by Boalt and Stebbins and quickly taking on passengers and freight. In bad weather the risks were greater, and so, at the captain's discretion, the Goodrich boats were authorized to pass by Ahnapee. It didn't happen often, but when it did, folks had good reason to grumble. It was a long and tedious ride by the stagecoach to Green Bay or Manitowoc to catch another steamer.

To feed all of these vessels their cargo took some doing, but Ahnapee was prepared. The warehouse at the end of the steamboat pier sheltered the perishable farm products, while the ties, posts, and shingles were piled wherever there was space. There were literally acres of them, piles accumulated throughout the winter, awaiting the new shipping season.[21] And as crews and local laborers put immeasurable sweat and toil into hand loading each vessel, more wood poured in from the surrounding countryside on river scows towed by one of two local tugs, *Betsey* or *Two Davids*. Ahnapee had become a "two tug town"!

One week it was reported that 55,000 ties and 12,000 posts had been shipped, and yet a person could "scarcely perceive any decrease in the size of the immense piles" stashed about the city's waterfront. Both the *Betsey* and the *Two Davids* were hard at work bringing scow load upon scow load down from Forestville. Youngs and Fetzers' mill in that village had twenty men working to keep the tugs in business. Farmers, too, contributed their share. Until seed time arrived, they busied themselves freighting the products of their woodlots to town on wagons. But still the hungry vessels kept coming and demanding their fill. In the last eight days of April twenty-three sailing vessels cleared from Ahnapee, taking 41,200 railroad ties, 27,300 posts, and 5,200 bushels of wheat. That was depleting the stockpiles at about twice the rate that the *Betsey* and *Two Davids* together could replenish them. And so, eventually, the spring rush was over. Vessels kept coming, and the tugs kept making runs to Forestville and back throughout the summer months, but extra hands went back to the farm to help with the planting, and the atmosphere around the docks was less frenzied until the fall, when the rush resumed to ship grain and wood before the snow and ice arrived again.[22]

EIGHT

CAPTAIN MCDONALD,
FORTUNE SEEKER

Now some folks are sailors but most are just dreamers
Held fast by the anchors they forge in their minds
When their hearts know they'll never sail over deep water
To search for a treasure they're afraid they won't find
So in sheltered harbors they cling to their anchors
Bank down the boilers and shut down the steam
And wait for the sailors to return with the treasures
To fan the dull embers and fire up their dreams.

—Eric Bogle, *Safe in the Harbor*

In 1880 an artist came to Ahnapee to do a portrait of the town. It was a good year for that project to take place. The resulting picture, entitled "Bird's-Eye View," shows Ahnapee at the zenith of its maritime life.

Bird's-eye views were all the fashion in 1880. Numerous towns, large and small, were depicted thus. The expectation of the printing company that hired the artist and produced many copies of the town portrait was that the company could sell more than enough of the portraits to cover the costs. After all, there was a guaranteed market at least as large as the population of the city, town, or village that was depicted. And the artists apparently took some pains to produce accurate portraits, but from a distance, of course, so that great detail was not demanded.

Comparison of this artist's rendition of Ahnapee with what is known from contemporary written sources suggests that it is a true depiction of the town in many regards. Of course, the importance of the river mouth and harbor is unmistakable. The size and type of sailing vessels, which are one- and two-masted, also reflect both the small size of the harbor and the limited business being done (in comparison to Manitowoc, Milwaukee, or Chicago). At the same time, the presence of the Boalt and Stebbins dock and the arriving passenger steamer with its side-wheels and walking beam, as well as the private docks upriver from the mouth, indicate that, for a small maritime village, Ahnapee was in its heyday in 1880, when there were several forwarding agents in addition to several industries near the river. Then, of course, there is that odd configuration of the piers at the mouth of the river, two built by the government flanking the river and defining the channel out into the lake and the third pier, the Citizens' Pier, sitting island-like in the middle of the stream. A short arm of the river can also be seen, just inside the piers and running parallel to the shoreline of the lake. Residents referred to it as the "bayou" (because it was a shallow and sluggish backwater), but it was, in fact, the channel of the original riverbed, which, in its natural state, had made a sharp right angle and run a short distance north along the lakeshore before crossing the sandbar and entering the lake. In the bird's-eye view it can be seen that this area on the north side of the river and around the bayou was then, as it still is, the location of the fishing industry.

Even the social structure of the town is reflected by the artist's depiction. The homes of the more prosperous merchants and professionals along Second and Third Streets near the lakefront are larger and more elegant. In contrast, the neighborhood on the other side (the north side) of the river, where houses are clustered around the Roman Catholic church on the hill, shows the separateness of the non-English-speaking immigrant community (mostly Germans). On the west side of town there are some large residential buildings that were multifamily dwellings built for laborers by the owners of the local industries.

A close look at the area around the river mouth shows still more

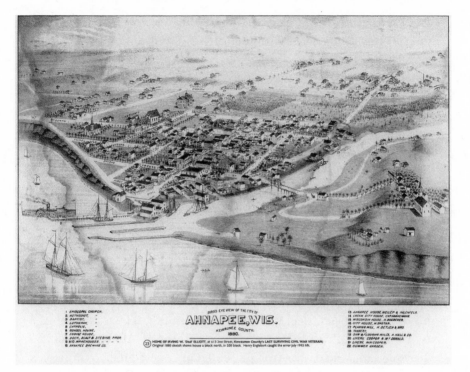

Bird's-Eye View (an anonymous artist's portrait of Ahnapee). (Reprint edition from the author's collection.)

interesting details. There is a ramp at the end of Steele Street (misspelled in the print as "Steel Street") that allowed wagons filled with grain to approach the Boalt and Stebbins warehouse at the level of the second story so that their cargo could be off-loaded. The bulk containers depicted on the pier, and the lack of anything like an external chute, suggest that grain was shipped in bags or barrels, rather than being loaded directly into the holds of vessels as was done at the ports where larger quantities were handled. Interesting, too, is the large wheel-like structure on top of the building just upstream from the grain warehouses. The building was the brewery. The wheel appears to be a windmill, which, of course, would create the energy needed to operate the machinery.

Above the Second Street bridge there are no lake vessels in the river, confirming the shallowness of the water and the inadequacy of the harbor even after a decade of improvements. The steam tug operating in this upstream environment has side-wheels and is towing a river scow. No doubt this is the artist's rendition of the tug *Betsey*, the vessel that was used to bring the products of the farm and forest down the Ahnapee River to the town, where forwarding agents would buy them and ship them to Milwaukee or Chicago.

The year 1880 was a propitious one for the bird's-eye view to be made because the artist caught the town right on the cusp of change. The appearance of the harbor at Ahnapee was about to be altered in a sudden and dramatic way. Never again would it have the bustle and busyness that the artist captured.

In October Lake Michigan was lashed into a destructive fury by the Alpena Gale (so called because of the dramatic disappearance of the steamer *Alpena* and the loss of the lives of all on board). During the gale the commercial pier owned by the clique was severely damaged, and the ice blockade that normally formed during the winter did further damage to all the piers at the mouth. The storm damage itself did not kill off the harbor development at Ahnapee. But the challenges that the destruction presented uncovered the community's unspoken sentiment that there was no longer a realistic hope that the goals for the harbor could ever be achieved. The people of Ahnapee had bought into the dream of becoming a maritime center. They had reached for the brass ring. But, by the end of 1880, they knew the dream would never come true.

The evidence is found in the way that people rose (or rather failed to rise) to the need to repair the damage done at the mouth. If Ahnapee's future as a trading center had been bright, investors would have been eager to set things right. But instead they stood by with their hands (and their wallets) in their pockets.

The first to publicly acknowledge that they would not take the plunge were the clique members Boalt and Stebbins and, by extension, Decker. In spite of the fact that their merchants' pier was the only place where the larger lake schooners could tie up, and in spite of the fact that their pier was the only place that could accommodate the large steamboats of the Goodrich line that brought both passengers and package freight to town, they announced, just three months after the gale, that they would not repair or replace the pier.[1]

Then, of course, there were the fellows with the really deep pockets—the federal government. Perhaps now that the merchants' pier was gone, the U.S. Army Corps of Engineers would get the go-ahead to pour their full resources into developing the inner harbor by blasting and dredging a still longer channel in the river to accommodate more and larger lake vessels. But even though work continued intermittently for years, it occurred in dribs and drabs and held out no promise for a new era of growth and prosperity. A delegate (De Wayne Stebbins) was appointed by the city council to go to Washington, DC, to lobby for more harbor funds, but it was clear from the start that it was a chancy mission. "Is it *sure* to be successful?" asked the editor of the *Record*. "No, it is not *sure* to be successful. But it is sure—'dead *sure*'—that unless some special effort be made we shall *never* have a harbor such as our necessities require."[2]

Stebbins came back from his "love errand" (that's what the editor of the *Record* called it) empty handed. From then on funds were never enough to pursue the work with the vigor that was needed. Over a decade later, the waterfront land was still in the hands of the clique, and the excavated channel was only two hundred feet long and seven feet deep. No doubt part of the disappointment for residents of Ahnapee was seeing that other towns were being developed with the funds that were taken away from them.

As time went on, it became abundantly clear that not only was the federal government not going to put large sums of money into the harbor but that other projects were considered much better investments. While Ahnapee was struggling with the question of what to do after the gale, Kewaunee, its sister city to the south, was attracting serious attention for the first time. Within a dozen years Kewaunee would have attained most of the goals that boosters in Ahnapee had been working the past twenty years to achieve. This Johnny-come-lately had a rail line connecting it with Green Bay and the West. With the rail line came the development of the port to accommodate cross-lake car ferries. And, with increased maritime traffic, Kewaunee won its own lifesaving station.[3]

In Ahnapee, an era had come to an end. All the boosterism, bluster, and bombast in the world could not reverse the tide of fate. The wager on the waterfront had been made and lost. It was time to look elsewhere for the promise of fortune.

Of course, this had huge implications for the sailors of Ahnapee. Not only could they not expect growth in maritime activity, they could only expect an inevitable decline. There would never be room for the sharp-prow, three-masted schooners in Ahnapee. And with the conclusion of the Sturgeon Bay Lake Michigan Ship Canal, and the stalling out of the Ahnapee harbor, even the local stone trade took a huge hit. Over the next fifteen years the fraternity of short-haul sailors broke up as the sailors had to look to other endeavors to make a living. But this dissipation did not happen all at once. There were still those who were ready to make their fortunes from the port of Ahnapee.

Captain William H. McDonald, a longtime resident, was one who held on. In the mid-1870s (when work was plentiful and optimism was running high) he got rid of the old tired scow-schooner *Venture* and purchased the schooner *Conquest,* making it the newest addition to the Ahnapee home "fleet." Even though the *Conquest* was a twenty-two-year veteran of the lakes, it was a step up for Captain McDonald. With a sharply pointed bow, a curvaceous though shallow hull, and a fresh coat of paint inside and out after the rebuild that Captain McDonald gave it, the vessel, while lying in the river next to the plain and boxy *Lady Ellen* and *Whiskey Pete,* would have caught the eye of any sailor

There was a hint of class and ambition in the schooner *Conquest* that was a reflection of its owner and master. He, like others, had found a degree of prosperity with the building of the Sturgeon Bay Lake Michigan Ship Canal. There he seized the opportunity to cut timber from canal lands and thus became the boss of a lumber camp in the winter and the captain of a lake schooner in the summer. One year he hired a crew of twenty local men to work in the woods for him, making him the kind of entrepreneur that the citizens of Ahnapee celebrated.[4]

Captain McDonald was a man who lived large. Mediocrity was not for him. He planned to make it big someday, and he was not afraid to take some risks to reach his goal. When he first moved to

Ahnapee, he was the keeper of the Ahnapee House Hotel, an institution that survives even to this day as the Stebbins Hotel. As the innkeeper he had his finger on the pulse of the town. There was a story told about him that likely contains elements of legend and myth but at the same time seems to capture a spirit that is consistent with all the other things we know about the captain's life. It was the spirit of a risk taker . . . a dreamer . . . a gambler.

As the story goes, "Bill" McDonald met a young stranger who had come to Ahnapee seeking work. The stranger was the gregarious type, and he made the Ahnapee House Hotel his temporary home. There he became acquainted with most of the other men in town who had an interest in business as they came into the barroom of the hotel for their occasional social libation. Of course, Captain Bill, who hosted these social hours from behind the bar, was privy to all the discussions that went on, and he struck up a friendship with the stranger.

Chadwick was the young man's name, and he, like the captain, had a touch of class. Years later he was described as "a rather sleek, smooth-faced, prepossessing young man, . . . quiet and reserved . . . [not] of the class of boisterous, hard-drinking and rough spoken woodsmen who sailed upon the lakes in the open water season and worked in the woods in towns along the shore during winter months."[5] After a winter spent working about town and ingratiating himself with the locals, Chadwick discreetly revealed that he had just learned that he was to be the heir of a substantial fortune. He even went so far as to quietly retain a local attorney for the handsome fee of one hundred dollars per annum to help him find some ways to invest his windfall in local projects. But, in spite of his supposed discretion, the word of Chadwick's fortune got out to the regulars at the Ahnapee House, especially when he settled on a plan to use his money to open a mercantile and gristmill in the community. At his mill, he promised, farmers could sell their grain for what it was really worth and use their enhanced profits to buy goods at reasonable prices. Of course, any prospect that the farmers would get more for their wheat and pay less for their store-bought goods was bound to grab people's attention. Soon the barroom at the Ahnapee House became the incubator for great expectations. Young Chadwick, with Bill McDonald's blessing, shared his plans with any who would listen and bought rounds of the captain's best liquor to toast the dawn of prosperity that his good fortune had brought to all.

Chadwick was so impressed with McDonald that he generously offered to make McDonald his business partner. It was only a matter of time before the inheritance money would arrive. Until then, Chadwick's credit with Captain Bill was golden. In fact, there were plenty of men who were willing to show their good faith by advancing him funds so that he could begin the work in time to start building that spring. All was coming together, and while Chadwick stayed in Ahnapee to formulate his plans and organize the funds of investors who wanted to get in on the ground floor, Captain McDonald went off to Chicago, where he was to meet Chadwick's father at the Sherman House and receive from him a promissory note for $10,000. With the money and signed documents from the beneficent Chadwick, the captain was empowered to buy from the wholesale houses in the city all the goods that they would need to open their joint mercantile business in Ahnapee.

But when Bill McDonald arrived in Chicago, there was no Mr. Chadwick staying at the Sherman House. There was no promissory note for $10,000. There was no way to buy the goods to start their business. And, when the captain arrived back in Ahnapee, there was no longer a Chadwick staying at the Ahnapee House Hotel! While Captain McDonald was absent, the very talented flimflam man had borrowed one of the captain's best horses and, taking the money that other residents of Ahnapee had given him to invest in the mill and mercantile business, had skedaddled, never to be seen again!

What gives credence to the story of how Chadwick took in the captain is the reputation that Bill McDonald had for gambling. He was, without a doubt, a man who was charmed by the beguiling looks and sweet whispers of Lady Luck. A fast horse and a fast track were what got his heart pumping. It was in the gentlemen's world of trotters and pacers that he loved to move, and it was on the ice, sitting in a sleek cutter with sharp and polished runners, that he loved to race behind his steed named Gold Dust Dick. He even took his horse to Chicago one summer to be properly trained as a trotter. This was one sailor who looked forward to the end of the navigation season. When the winter came, the captain could be found as soon as the ice was solid, racing Dick against the best horses that could be found between Kewaunee and Sturgeon Bay.[6]

Perhaps the name of Bill McDonald's favorite horse—Gold Dust Dick—was a sign of prescience. It most certainly was a sign of wishful thinking, for the captain ultimately went looking for much greater fortune than he could win on the ice of the Ahnapee River.

With the spring thaw, the captain's adventuresome ambition carried him far from Ahnapee. He was not satisfied to stay around his home territory trying to squeeze a meager living out of a declining trade. He could envision much greater things. Beginning in 1884 Lake Superior was where he staked his claim. He found a lucrative and plentiful cargo there to fill the hold of the *Conquest*. The cargo was stone once again but not the limestone found about Door County and used in foundations and piers. Captain McDonald was after the hard igneous rock of the great Canadian Shield, rock that was suited for the heavy duty of providing the roadbed for the street railways of Sheboygan and Milwaukee. To find it he would have to leave the waters of Lake Michigan and sail east through the Straits of Mackinac and then north into Canadian waters, past the rocky coves of northern Lake Huron, up the canal paralleling the Saint Mary's River and into Lake Superior. On the Canadian side of the border the region was called Algoma. And it was in this wilderness that Captain McDonald made and lost his greatest gamble.

The story begins with another chance friendship that sounds far too good to be true. This time it was between the captain and a good natured Native American, who, it seems, was so subservient to Euro Americans that he was willing to show Bill McDonald a vein of copper so wide and so long that it promised to make the already established mines of the Algoma region look paltry. But the captain was not going to be duped again. He was said to be "skeptical" at first but was convinced by his "dusky friends" of the Chippewa tribe to investigate the claims for himself. Supposedly what he found was not one but several potential mine sites, and, best of all, his Native American guides were willing to sell their title to the land for a "moderate" price.[7]

The story of the captain's good fortune stretches one's capacity for belief. Was Captain McDonald the flimflammer or the flimflammee? Men of good faith and sound reason have again and again shown what risks they are willing to take when the prospect of a vein of copper twelve feet wide, or a discovery of gold-bearing quartz, comes to their attention. Assays of ore samples were done in Milwaukee. A syndicate was formed and named the Imperial Land and Mining Company. Two hundred thousand shares were placed on the market for a potential capitalization of five million dollars! At one point the captain and his son, Alva, had three vessels in operation—the schooners *Conquest* and *John Raber* and the little steamer *Vesty V.* It seems that the newspaper stories were correct. "The captain has got things solid for a life of gilt-edged ease, and . . . during the remainder of his happy existence he will be able to butter his bread on both sides, to go to the circus every day and to the matinees on Saturday afternoons."[8]

Nonetheless, that year, and in the years to follow, the McDonald vessels came down from the north carrying nothing more valuable than cobblestones. The captain continued to visit the Algoma region of Ontario for several seasons after the first discovery was announced, but the activity of the mining syndicate skyrocketed gloriously and fizzled ignominiously all within a year's time. Seven months after the Imperial Land and Mining Company was formed, the *Milwaukee Sentinel* published an announcement that the syndicate owned eleven hundred acres of land in Canada and had good prospects for mining gold, silver, and iron, as well as copper. One vein of "gold-bearing quartz" was said to be twelve feet wide and two and one-half miles long! Yet investors did not come flooding in to join the bonanza. Just five months later, the same newspaper printed the mysteriously terse announcement that the Imperial Land and Mining Company had filed a resolution of dissolution.[9] No explanation was offered. And, even though Captain William H. McDonald continued to sail out of Ahnapee for years after his mining deal went up in a puff of smoke, there was never another word about his mining days in the press.

One summer Captain McDonald was on the quarterdeck as *Conquest* was towing through the St. Mary's River between Lake Superior and Lake Huron when a large black bear was spotted swimming across the river. The captain immediately decided to go for the prize. He hailed the tug's master and asked him to slow while he put his ship's boat in the water and manned it with four hale and hearty sailors from the deck of the *Conquest*. While the sailors pulled for the bear, Captain McDonald took aim with a hand gun (not the kind of gun that was usually used for bear). Three bullets did not slow the bear down, and another bullet at still closer range only served to enrage the beast. For a short time it looked as though the bear, which by then had turned on its pursuers, was going to tip the yawl over. It managed to break an oar that one of the sailors was using to keep the bear at bay while the captain reloaded his gun. Altogether, the captain is said to have put eleven bullets into the bear before they thought it safe to get close enough to put a rope around its neck and pull the seemingly lifeless beast back to the schooner. Still, the bear revived long enough to make one last pitiable lunge at the captain as they hauled her aboard. Bill McDonald's bloodlust for bear is not surprising. After all, he lived at a time and in a place where wild game was a normal part of the human diet. His impetuousness, however, is a different story. It seems the captain just could not let a chance at a good thing pass him by. In the end, he won some and he lost some, but in the high stakes game of mining for precious metals the captain only lost.[10]

Among other things, Captain McDonald lost the schooner *Conquest*. In 1887, he had used it to take a cargo of Christmas trees from Ahnapee to Chicago, where the trees were loaded on railroad cars and shipped to market in St. Louis.[11] But the next year, the same year that the syndicate folded, he sold the *Conquest*.[12] In 1888 the captain still was in the market for Christmas trees, but that year he took them to Chicago on the little steamer that he had bought near Sault Ste. Marie, *Vesty V.*[13] Eventually he would sell the steamer, too, and briefly try his hand in the ship's chandlery business, where equipment for vessels was sold, before purchasing the old schooner *Surprise* in 1889.[14] Everything seemed to go wrong in the captain's life after the failure of his mining scheme. His wife died the year after he bought the *Surprise*.[15] A year later he lost the *Surprise* in a shipwreck at Charlevoix.[16] He invested in a fish tug and tried hauling nets briefly, but a year later he had given up fishing to become the master of the decrepit old schooner *Sassacus* when it was wrecked on the coast of Door County. He was on a losing streak. "It seems that the Captain has been having more than his share of misfortune during the past 3 or 4 years," opined the editor of the *Record*.[17]

As was the case with so many of the boosters of Ahnapee, Captain McDonald went for the brass ring of fortune, and he missed. In the end he slipped from public view, and his last days passed unrecorded.

NINE

Captain Armstrong:
Working for "the Man"

Life aboard the old schooners was a dog's life. In fact, no one now would make a dog live in the quarters we had, nor eat the food we ate. And often we had only snatches of sleep day after day during bad weather. But, by God, I'd do it again if I had the chance! A vessel under canvas is alive—you'd feel it, an' how we'd drive 'em! But them damn steamboats are just lifeless machines with no personality.

—Captain William R. Dunn
in Ivan Walton's *Songquest*

*C*aptain McDonald's disappearance from the public record should not be a surprise. As the nineteenth century was coming to a close the generation of sailors who had crewed the great white-winged fleet of sailing vessels in their heyday was dispersing. Within a single generation a distinctive and colorful era came and went. For forty years after the great rush westward across the lakes began, sailing vessels dominated the waterborne trade in tonnage of cargo carried, in spite of the fact that competition from steam vessels began very early in the century. Even after steam vessels surpassed sailing vessels in the interlake trade, sailing vessels continued to dominate the intralake trade almost to the end of the century. But, gradually even that trade was being absorbed by railroads and steamers. Sailors like William H. McDonald were relics of the past, of interest for the stories they could tell but no longer relevant in shaping the future. On Lake Michigan the niche remained for them only as long as there were small and isolated ports that needed transports or the presence of coastal resources at the northern reaches of the lake that could not be easily moved by road or rail.

As the importance of sail craft to the commerce of the region was being surpassed, sentimentality and idealization helped keep interest alive in the stories of these vessels and their captains and sailors. Romantics reveled in tales of life on the lakes, while the harsh realities of nautical life were taking sailors to ever more obscure and bleak places—the backwaters of maritime commerce—where they were exposed to hardship, danger, poverty, and death. One sailor who knew those realities well was another resident of Ahnapee, a man who had served as first mate under Captain William H. McDonald during the prosperous days on board the schooner *Conquest*. His name was William Armstrong. Like his former captain, Armstrong continued to live in Ahnapee, but as the town's maritime business began to dry up, he had to look elsewhere to make his fortune.

Captain Armstrong had worked his way up through that unofficial mentorship system that bred so many other Lake Michigan short-haul sailors. No one could have loved the life of a lake sailor any more than he did. He fit the image of the "rock-'em sock-'em sailor"—the two-fisted drinker for whom brawls were a sport to be enjoyed rather than an ill to be avoided. When Billy Armstrong showed up at a party, folks knew that the marshal was likely to be called to restore the peace before the night was over. A night in jail, a tongue-lashing by the justice of the peace, a fine to be paid, and all was forgotten.[1]

In the fulfillment of his nautical duties as well, the feisty sailor suffered more than his fair share of bumps and bruises, only to keep coming back for more. He sailed Lake Michigan for years to the total neglect of opportunities to apply his skills to jobs on land where he could have made more money under better conditions and with shorter hours and to the total neglect of his personal health and well-being. Indeed, his body was beat up and bruised in his profession every bit as much as were the old floating workhorses that he served on. And when death finally laid claim to him, it found him in the cabin of a little gunwale-built scow-schooner, the *Charley J. Smith,* moored dockside at Sturgeon Bay, not far from his home of Ahnapee.[2]

For some savvy sailors the key to survival in the waning years of sail craft was to associate with one of the large companies that dominated maritime transportation. William Armstrong's chance to go to work for just such a company came after the Alpena gale in 1880. The success of a company then, as now, depended on it being big enough to command a market, flexible enough to change with the demands of consumers, and diversified enough to cover liabilities in one area with assets in another. The men whom Captain Armstrong went to work for were in the process of developing just such a company. Starting with the indigenous industry of cutting down trees, they expanded to own sawmills, shipyards, steam and sail vessels, salvage equipment, rescue tugs, dry docks, and stone quarries. Two entrepreneurs, Thomas Smith and John Leathem, capitalized on the demand created by the growth of the cities at the southern end of the lake, the abundance of raw material (both wood and stone) on Green Bay, the availability of experienced mariners, a surplus of marine property, and the shortcut between Lake Michigan and the pineries of northern Wisconsin and upper Michigan provided by the new Sturgeon Bay Lake Michigan Ship Canal. With the help of another early lumberman, Charles Scofield, they established a company that thrived halfway through the twentieth century.[3]

Leathem and Smith began their business by buying old maritime property and restoring it to usefulness. One of their early acquisitions was the schooner *Peoria,* which had gone on the beach at Bailey's Harbor in October 1880 along with several other vessels. The *Peoria* was "hard on" and had already seen twenty-five years of keel-busting service. Its owners were only too glad to take what they could get for it from some Door County salvagers. The total paid was a mere $100, and the local salvagers turned around and sold the vessel and its cargo for $750 to Scofield & Company of Sturgeon Bay even after the two-masted schooner had been hung up on the rocks throughout the winter of 1880–81. Scofield had the means and John Leathem had the technical expertise to get the *Peoria* off the beach. A wrecking tug was called in from Milwaukee to help—another expense. But before they attempted to free the schooner it was loaded with sixty thousand feet of lumber and three hundred railroad ties, which seems counterintuitive until it is recalled that soft wood floats. Even with the added buoyancy in its belly provided by the cargo, the *Peoria* barely made it to Milwaukee with the steam tug *Leathem* at its side. It could not be trusted to a tow line. With the tug on its beam, its deck was a foot and a half under water when it came into the Milwaukee River. When the *Peoria* reached the shipyard, repairs were done post haste. John Leathem stayed with the vessel to supervise the work and shelled out over $1,000 more before it was all done. But, even with all that, the new owners got their money's worth. The *Peoria* proved to be a stout sailor.[4]

When the *Peoria* came off the boxes in Milwaukee and was put back to work for Scofield & Company, it began to earn its keep right away, carrying 1.8 million shingles on its first trip from the company's mill on the Door County Peninsula to Milwaukee. A couple of captains took turns serving as its master until late that same summer First Mate William Armstrong was hired away from the schooner *Conquest* to assume his first command on the *Peoria*'s quarterdeck. In the fall of 1881 he brought the *Peoria* into the river at Ahnapee, his hometown, where it would stay for the winter. No doubt he stood tall as he dropped anchor in the river (and headed for the saloon). The papers had recently carried a story about a trip the *Peoria* had made under his command between Chicago and Sturgeon Bay in twenty-three hours. Two weeks later it was boasted that the *Peoria* had shaved another hour off its time on the same run. Very fast sailing, indeed![5] But there may have been something else behind the headlines— something that would have been less welcomed by its crew—something of a more ominous nature. Perhaps it was not the daring of riding the waves and the skill of mastering the wind that account for the *Peoria*'s speed. Perhaps it was the demands of meeting a deadline by which the cargoes needed to be shipped. Was Captain Armstrong showing off what he could accomplish with a twenty-five-year-old schooner, or was he feeling the pressure from the "home office" to make a fast transit so that they could get one more trip in before the harbors froze up? Was it the search for adventure or the need to improve the bottom line that Captain Armstrong was answering to?

The years came and went: 1882 . . . 1883 . . . 1884. . . . Captain Armstrong had regular work with the owners of the *Peoria,* making runs up and down the western shore of Lake Michigan from Green Bay to Chicago and Milwaukee. Life was good. Billy was in the big leagues. He was able to build a house for himself and his wife in Ahnapee. Sometimes Mrs. Armstrong sailed with him, making his career a family affair and allowing them to pocket the money that would have gone to pay a cook. The captain hired a number of sailors from Ahnapee to work on "his" boat, raising his status still further in town. But then, in 1885, there was a dramatic change in the career of the schooner *Peoria* and its captain.

Companies that carried large quantities of bulk cargo like lumber, grain, stone, or ore had discovered that they could move more product in shorter times and for less money if they used barges. A single steam-powered vessel could pull a string of barges—called consorts—thus transporting double, triple, even quadruple the amounts of cargo in a single voyage. The barges were primarily towed, and so they did not need engines of their own. They had small spars that could carry just enough canvas that, if they should become separated from their tug, they would not be left totally dead in the water. With no need to actively sail the barges, they could carry a skeleton crew (a two-man crew was not unusual), thus reducing labor costs tremendously and leaving more room above and below decks to carry cargo.[6] Not only that, but many company owners thought that untrained laborers, rather than experienced sailors, were adequate to man the barges. In 1881 the tug *Favorite,* towing three barges, made fifty-three round trips with an average cargo of 1.25 million board feet of lumber each and every trip, amounting to 66.25 million board feet (12,550 board miles) of lumber carried in a single year by a single steamer and its consorts![7] That is one-tenth of all the lumber shipped from Muskegon, Michigan, in 1887, the year of that town's peak output.[8]

So, 1885 was the year that William Armstrong went from being a schooner captain to a barge captain.

The steamer *Edward Smith* towing two sail barges, or consorts. (Emmett R. Dowdell photo, Labadie Collection, Thunder Bay Sanctuary Research Collection at Alpena, Michigan.)

Barges could be built in the shipyards of Wisconsin and Michigan, and, of course, many were. But it was less expensive to take an old wooden hulled vessel and strip it. Such was the fate of the schooner *Peoria*. In 1885 it became the barge *Peoria*. No more would it set its own course. It would be the consort of the Leathem and Smith steamer *Thomas H. Smith*. No more would Captain Armstrong decide when to cast anchor or how close to the wind to sail or even when to head out and when to run for shelter. The life of a barge and a barge captain was a life of following in someone else's wake, both figuratively and literally. Some captains chafed under the change in their duties. They were not in charge anymore. And even landsmen lamented how the barge was driving the schooner from the face of the lake and dismasting many a once proud sailing vessel.[9] On a societal level questions were being raised about how safe barges were and whether barge operators were exposing their crews to unnecessary risks, especially because the barges were so frequently overloaded. In 1883 Richard Powers, president of the Lake Seamen's Union, appeared before the Senate Committee on Education and Labor to testify about working conditions on Great Lakes vessels. While addressing the use of barges on the lakes, Powers told the senators that not only were barges undermanned but that qualified sailors were replaced by common deckhands who did not have the knowledge or the skills to be able to handle the vessel in the event that it had to be cut loose from its tow vessel and fend for itself.[10]

Sailing vessels "de-mast-ulated"? Captains emasculated? Captain Armstrong certainly had an opinion about these changes. Unfortunately, he did not record it in such a place that it was vouchsafed to us. It is certain, however, that he experienced the downside of being a barge captain.

Two episodes provide some fodder for the imagination to chew on, windows into Armstrong's life as the captain of a barge. The first occurred in the stormy month of November 1885. The *Peoria,* fully loaded with lumber, was following the steamer *Thomas H. Smith* up Lake Michigan at the end of a hawser. Twice, they sought shelter from the tempest. Each time the captain of the *Smith* headed back out into the raucous lake before the storm had blown itself out. It was not a comfortable trip, but they made it almost to their destination without mishap. Then, all of a sudden, off Grosse Point, north off Chicago, the towline parted . . . the *Peoria* was adrift . . . without warning! With no time to prepare, the *Peoria* was given back its right to find its own way in the world. Instantaneously, Captain Armstrong had his command back, although, no doubt, not as he hoped it would be! The barge did not sail well. It certainly did not sail like a fully rigged schooner would, and it did not go well for the *Peoria* in the midst of the storm. The vessel held its course to Chicago and stayed off the beach, but when it got to the mouth of the Chicago River, it was steering erratically. While the steamer *Smith* sat safely inside the harbor with its captain and crew warm and dry, the barge was dashed against the breakwater by the force of the waves, losing its bowsprit, jibboom, and headgear and suffering damage to its bulwarks.[11] The accident was not fatal for either the *Peoria* or its crew, but one cannot help but wonder what it was like to be left in the lake—so vulnerable and, apparently, so expendable. And what would feisty Captain Armstrong have to say to the captain of the steamer that had left them to their own fate—the captain who sat safe in the harbor while Captain Armstrong tried and failed to make it through the narrow passage between the piers, at the risk of everyone on board?

Eleven months later another mishap occurred. The barge *Peoria* was once again out on the lake as the consort of the steamer *Thomas H. Smith* when Captain Armstrong suffered a fall and injured his left leg to the extent that he was incapacitated for weeks thereafter. What makes this an even more noteworthy event is that at the time of the injury, the barge *Peoria* was on fire! The logbook of the lifesaving station at the Lake Michigan end of the Sturgeon Bay Lake Michigan Ship Canal contains the following cryptic note for October 10, 1886: "At 1130 PM Surfman Dinone who was on watch reported a schooner on fire[.] I ordered the Surf boat out and the tug Spalding was laying here at the time and got the crew out and he took our line going out[.] on arriving we seen it was a scow in towe [*sic*] of the Steamer Smith loded [*sic*] with cider tise [*sic*—cedar ties] on fire, signed Wm. Nequette, Keeper."[12]

Once again, no one died, but the plight of the barge captain is graphically illustrated. The most likely explanation for the source of the fire was cinders from the stack of the steamer landing on the deck cargo of the barge. Imagine that steamer and barge charging straight into the wind. Imagine sparks from the *Smith*'s stack streaming back toward the *Peoria,* where they caught in the dry cedarwood piled high on its deck like so much tinder. Imagine a fire starting—not a benign and tame fire but a fire made voracious by the infusion of oxygen that came with the howling wind and by a ready supply of highly flammable fuel. The fire would most likely have started forward of the quarterdeck, straight upwind of where the captain would be standing near the wheel. Imagine Captain Armstrong with his back to the *Peoria*'s taffrail, looking directly into the face of the intensifying fire as it advanced inescapably toward him. This was not an enviable position. It was fight the fire, jump ship, or perish. Apparently, the captain chose the first of these options, as he was found injured and on deck when help arrived and the vessel survived to sail again without a serious interruption of service.

At first the injury to the captain sounds relatively minor. One report states that it was his "great toe" that was hurt while he was running on the deck to avert a catastrophe. But this was more than a painful stubbing of a toe, more even than the breaking of a bone. Two weeks later it was reported that "the entire limb below the knee was affected" and he was "hardly able to get out of the [schooner's] cabin." A month later he was still "unable to get around," and the command of his vessel had been given away. From that point onward the captain had a series of critical health problems. In 1887, after he had regained command of the *Peoria*, he had an "attack of paralysis" and had to turn the quarterdeck over to William Bie, a younger Ahnapee sailor who crewed for him. This health crisis was the end of his career with Leathem and Smith, and the *Peoria* passed into the hands of his rival, John Patrick Clark.

In spite of harsh working conditions and risks that would not be tolerated in the United States of the twenty-first century, captains like William Armstrong did not complain. The movement for improving the conditions for the laborer was an important influence shaping urban communities where industry operated on a large scale. Sailors were trying to make their voices heard and to gain negotiating power with the owners and masters of the lake boats by forming a seamen's union.[13] While unionization initially had a beneficial effect on wages and working conditions, the influence of the union soon began to wane. Union sailors could refuse to work with nonunion men, but they could not prevent owners from bringing "scabs" on board who were willing to tolerate bad working conditions and great risks of personal harm just to have a place to sleep, free meals, comradeship with others, and a little money in their pockets for a fling when they were done.

Within the "mosquito fleet" of small vessels that were independently owned there was very little sympathy for organized labor. Captains like William Armstrong, who were often owners or part owners of their boats, operated with a businessman's mind-set. As such they had a natural feeling of commonality with the management side of the battle between business owners and their workers. The captain of a vessel was responsible for hiring the crew, maintaining discipline on board, and getting the boat to the desired location and back safely. But he was also responsible for decisions that affected the bottom line. It was the captain who would negotiate rates with shippers and wages with sailors. He would also be the one who would have the most direct and immediate effect on the working conditions of sailors: the hours they worked, the jobs they were assigned to, and the amounts they were paid.[14] With so much responsibility for the profitability of the boat, the captain (and even more so the owner-captain) would not be tolerant if he heard bellyaching from his crew, and he would certainly not be an activist for labor rights himself. This was likely even more the case when the economic security of the captain-owner and his family was hanging in the balance.

Of course, finances were a major point of friction. To save money a captain-owner would offer to pay his crew a set amount for a voyage rather than the customary daily wage. If the passage was a fast one, the sailors could make more than they would if they worked at the per diem rate. But when the passage was slow, the sailors ended up working for much less. Such was the case when the scow-schooner *Coaster* arrived at Sturgeon Bay in April 1886. Captain Jacobson had offered the sailors $8 each for the round-trip and felt perfectly justified by the law of supply and demand. He pointed out to the labor sympathizers that there were so many men in Chicago looking for work that he could have hired any one of a hundred others if these had refused the job. The *Door County Advocate*'s marine editor sympathized with the captain. It did not matter that foul winds had delayed the schooner so much that they were likely to spend "upward of two weeks . . . in making the round trip." "This [$8]," wrote the editor, "may seem small pay, but the men have all they want to eat, which is probably better than they would have fared had they remained on shore."[15]

For the most part unionization was not a threat for the masters of the small schooners and scow-schooners that frequented Ahnapee and the Door County–Green Bay area. There were fewer sailors in the small ports, and so there was less synergy working toward organization. Nor did sailors have a place (such as a union hall) where they could congregate and plan united action. Then, too, many of the small and locally owned vessels were crewed by a hand-picked group of local residents, friends, and family. The personal relationship between the captain and the crew was a significant factor in limiting the likelihood of labor disputes. Because there were few confrontations, there were few occasions for captains to show their animus toward the labor movement. A couple of examples can be cited, however. When the cargo handlers at Langworthy Pier (a short distance south of Ahnapee) were striking for a better wage, the schooner *U. S. Grant* came along expecting to pick up a cargo. Captain W. H. Decker was told that there would be no loading that day at Langworthy, but rather than take no for an answer, Captain Decker hired a new crew and then confronted the protesting strikers while brandishing a gun. This resolved the strike . . . at least for the moment.[16] Another instance is taken from the report of the captain of the steamer *Thomas Smith*. The *Smith* arrived in the Chicago River the day before the Haymarket Riot in May 1886. There the vessel was detained for almost three weeks, first because the captain was afraid to approach the lumberyards because it was rumored that the rioters were planning to set the lumber district on fire; and second, because there were not enough lumber shovers willing to work at the off-loading and boats were backed up waiting their chance to disgorge their cargo.[17]

Given the pro-management (the term used in the 1880s was *pro-capital*) atmosphere and Captain Armstrong's position as the ranking officer on the *Peoria,* he probably did not protest, but if he had, it would have been for good reason. He was typical of the short-haul sailors who accepted their afflictions as their fate.

But for all of the risk and hardship, tedium and loneliness, and all of the swallowing of orders from other men, Captain Armstrong's time aboard the *Peoria* was not without its enjoyments. Depending on the needs of the company, the vessel went back and forth between being towed as a barge and sailed as a schooner. And where the *Peoria* was, the schooner *Westchester* wasn't likely to be far away. The *Westchester* was another reclamation project by the frugal owners of the firm, and as soon as they got the vessel off the bottom of the Milwaukee River and gave it a makeover in the shipyard they placed that "prince of good fellows" J. P. Clark, the Falstaff of Lake Michigan's maritime community, in charge.[18] Comradery and competition were the by-products of putting Captains Clark and Armstrong in close proximity to each other. They came out of the same mold. Both enjoyed drink, and both enjoyed a contest. No sooner had Captain Clark assumed command of the *Westchester* than he began to look around for somebody to beat, and he settled on the *Peoria*. The challenge went out in the newspaper when Captain Clark boasted that he had made two runs to Chicago from Red River (on the east side of Green Bay) in half the amount of time that it took Captain Armstrong to make two trips with a similar cargo from Whitefish Bay, eighty miles closer to their destination. "I can't say whether it was luck or fortuitous winds," said Captain Clark, "but good sailing has a great deal to do with quick time."[19] No more needed to be said. Captain Armstrong had to defend his honor. The quest for the broom was on. (The vessel that won a race on the lakes in those days was entitled to tie a broom to its topmast as a symbol of having made a clean sweep of its competition.)

The two captains found joy in their friendly rivalry. While Captain Clark may have won the bragging rights first, Captain Armstrong would have his chance. The next season the *Advocate* carried a notice that Armstrong and the *Peoria* had made four round-trips between Door County and Chicago (over twenty-two hundred miles) in twenty days, including the time that it took to load and unload the vessel. "Allowing for time consumed in loading and unloading," opined the editor of the marine news column, "this is acknowledged to be the fastest time ever made by any sailing vessel on Lake Michigan."[20]

Captain Armstrong proved that he could sweep his competition. But the cloud of poor health still hung over his head, and it was becoming darker and more threatening with age. The last time that Captain Armstrong walked the deck of the *Peoria* was in the summer of 1887. After a busy start to the shipping season came the dog days of summer. The captain was at his command when he was struck down and rendered helpless by a stroke. Totally incapacitated, he returned to Ahnapee, where he needed help to accomplish the simplest of tasks. Over the next couple of months, the captain was said to pass in and out of consciousness, and family and friends feared that he would languish and die.[21] But, like the vessels that he had served on, he weathered the storm. The captain's period of rehabilitation was long and without the benefit of physical therapy, speech rehabilitation, or workers' compensation. Amazingly, he went on to sail again, although it was over a year before he was well enough to take the helm of a vessel. Perhaps it was passion for the sea that brought him back. Just as likely, if not more so, it was poverty or the fear of it. William Armstrong would work until he died. He had a family to support.

After his stroke, however, Armstrong did not have a job to return to. Other captains in the employ of Leathem and Smith had taken over the *Peoria,* and either Captain Armstrong was not rehired or he chose to make his way on his own.[22] At any rate, when he did return to the lake, it was in command of his own vessel, the schooner *J. W. Wright.*[23] The marine columns frequently refer to the *Wright* as the "little" schooner *J. W. Wright,* and it certainly was small. At 52 feet length of keel it was less than half the length of the schooner *Peoria.* With a beam of 13.7 feet and a depth of hold of 5.6 feet, the vessel was measured to be a mere 26.24 gross tons. (The *Peoria* was 172 gross tons.) No longer would William Armstrong be a company man, and no longer would his boat be relegated to the end of a towline. He rejoined the mosquito fleet and resumed working for himself. The only tethers that could hold him were the tethers that he tied himself.

The little schooner *Wright* had been built at Oshkosh, Wisconsin, on Lake Winnebago in 1869, and in the early 1880s it was a frequent visitor to the port of Ahnapee, where it was well suited for the shallow harbor. The *Wright* took out cargoes of wheat, potatoes, and cedar posts and brought back cargoes of manufactured freight. Its petite size is reflected in the size of the cargoes it carried. For instance, it sailed from Ahnapee in April 1882 carrying 53 bags of wheat and 315 bags of potatoes.[24] Perhaps it was seeing the *Wright* come in and out of Ahnapee that left Captain Armstrong with a favorable impression. Maybe its size was the deciding factor. A smaller boat was less to handle. A propos, the nature of the trade that Captain Armstrong engaged in changed dramatically. If the term had been invented at the time, he might have been called a *boutique captain.* The cargoes that he shipped were the goods of the microeconomy that existed between towns and villages around and across Lake Michigan. When fruit was in season, it was apples, peaches, or berries. When haying was in progress, it was fodder for the draft horses that crowded the busy streets of the cities around the lake. When the men went north to the lumber camps, it was tools and clothing and grub . . . lots of grub. And when the end of the year arrived, it was, once again, Christmas trees.[25]

In one of his dockside talks with the editor of the *Door County Advocate* William Armstrong provided some of the best glimpses into the realities of the maritime Christmas tree trade. "When will you lay up?" asked the reporter in the fall of 1889. "I don't know exactly," said the captain. "I have a notion to go to Chicago with a load of Christmas trees if I can make a strike. If I do I won't get around home much before New Year, if I get back at all with the schooner before next spring."

"Is there much money in the Christmas tree business?" he was asked. "You're right; if you happen to strike it and there aren't too many ahead of you. . . . Some of the owners of hookers frequently make more money out of Christmas trees than they do out of their entire season's work, but these instances are not very numerous. I have been with captains whose sales would foot up from $80 to $125 a day for a week, and more than half of it profit."[26]

Eventually, Captain Armstrong moved on to own the classic little two-masted gunwale-built scow-schooner *Charley J. Smith*. Like the captain, it had seen its best days already, but it was his. So it went for well over another decade. When the end came for the veteran sailor, it was on board the *Charley J. Smith*. (He had sold it to George Wing two years before, but it was still *his* boat.) He suffered a second stroke, this one fatal. His last cargo was Christmas trees.[27]

Both Captain Armstrong and Captain William H. McDonald were gamblers, and in the end, fortune eluded both of them. But both men took pride in the fact that, when the end came, each could say he was his own man.

THE END OF THE
MARITIME COMMUNITY

There is no sense . . . in being bemused by the backward glance. The world we have lost might be a nice place to visit, but we would not want to live there. . . . Our chances of building a good future may be poor, but they vanish altogether if we keep facing in the wrong direction.

—Bruce Catton,
Waiting for the Morning Train

So, "once upon a time," Ahnapee was a maritime community—a town that owed its existence to the schooners that plied Lake Michigan.[1] But within a half century the maritime village (designated a city but hardly big enough to justify the title) grew and prospered and was eclipsed. As the century ended, Ahnapee turned its back on the lake, which gave it birth, and faced inland in search of its future.

In the spring of 1893, one might have thought that something of a maritime renaissance was occurring in town. A brand-spanking-new vessel was being built on the banks of the river—a scow-schooner named *Emily Taylor*.[2] The sound of saw and hammer, adze and caulking mallet, was heard throughout the late winter months and well on into the summer. The builder was Captain Johnson from the town of Carlton, in the same county. The wood for the new hull (tamarack and maple) was brought down the river from a sawmill at Forestville just as in the good old days of two decades earlier. The schooner's model was another little scow-schooner, the *William Finch,* a product of another small maritime community, South Haven, Michigan. (By 1893 the *William Finch* was a resident boat that had been doing a brisk business under the command of Ahnapee native Michael Wenniger since 1887.) The *Finch* was part of a small cohort of vessels that still made Ahnapee their home and had been regulars in the port, and the Wennigers were busy that spring giving it a new coat of paint. Nearby, a little steam barge, the *Mary Mills,* was being fitted out. Yes, Ahnapee had its own resident lake-worthy steamboat. The *Mills* was undergoing some pretty serious renovation. With its hull stripped down almost to the waterline, it was being strengthened with new timbers and reconfigured so that it could carry more cargo. Elsewhere on the river the masters of the schooners *Industry, J. W. Wright,* and *Georgie Brown* were hastening to be ready for the first opportunity to sail. But the most important reminder of the golden decade for Ahnapee was the beginning of another year for the scow-schooner *Lady Ellen.*[3]

Ahnapee was indebted to no vessel more than to the *Lady Ellen.* Built by Major William I. Henry, boatbuilder, fisherman, Civil War hero; launched into the Ahnapee River to the celebratory huzzahs of the townsfolk; captained by its builder's son, William I. Henry Jr.; the vessel was witness to just about every seminal event in the maritime history of the town. The *Lady Ellen* helped to improve the harbor into which it had been born as a stone hooker and, when it was not busy there, went on to assist in the building of the Sturgeon Bay Lake Michigan Ship Canal. (While working at the canal the *Lady Ellen* labored beside that "bad boy" contemporary, the *Whiskey Pete.*) It brought in the foundation stone for the county jail built at neighboring Kewaunee; took the building materials and steam engine to Jacksonport, where the nephew of Ahnapee's earliest businessman, Samuel Hall, was building a new sawmill; and brought back the lumber for building a new bridge over the river at Fourth Street. The vessel's side job was salvaging cargo and equipment from vessels that had the misfortune of being wrecked along the nearby coast, but apparently it was never accused of being a "pirate" ship or a "wreck picker." The *Lady Ellen* was a pioneer in taking Christmas trees from Ahnapee to Chicago. Its first such voyage was in 1876, but the vessel's captain, Captain John McDonald, discovered when he got there that others had the same bright idea and the market was flooded. The space not taken by fresh cut pines on that first trip was filled with barrels of fish. (That must have been an olfactory smorgasbord!) The *Lady Ellen* survived the Alpena Gale only to be chased up onto the beach by a storm the following fall. It was too late in the season to repair and relaunch the vessel, and so it spent the winter onshore at Foscoro. The next year the schooner was sold to the son of its builder, William I. Henry Jr., and his partner, Orin Vose. They raised the roof, literally, rebuilding the vessel's cabin, lengthening its keel, and increasing the depth of its hold to accommodate larger cargoes. It did the heavy lifting needed to bring machinery and supplies for some of the town's earliest factories. It took salted fish and potatoes to Milwaukee and came back north with coal for the winter and "M. T. [empty] barrels" for the fishermen. One December, much to the joy of local boys and girls, no doubt, the crew played Santa's helpers by chopping a channel through the ice to reach the dock so that the ship could deliver its load of Christmas goods. The *Lady Ellen* was the only commercial sailing vessel to spend its whole career with Ahnapee as its home port. No other vessel could compete with it as a symbol of the town's connection to the lake. Perhaps its demise was so quiet and unheralded because there was no one who wanted to accept it. There was no good-bye. The schooner simply sat in the river and went to pieces, until by the end of the 1890s it had become an eyesore.[4]

In 1893, however, the *Lady Ellen* was not yet considered a blight upon the landscape. As the days lengthened and temperatures rose, it seemed that the rituals of the maritime community would repeat themselves as they had for decades and would for untold years to come. But before the century came to an end the *Lady Ellen* had completed its slide into relic status, and its cohorts had dispersed. The *Industry*, the *J. W. Wright*, the little steamer *Mary Mills*, all were gone. Even the newcomer the *Emily Taylor* moved on. In fact, it left its birthplace soon after its launching, never to return. And, when it met its fate, it was on the shore of Lake Superior, not Lake Michigan, that its bones became dried and bleached. The year 1893 was not a renaissance of maritime life for Ahnapee; it was the last gasp.

Because there is good documentation of the harbor activity in 1879, it is a convenient reference point by which to gauge the state of decline in 1893.[5] And what a difference fourteen years made! In 1879 there were 261 clearances from the harbor made by eighty-six different vessels. In 1893 there were 100 clearances, and only thirty-eight vessels visited the harbor.

In both years the vessels visiting frequently were in the minority, while the great majority of vessels only came into the harbor one or two times in the entire season. Putting it differently, a relatively small proportion of the vessels accounted for a very large proportion of the clearances. In 1879 six vessels (out of eighty-six) made 50 percent of all clearances, while thirty (out of eighty-six) vessels made 75 percent of all clearances. In 1893, however, it only took two vessels (out of thirty-eight) to make 50 percent of all clearances and only twelve (out of thirty-eight) vessels to make 75 percent of all clearances. By these measures it is fair to say that the maritime activity in Ahnapee in 1893 was roughly one-third of what it had been in 1879.

The contrast between the two years is even starker when it is seen that fully twenty-two of the thirty-eight vessels that are recorded as entering and clearing the harbor at Ahnapee in 1893 were there only to seek shelter or for an overnight layover while in transit to some other destination. Thus, only sixteen vessels actually came in to transact business in 1893, whereas in 1879 almost all of the 261 visits by the eighty-six vessels were either to load cargo, to unload cargo, or both.[6] While the record kept of arrivals and clearances is not detailed enough to quantify the amounts of cargo carried, it is obvious from this information alone that the amount of material passing through the harbor on sailing vessels was drastically smaller. Conservatively, it could be estimated that less than one-tenth the amount of cargo coming in or out of the harbor in 1879 was carried in 1893.[7]

Another graphic indication of the change in the economy of the harbor is illustrated by a change in the types of cargoes that were being shipped in and out of Ahnapee. In 1879 wheat was the primary cargo in 49 clearances, while in 1893 there was not a single shipment of wheat. In 1879 there were 118 recorded shipments of large quantities of posts or railroad ties, while in 1893 posts and railroad ties are only mentioned in 4 shipments. And, while finished lumber was not a frequent commodity shipped, in 1879 Ahnapee was exporting at least a modest amount of it, while in 1893 the only cargoes of lumber were those that were being imported. (The only woodland product that is mentioned more often in 1893 than in 1879 as an export from Ahnapee was bundled shingles.) Agricultural shipments in 1893, both in and out of port, helped to make up for a small percentage of the shortfall of other kinds of freight. Fruit (from Michigan's Lower Peninsula) is listed as the primary cargo of a number of vessels arriving in Ahnapee in 1893, while it is never listed as the primary cargo in 1879. Farm produce such as potatoes, eggs, and butter is given as a primary cargo being shipped out of Ahnapee in 1893, while in 1879 there is not a single instance of farm produce being mentioned as part of a cargo.

As for the kinds of vessels that visited Ahnapee in 1893 as opposed to 1879, there were also some noteworthy changes. In the earlier and much busier year there was only one visit by a steamer at Ahnapee (excluding the scheduled visits from the Goodrich Transportation Line steamers) to load or unload freight. Fourteen years later, steam vessels had a much greater role. There were fifteen visits to the harbor by steam-powered freight carriers (again, excluding the Goodrich boats). But while steam was much more in evidence, the size of the cargo vessels went down dramatically in the last decade of the century. The median size of the vessels in the 261 clearances of 1879 was ninety tons, while the median size of the vessels in the 100 clearances of 1893 was only fifty tons.

In short, the bubble of maritime activity had burst.

The scows and schooners that traded at Ahnapee throughout the latter half of the nineteenth century had always been smaller than the norm. "Crudely built" or "primitive" might also be apt descriptors for some of them, but it should not be assumed that they were poorly made. The quality of the workmanship would have varied greatly from one vessel to another depending on the skill of the shipwright and the materials that were available at the time of construction. Those who did good work gained a favorable reputation and were sought out by those who invested in boats. Often they would pack up their tools and move to a location where a boat was wanted. There they would improvise a shipyard and work with local materials. Nonetheless, the small schooners and scow-schooners were the opposite of technologically sophisticated. Simple to make, lacking in frills, lacking in grace and speed on the water, they were devoid of creature comforts for crew or passengers. Those with the shallow and boxier shaped hulls were also considered less stable on the water and therefore less safe, and the marine underwriters would not give them higher than a "B1" rating, thus lowering their insurability and their attractiveness to shippers of more valuable cargoes.

It is logical to assume that the primitive would precede the sophisticated. So, the simplicity of design and ease of construction might suggest that scows were an early phenomenon on the lakes that would eventually be replaced by the larger and more sophisticated schooners that had compound curves and large spreads of sail. But, in fact, scow-schooners were the late arrivals on Lake Michigan, being built in numbers only after some of the most sophisticated and well-built vessels had already been launched and put to work.

It might be tempting to conclude that scows were a hull type that simply had not yet been introduced on the lakes, but that would be a mistake. On Lake Erie scows were being built as early as the 1820s.[8] They were put to work in such efforts as taking limestone from Kelley's Island to Cleveland and other communities. Further east, scow-schooners had been used by then on Lake Ontario in the Bay of Quinte region and on the upper Saint Lawrence River.

The smaller (sometimes cruder) vessels coexisted with their more comely cousins because they filled a specific niche. They were the vessel of choice for serving the needs of regional trade even though maritime technology made so-called better craft available. They were just the right tool for Lake Michigan when the economy began to demand more short-haul vessels for the commerce that was occurring on a regional scale (intralake, rather than interlake).

The popularity of the scow-schooners is often attributed to the natural state of the lakes where harbors were shallow and inaccessible to the larger vessels. Their draft was said to be so shallow that they could "float on a heavy dew." But, even though it is obvious that the smaller craft of the independent sailors could navigate in and out of tight places more easily, this was not the main reason for their popularity. The evidence for this conclusion is that when harbors were in their most natural, unimproved state on Lake Michigan—the very time when smaller schooners and scows would be expected in great numbers—they were practically nonexistent even though the design was known and the technology to build them was easily ascertained. In 1838 there were 413 arrivals recorded at Chicago between the beginning of June and the middle of November, but not a single one is identified as a scow.[9] In the 1850s a marine architect named William Bates was building schooners at Manitowoc, Wisconsin, that were known internationally for their design. Bates is widely recognized as having been the preeminent builder on Lake Michigan.[10] Yet when a tally of vessels on Lake Michigan was made in 1855, there were 161 vessels owned at Chicago, but only 3 were scows. The same year there were 21 vessels owned at Racine, Wisconsin, but none were scows.[11]

Although counterintuitive, it is nonetheless true that in the early days of commercial development when high volumes of maritime traffic were building up at Chicago and Milwaukee and a number of secondary ports around the lake, the principal wind-powered sail craft were schooners, brigs and barks of substantial size (one hundred to three hundred gross tons). The humble scow-schooners came later and first appeared at secondary and tertiary ports like Ahnapee that exported their goods within the region to the primary ports from whence they would be redistributed across the nation.

The corollary to this assertion is that as new means for shipment of short-haul cargoes were developed (i.e., regional rail connections and improved roadways) the need for small schooners and scow-schooners no longer existed, and they inevitably went the way of the dinosaur. But they did not go without a fight. They hung on as long as they could. When they were no longer needed in one place they moved to other places where they could still eke out an existence. And, because they had filled a purpose for smaller communities where other means of transportation had not arrived, they tended to

The scow-schooner *Essie Thompson,* abandoned and decaying, shared the fate of most wooden-hulled sailing vessels at the end of the nineteenth century. (Courtesy of the Wisconsin Maritime Museum, Manitowoc, Wisconsin.)

migrate north on Lake Michigan to the more remote and less accessible areas. The Door County–Green Bay area was one such region. (Ahnapee is located at the base of the peninsula, although it is in Kewaunee County.) There scow-schooners were able to hang on for a few more years as a sort of "mom and pop" business.

Eventually, the railroad even came to Ahnapee. Years of effort and debate, frustrated plans, and many false starts occurred before the tracks were laid into town. At other locations around Lake Michigan the combination of lake boats and railroads had led to creating transshipment points where railroad freight could be loaded onto steamers and taken across the lake, thus saving the railroads in Michigan and Wisconsin from having to bring their freight all the way around the southern end of the lake, avoiding the busy rail hub of Chicago, and providing a more direct route eastward for the burgeoning shipments of grain from the plains states. Eventually, car ferries were built so that railroad cars could be loaded directly onto boats and sent across the lake to be picked up on the other side without the time and expense of unloading on one side of the lake and loading on the other side. The idea of Ahnapee being a port for such transshipment of goods had been proposed early in the planning as part of the rationale for bringing the railroad to town. But by the time that the road was actually built, a water-to-rail link was a dream that had long since vanished. Kewaunee, Manitowoc, and Milwaukee had already filled that need. The Kewaunee Green Bay & Western Railroad (KGB&WRR) connected the port city of Kewaunee with Green Bay and from there enabled access to routes west to the Mississippi River and beyond. As a link in the unbroken connection from the wheat belt of the Great Plains to railroads on the other side of Lake Michigan that ultimately extended all the way to the East Coast, the KGB&WRR was a viable enough enterprise to attract investors from the East.

Presumably, the builders and investors of the Ahnapee & Western Railroad (A&WRR) had other incentives for putting their road through, but it is hard to imagine what economic prize was to be won when the A&WRR opened its spur from Casco Junction to Ahnapee, other than to fulfill the ambition of the man who had labored so long to get the road built—Edward Decker.[12] Decker supplied the lion's share of the private money needed to build the thirteen miles of track from Casco Junction, where it connected with the KGB&W. Other men who had experience in building and operating railroads were unable to see the business sense of the project and certainly could not commend it as a good investment to the eastern financiers whose money was essential to build most railroads. "I am very much in doubt as to their success in a financial way," said the president of the KGB&WRR. "If the road is built at all it must be built by capital furnished by parties living up there. The local business is not sufficient to warrant outside capitalists in investing their money in the scheme."[13] But the Ahnapee men pressed on, boasting that the lack of outside investment was actually an advantage. In promoting the road to the general public the officers of the railroad touted the fact that their proposal would "not sacrifice home interests to the dictation of outsiders." It would be built and controlled by persons "whose interests are identified with the interests of all of us."[14]

This power-to-the-people appeal worked. The citizens of both the city and town of Ahnapee voted to support a bond issue to raise money for the construction of the road. Local businessmen, too, reached deep into their own pockets to contribute money to the cause. So, while the A&WRR was mainly Edward Decker's baby, he had gathered his allies around him as he had in the past.[15] The names of the officers of the railroad will be familiar: Edward Decker, president; Charles G. Boalt, vice president; and De Wayne Stebbins, secretary. The clique was still intact and still had influence in the town. It is noteworthy, however, that when the iron horse did reach Ahnapee there was no public celebration whatsoever. In Kewaunee and Sturgeon Bay the arrival of the first train was feted with speeches, banners, parades, and concerts. When it reached Ahnapee there was none of this. It leaves one wondering how much popular support there really was for the A&W.

Of course, local businesses made use of the railroad, especially the furniture factory that made shaped furniture from the newly invented material called veneer. Some entrepreneurs became more venturesome in hopes that a rail link would give them access to a much larger market in which to buy material and sell their product. But to say that the Ahnapee & Western Railroad sparked a new era of growth and prosperity would be wrong. The potential for growth in the area had been met. Timber products were gone; land had been apportioned and occupied; population growth was stable; cheese had replaced wheat as the hot agricultural product. Ahnapee was learning to accept what it was, a small town (née city) on the shore of the lake. Never again would the harbor be host to a half dozen and more "white-winged" schooners at a time. As the new century loomed just ahead the Goodrich steamers became the main waterborne carriers of passengers, merchandise, and freight to and from Milwaukee and Chicago, and the very occasional freighter paid a call with a bulk cargo such as coal.

Anxious about its future, Ahnapee would try to redefine itself, changing its name to the more euphonious Algoma in 1897 with the hope of attracting tourists from the dirty, hot, and crowded cities with promises that it was "cooler by the lake" and the fishing was always great.

The schooner men either went away or found a new place within the community. The ebbs in the ebb and flow of the economy had already taught some of the Ahnapee sailors that they needed to have a backup to sailing. Some went to commercial fishing. Others moved out to the farmland. One built and operated a roller skating rink. Several of the most enterprising migrated north to places on the Door Peninsula (Jacksonport, Egg Harbor, and White Fish Bay) and the west side of Green Bay (Cedar River and Menominee) where the land or the water would still support the kind of work that they had once done in Ahnapee. Others were venturesome (perhaps desperate or foolhardy?) enough to cast their eye on things much further off. Even the wheatland of the Great Plains and the gold fields of Alaska claimed a few.

The lucky ones were the ones who had another trade or enterprise to go into when the lake trade dried up. But what of the few who did not move on—the ones who either had nowhere else to go or were too stubborn to give up their lifework? They were not so lucky. They certainly did not find their fortunes, but, if only because they were the last of a dying breed, some of them found notoriety, and a few even found brief moments of fame.

ELEVEN

The Last of the
Short-Haul Sailors

Do not go quietly into that good night, . . .
Rage, rage against the dying of the light.
—Dylan Thomas

$\mathcal{A}$s often happens as an end approaches, people became more senti-
mentally attached to the remnants of the age of sail when they realized that the time of the sailing ship was past and the objects of their
interest were soon to be lost. All around the lakes people were seeing
an era come to an end, and they sought to record the stories of the old
days on the lakes. What they put down, however, were often reminiscences tinged by longing for the past and a desire to glorify the days
gone by. And, because there was not a whole lot of the "high life" to
speak of, the stories often glorified the "low life." Consequently, the
pictures of the sailor's life at the end of the nineteenth century that
have survived until today are of the more colorful aspects, often
embellished to the point where the line between fact and fiction is
blurred. As Ivan Walton, a folklorist who spent several years traveling
all around the lakes interviewing old sailors and looking for stories and
songs from the sailing-ship days discovered, the only person who can
stretch a story further than a Great Lakes fisherman is a Great Lakes

sailor. Distortions were all the more likely when these stories were shared in a state of inebriation, which Walton found so often in his travels as to leave the impression that the same gene must be responsible for both the love of sailing and the love of alcohol.[1]

So it is that we are left with the stories of men like Dan Seavey, the "pirate" of Lake Michigan, for he was one sailor who certainly did not go "quietly into that good night." One of the escapades that won him the title of "pirate" occurred in 1908 on Lake Michigan. Little is known for sure about Seavey's life before and after this event, but, it seems, the lack of knowledge has been compensated for by a superabundance of imagination, speculation, and educated guesses. Depending on which story you read, Seavey was in the navy; worked as a lumberjack; was a fisherman; went to the Yukon during the gold rush; was an ocean sailor, a saloon owner, a farmer, a deputy federal marshal, a movie actor, and (of course) a Great Lakes sailor. Those are the titles that belong on the positive side of his resume. On the other side, he was a thief, a bully, a brawler, a perpetual drunk, a promoter of prostitution, a violator of game laws, a perpetrator of manslaughter, an arsonist, and a wreck picker. With all of these "accomplishments" claimed for his life, it is likely that one other might be missing—storyteller. But Captain Seavey did not have to promote his stories alone; there have been plenty of others who have been willing to repeat, or spin, a good yarn about him.[2]

One of his magnets for attention was the schooner *Wanderer*, which he owned in the 1900s. At fourteen gross tons it was small (41 feet long, 10.5 feet wide, and 4.5 feet deep). Although the vessel was a topsail schooner, its hull presented a distinctly different profile. Aft of the main mast, where the cabin for the master would have been, there was an open cockpit with stylish curved combing around its edge. Between the main mast and foremast was a large cabin where the cargo hold would be on a vessel meant to carry freight. The profile of the cabin was that of a luxury yacht, and it was obviously built for passengers, not freight. The bow stem was very plumb, but also very sharp, giving the schooner a racy look. Other, even more dramatic, differences were below deck, where the vessel had the plush appointments that were usually reserved for the wealthy. This was no lumber schooner, and it was a far cry from the humble scows of the short-haul sailors. The *Wanderer,* in fact, had been built in Chicago as a luxury yacht for the Pabst family, a Milwaukee family that made its wealth in shipping and brewing beer. How Dan Seavey got ownership is a mystery, but the *Wanderer* was the right boat for a rakish raconteur like him. Captain Seavey used it, at least part of the time, to carry parties of hunters to remote points at the northern end of Lake Michigan, where (some said) they could stalk their prey without regard for the hunting laws. In all likelihood, Dan found some gentlemen in Milwaukee or Chicago who were the sporting type and in a position to pay well for taking them far beyond where work and family could reach them so that they could act on their primal urges and vie for boasting rights about their adventures in the northern wilderness. The fact that they could do so in a boat associated with the wealth of the Pabst family and still bearing some of the luxury in its accommodations would have given Captain Seavey at least a few friends who were more highly placed in society than he could ever hope to be.

Appealing to appetites of male customers was a sidelight for other sailors as well. But some of the appeals were of a downright salacious kind. There were a number of ports, both large and small, where boats would anchor offshore and offer an opportunity to gamble, drink, or find sexual favors. Dan Seavey's operation was of this ilk, although perhaps not offering all the "services" that some boats did.[3]

The best known of the Seavey stories, the tale of an event that occurred in 1908, has been no less embellished than any of the others. Everyone agrees that Seavey stole a schooner, the *Nellie Johnson,* right out from under its master's nose. Some say that it happened in Chicago, others Grand Haven. Some say he got the captain and crew drunk, put them on the dock, and sailed away single-handedly. Others say the captain was off on his own spree when Seavey, who was a member of the crew, convinced his fellow crew members to mutiny and steal the vessel. Some say he went to Chicago to sell his cargo, others say Frankfort, and still others say that he went into hiding among the islands of the Fox and Beaver chains. Some say that he was still in the *Nellie Johnson* when the federal revenue cutter caught up with him, while others say that he was fleeing across the lake in his own little sail yacht, the *Wanderer.* Some say that he tricked the revenue cutter *Tuscarora* into running aground by moving the channel markers, while others say that the revenue cutter gave chase and brought him up short with a shot over his bow. From the time that the newspapers first reported the story up until the 1960s, when a reporter wrote several contradictory stories after visiting the aged Seavey in a retirement home in Peshtigo, Wisconsin, the story of his "piracy" was a living thing, constantly evolving and changing shape.[4]

There is, however, at least one record of the event that was written at the time that it occurred and by persons who had direct access to the main characters as well as good reason to be truthful and objective. The report is the log of the revenue cutter *Tuscarora,* and it tells of the trip that began in Chicago, where a U.S. marshal and the owner of the *Nellie Johnson* came on board, and ends with the capture of Dan Seavey when the cutter overhauled his ketch, the *Wanderer,* seven miles from the mouth of the river at Frankfort, Michigan.

The logbook provides some important indications of what really happened. First, it makes it clear that Seavey did not act alone, and it confirms that Seavey had been a crew member himself on the *Nellie Johnson.* So, when Marshal Thomas Currier arrested Seavey, the charge was "mutiny and revolt" for inciting two other men to help him. They had an unspecified gripe against the captain and decided to take the law into their own hands. It was not the schooner itself that they wanted but the schooner's cargo, the load of lumber, which they proceeded to sell. Once they had done that, they abandoned the schooner. All this suggests that the dispute was over money—perhaps money that the captain owed the crew for wages. The sailors had no patience with the courts of law. They wanted satisfaction of their claims. They would be judge, jury, and enforcer. The captain of the *Nellie Johnson,* however, had the law on his side and so enlisted the help of the revenue cutter *Tuscarora* and the U.S. marshal in finding his lost ship and cargo.

Alas, almost all of the more dramatic parts of the story are not corroborated by the ship's log. The *Tuscarora* did not go aground, Dan Seavey was not playing hide-and-seek among the islands, and the *Tuscarora* did not fire a warning shot across the bow of the *Wanderer* in order to bring Seavey's flight to a sudden halt.[5]

Seavey was indicted in federal court in Chicago, and a date for his appearance was set, but the case never came to trial. The missing court case could simply mean that the plaintiff failed to pursue the case, a not unreasonable supposition, especially because he got his schooner back. The truth will never be known.

The very idea of running away from the law as Dan Seavey did is absurd to twenty-first-century minds. The long arm of the law can reach almost anywhere to bring someone to justice. Maritime law is enforced by the federal government, and so fleeing to another state would be no protection for a "pirate." Yet, there is case after case of sailors trying to evade the law by running from it in the nineteenth century.

The scow-schooner *Supply* provided a particularly picturesque example when its captain tried to run away from the law. Two weeks earlier the schooner had missed the channel between the piers while trying to enter the Milwaukee River in a storm and was driven onshore. Although not badly damaged, it had to be hauled off and brought to the Alan McLeland shipyard for repairs. When the captain could not pay the expenses incurred, the Alan McLeland Company held onto the vessel in lieu of payment. Days turned into weeks, but still the cash-poor captain was not able to come up with the money. Then one day, the captain and his crew managed to break his scow-schooner out of "jail." They sneaked aboard where it lay in the Milwaukee River, and as soon as they reached the lake they headed south. Meanwhile, on the shore the alarm went out, and the federal marshal was called. Marshal Burke, having commandeered a tug, went in pursuit and caught the *Supply* off the harbor of Racine. About two weeks later the vessel was sold at a marshal's sale in Milwaukee for $1,300, still far short of the $2,500 of claims against it.[6]

Did the captain of the *Supply* (or, for that matter, Dan Seavey) really think he could get away with the heist? And where did he think he could go that he would not eventually be caught and brought to justice? Did he expect that no effort would be exerted to catch him? Did he think that if he crossed state lines the law could not follow him? Did he actually think that he could retain command of the scow-schooner by fading into the fleet? How do you hide a schooner from the law and still make a living with it?

Yet it seems that this kind of blatant thievery was not unusual, especially among the independent captains on the lake whose livelihoods rested so precariously on the ability to find a cargo and make another passage. In 1900, as the era of sail was ending, a little known, but no doubt colorful, captain named Henry Cota (also found as Coty and Cody) was supporting his family by sailing a series of old and tired schooners and scows carrying general freight on Green Bay. In 1900 he had already been arrested and jailed a number of times for criminal behavior, yet he was caught once again red handed taking on a load of fruit at Sturgeon Bay, where he knew full well his vessel would be seized if the sheriff saw him there. It was almost as though he sailed right into a trap. Arriving the first time, he anchored offshore but within easy reach of a pier where there was a cargo of fruit that he could make some money on. He and his crew took the fruit on board their ship's boat and rowed out to their schooner in the bay to load it. Not having been interfered with by the authorities, Captain Cota became bolder on his second visit to the pier. This time he brought his schooner right up to the dock, where the cargo was waiting. But, he had tempted fate one too many times. This day Sheriff Washburn was swift to act, and, with court order in hand, he seized the little schooner. The offense that caused this legal action was failure to pay a debt of $12. The amount might as well have been $1,000. The captain did not have the money.

Still, Captain Cota had more cards in his hand to play. Until the matter was able to be settled the sheriff put a watchman on the vessel to make sure that it did not disappear into the night. Captain Cota, however, proceeded to schmooze the watchman. Cota then pretended to go off into town to sleep, leaving the watchman on board. The watchman, believing that Cota was out of commission, seized this opportunity to leave the vessel himself and go in search of a meal. When he returned a half hour later, the little schooner was gone.[7]

The more of these kinds of stories one finds, the more it becomes clear that in each case they are about men whose economic security was hanging by a thread. These are the actions of desperate men, not carefree vagabonds. These were men for whom $12 was worth a fight that could very well end up with them in jail with their most valuable asset, their vessel, sold out from under them. And, all too often,

The schooner *Conquest*. Its cargoes of stone helped to build Milwaukee. (Historical Collections of the Great Lakes, Bowling Green State University, Bowling Green, Ohio.)

they were also men whose judgment and perspective had been changed for the worse by chronic alcohol abuse. Indeed, poverty and alcoholism were powerful forces among the last of the independent sailors on the lakes.

George Doak, one of three brothers of Captain Johnny Doak, fit the stereotype of dissolute alcoholic to a tee. Even in his own day, the painfully sad life that he lived was recognized widely, and his fellow sailors would not have wished his fate upon anyone in their fraternity. He worked on boats in the same waters as his brothers, rising to the rank of first mate onboard the schooner *Belle Walbridge* in 1877 and captain of the schooner *Ardent* the next year.[8] Yet at the same time his illness of addiction was progressing relentlessly and in full view of the community. The fact that his behavior was hard to overlook is illustrated by an incident of drunk and disorderly conduct on the streets of Ahnapee that would have gotten him thrown in jail if he had not had the sense left to calm down when the marshal showed him his gun. That particular night he ended up sleeping it off in the forecastle of Captain McDonald's schooner *Conquest,* where a doctor visited him to tend to his "abrasions." A month later the *Door County Advocate* ran a luridly detailed story about George's sorry state. "Fifteen years ago he was a young man of considerable promise, but he fell into dissipated habits, and it is said that no one has seen him when he was entirely sober for many years." He was a drifter, said the *Advocate* reporter, "only working enough to keep himself constantly under the influence of alcohol." A rather pitiful figure, he was described as wandering about the South Water Street district of Milwaukee, asking directions to a boat downbound to Lake Erie that did not "tip" too much.[9]

The next summer a man who was a nineteenth-century version of a motivational speaker came traveling through the area holding rallies for sobriety. George was on board the schooner *Lettie May,* and one night during his shore leave he went to hear the speaker. There, in front of God and everyone, he took the pledge for sobriety and actually managed to put down the bottle. A short time later the *Lettie May* spent a night in Ahnapee, and the locals got to see something they had never seen before—a sober George Doak. They liked what they saw. He was once again, in the spotlight, and the Ahnapee newspaper pronounced him to be "straight as a string." Unfortunately, his abstinence from alcohol was a temporary state.[10]

Either because his erratic behavior made him unwelcome on board ship, or because he himself decided that he needed a change of vocations, George eventually took up a new job as a painter, specializing in painting in high and precarious places. It was a logical extension of his skills as a sailor accustomed to handling block and tackle and sitting in a boatswain's chair as he was raised to do work on the rigging high up among the topmast and cross spars. But, because of his chronic alcoholism, George more or less had to work drunk. If he stopped drinking too long, he would get "the shakes" and be in no condition to do his job. So with steady hands but a fogged mind, he continued to work at his trade. In 1889 he fell eighty feet from a smokestack in Oshkosh, Wisconsin, and was injured quite badly. That would have been enough to warn most men off but not George Doak. In 1890 he was hired to work on a smokestack in Kewaunee.

This year he was not so lucky. Death was attributed to a fall from a great height, but the real cause of death was alcoholism.[11] The last remaining Doak brother, Alex, and his sister, Eleanor, came to claim the body and take it to Sturgeon Bay for burial. George was the third of the six Doak children to die at an early age (he was thirty-nine). Johnny had been forty-four when he died of cancer, and Catherine was twenty-five when she burned to death at Williamsonville, Wisconsin, in 1871.

There are pathos and poignancy that cannot escape notice in the lives of these men and their families. Their lives were short, hard, and touched by tragedy. They were also full of comradery, humor, and warm sentiment.

It was mid-October 1909, and Henry Cota's son, Ed, was the master of the scow-schooner *Una*. He had loaded cordwood at Horseshoe Bay at the tip of the Door County Peninsula just inside of Death's Door and had sailed the vessel single-handedly down to Sturgeon Bay. There he took on a crew of one and continued through the canal and on to Ahnapee (by then, Algoma), where the *Una* had been a familiar sight for over two decades under a couple of different masters. Three hours after leaving the canal they had traveled a modest eleven miles in light winds and were three miles from Algoma. There they struck a reef six feet below the surface of the lake. The *Una* sprung a leak and filled with water. The good news though, was that it was firmly hung up on the reef so that it would not sink.

It took the effort of many people working together to save the *Una,* which eventually ended up sitting in the Ahnapee River by the Second Street bridge. Algoma fishermen tried to pull it off with their gasoline-powered boats. When this failed and the boat from the life-saving station at Sturgeon Bay arrived, these same fishermen worked for hours to take the cargo off the *Una* in hopes that it would float. Eventually, the Kewaunee lifesaving crew had to be called out, too, in order to get the little schooner off the reef.

By the time that the Sturgeon Bay lifesavers arrived it was too dark to work on the schooner, and it was decided that they would spend the night in Algoma and resume the rescue work the next day. But when the captain of the lifesaving crew, Carl Anderson, inquired at

Algoma for the captain of the stranded schooner, he was told by the one and only crew member, John Devine Jr., that the captain was still on board the *Una* and had refused the opportunity to come ashore for the night with the fishermen who had lent them aid. Out of concern for Captain Cota's safety, Captain Anderson went back out to the *Una* in the darkness of night, risking his own encounter with a reef. He tried to reason with Cota. It was not safe to stay out there. The wind could change. Waves could threaten the stability of the schooner, and with a hole stove in its hull, it could sink with him aboard and no help available. Captain Cota's response expresses the anguish of independent captains of his day. As the report of the life-saving crew would later state, "The Captain was very discuraged [*sic*] and saying that he preferred to go down with his vessel." It took all of the persuasive powers that Captain Anderson could garner to convince Ed Cota to spend the night onshore.[12]

Captain Cota's refusal to abandon his ship implied at the very least spending a long, lonely, and cold night exposed to the elements on the deck of a schooner that had filled with water. At the most, it implied that he was willing to risk death rather than abandon what was, perhaps, the only piece of property he owned—his vessel. In his stubbornness he is a symbol of all those independent captains who just could not change with the times. Like the vessels they mastered, the sailors were facing their own obsolescence, but they would not give up without a fight.

To the public who only knew the stories and never met the people, Dan Seavey was a "pirate" on the inland seas, George Doak was a free spirit who did as he pleased unfettered by the constraints of time clock and rent payment, and Henry Cota was the "Old Man of the Sea." Their lives were full of romance and adventure. They kept alive a way of life that was fabled. But behind the story were real people who were living on the edge of poverty even by the harsh standards of that day. Their most notorious acts were often acts of desperation or wantonness driven by a need to hang onto what little they had and an inability (or refusal) to change their way of life.

The prize that they defended most fiercely was the illusion of their independence. They took pride in their ability to make their own way, defying any who would regulate them, whether it was for their good or ill. They joined no unions, formed no associations, sought no legal protections, and accepted no charity. Sometimes addled by alcohol, and always frustrated by the economic and social progress that was quickly making their way of life untenable, the diehards stuck to a way of life, eking out an existence. They clung to the shorelines of areas like Green Bay, Wisconsin, where small communities remained untouched by railroads or improved highways, and most of their voyages were short hauls.

Some accepted their obsolescence with grace and aplomb, while others fought it to the bitter end. In the public eye the acceptors faded into the past, and what have survived are the images of the fighters. When they got into a real jam, they bent the law to suit their own purposes. When they ran out of money, they sailed away just before their bills came due. And, when the law caught up with them, demanding justice for their crimes of delinquency, they had nothing to give in recompense. From all their hard work and reckless adventure they gained little, except that coveted feeling of independence and, of course, good stories of daring defiance of society's laws and narrow escape from nature's fury.

It has already been well demonstrated that at the end of the nineteenth century there was a great irony in the way Americans viewed their own society. Just as the image of the small family farm was becoming the dominant image of the lifestyle of Americans, that way of life was quickly disappearing—being replaced by an increasingly urbanized and industrialized society. Mechanization was taking over farming. Fewer hands were needed to do the work. Big farms were replacing small. Railroads and refrigeration made the proximity of farms to the markets increasingly irrelevant. Most of the prime agricultural land was claimed. The inevitable result was a flight to the city, where industrialization promised new jobs and new prosperity. For the rural laborer the future was in the city.

A parallel process was occurring in the maritime community. The future was in the city, too, for at least some of the short-haul sailors. Most got lost in the metropolitan areas, taking jobs of low status and fading into the population. But a few were like the Schuenemanns. They moved to the city and found a place in society that made them stand out as exemplars among their peers.

TWELVE

THE SCHUENEMANN BROTHERS

This is the Napoleon of cities. A city of colossal vices and
colossal virtues. It is now devouring, one day it will begin
to send back its best arterial blood into the nation. My
metaphor is a bit questionable but that is due to my two
minds concerning this salad—I alternately curse and bow
down in wonder before this city.

—Hamlin Garland,
Rose of Dutcher's Coolly

*I*n the era of urbanization Chicago was determined to be the most
perfect realization of urban grandeur. The phoenix that arose from
the ashes of the Great Fire, the city that survived its personal apocalypse, Chicago was full of itself. Grandiosity and bravado were the
prominent traits of the city. Chicago was the place where all that was
new to the age was unfolding before one's eyes. Railroads? Chicago
was the continental hub. Marine traffic? Chicago was the busiest port
in the nation. Grain? Pork? Beef? Lumber? Chicago could claim to
be the busiest marketplace on the continent. Building? Chicago took
the New York skyscraper, mixed it with the Otis Elevator and steel
from the mills on the Calumet, and ran with it. If some other city
could do it, Chicago would do it better. The proof, for all to see, was
the White City, the grounds of the Columbian Exposition, raising

palaces of ancient elegance to house all the things that promised a future where everyone would have a life of ease. People came from all over the country and all over the world, and they were impressed—not always positively—but impressed nonetheless.[1]

Anxious to forget that it was ever a frontier town built on a swamp, Chicago turned its back on its past. The true fathers and mothers of the city, the old pioneers, as they called themselves, were long since relegated to the pages of history books. The new leaders of the community were, almost to a person, new arrivals. In fact, it seemed that everyone who lived in the city came from somewhere else—flooding in from small towns, East Coast metropolises, southern sharecropper farms, northern timberlands, European countries—especially European countries—the German states, Ireland, Italy, Poland, Bohemia, Scandinavia.

Everybody brought a dream to this city of newcomers. Ambition was the fuel that made it run. Some came to buy and sell, while others aspired to political power. Some sought fulfillment in the arts, while others strove for reform. Some built buildings, while others imagined the perfect urban landscape. Some would become literary lights, while others would create great institutions of learning. From Jane Addams to Phillip Armour, George Pullman to Beatrice Potter, Ida B. Wells to William Ogden, and Louis Sullivan to Carl Sandburg, in Chicago could be found every kind of human ambition imaginable. But for every one of these luminaries there were thousands upon thousands of others: those who stocked the shelves in the emporiums; spilled the blood in the slaughterhouses; drove the rivets into the skyscrapers' steel skeletons; dug the tunnels and canals for the sewer system; sold their bodies in houses of prostitution; fought the traffic as draymen and teamsters; provided hospitality and distraction as saloonkeepers and vaudevillians; endured the tedium of the office as typists, clerks, and messengers; approximated civic order as policemen and firemen; and toiled, endlessly toiled, as streetcar conductors, garment makers, boiler stokers, cigar makers, lumber shovers, dockwallopers, street cleaners, icemen, domestic servants . . . et cetera, ad infinitum.

Chicago was in its adolescence. It was a time of great aims and expectations, of physical and intellectual prowess, and of boundless energy. But it was also a time of hidden appetites, uncontrolled impulses, and shadowy motives. Bright and optimistic prospects for progress seen in architecture and industry stood in juxtaposition to dark and deplorable realities of urban slums, cholera, and exploitation of immigrant workers. The grittiness of urban life inspired some of the best prose of the age. So Chicago was described as "a hideous monster—a piteous, floundering monster, too."[2] It was a place beyond comparison: "Nowhere a more tireless activity, nowhere a more profuse expenditure, nowhere a more determined striving after the ornate, nowhere a more undaunted endeavor towards the monumental expression of success, yet nowhere a result so pitifully grotesque, grewsome [*sic*], appalling."[3]

The polarities of the city were reflected, too, in the way that class was pitted against class. "Nowhere in America," wrote one of Chicago's best biographers, "was the division between rich and poor greater; nowhere were the enemies of labor more solidly united; nowhere was nativism more pronounced."[4] While the elite of society were able to surround themselves with comfort and splendor, the anonymous mass of people lived among every form of squalor, misery, and hardship imaginable. Only the refuge of a developing middle class—comprised of those who could compete in the marketplace because they had well-developed skills—could offer hope of economic and social security to those who had gambled their futures on moving to the city. But for most citizens of Chicago the barriers to reaching that social plateau were imposing—the language gap, a paucity of opportunity, and a lack of education. To these barriers must be added racism, classism, sexism, and nativism, which had the effect of excluding even the most qualified from achieving success. But even if these walls could be breached, there was far too little room in that so-called middle class to accommodate all who wanted to be there. So, while men and women who rose to the forefront of society and were rewarded with wealth and fame are adulated, the achievements of thousands of others who rose from poverty and hardship to carve out a space for themselves in the middle class are no less worthy of laud.

Sailors, as a group, were not known for their middle-class aspirations or achievements. Often they were transients for whom Chicago, like other port cities, was a temporary home where they could find a night's rest in a boardinghouse, an hour of distraction in a brothel, a fatalistic wager in a gambling den, or succor for their aches and pains in the Marine Hospital. When the ice was off the lake or the vessel was fully loaded they would be off again. Only a few found a home in the city, and even fewer rose from the ranks of "the great unwashed" to the ranks of the middle class. But among these few were two sailors from Ahnapee, Captain August Schuenemann and his brother Herman, the only two of their hometown peers who gained notoriety in their own time. While other sailors of the "mosquito fleet" retreated northward and westward, where they found a way to maintain their physically demanding and rigorously independent lifestyle, the Schuenemann brothers sailed to the metropolis, where they became the main actors in one of Chicago's great legends.

Between 1884 and 1912, when the Schuenemann brothers lived in Chicago, the number of German residents hit an all time high. The peak year was 1904, when there were just over two hundred thousand German citizens in Chicago, a city of almost 2 million people. To put these figures in perspective, there were less than a hundred thousand Irish, the next largest immigrant group, in the city that year.[5] The German population was not only very large, it was also very diverse. The German residents are most often remembered for their role in the labor movement, their efforts to move the United States toward socialism, and the presence among them of a few renowned anarchists. But these few facts create only a caricature. It must also be remembered that there were vast numbers of Germans who blended into the urban scene by embracing the political and societal norms of the city. Some of these were laborers who did the most base and vulgar jobs for minimum pay. Others were semiskilled laborers and skilled craftsmen who brought with them the know-how to help build the manufacturing capacity of the city. Still others arrived with both capital and experience in service based jobs and were able fairly soon to establish the kinds of businesses that were integral to their own neighborhoods, such as grocery stores, butcher shops, retail stores, and saloons. Finally, there were a substantial number who came with the advanced knowledge and skills needed to be leaders in the arts and industries of the city.

When the Germans came to Chicago they had everything they needed to establish a functioning community unto themselves. They could plant their own churches, print their own newspapers, retail their particular kinds of foods and goods, form their own musical groups and singing societies, launch their own venues for entertainment, staff their own schools, build their own craft shops and manufactories, and form their own charitable organizations to look out for the interests of those of their own who were less fortunate. The vibrancy and diversity of this community made it easier for newly arriving German immigrants to find a secure place where they could live and work among other Germans while they figured out what it meant to be an American.

It was to this community that August and Herman Schuenemann came when they moved to Chicago. August had lived part-time in the metropolis before—he worked as a streetcar driver during the winter of 1881 until he returned north to take the helm of the scow *Sea Star* when the navigation season began. But he only took up residence there in 1884, when he moved into a German working-class neighborhood, living at 449 West Twelfth Street. By that time he had been sailing on Lake Michigan for approximately a decade and had earned the title of lake captain.[6] But the business of sailing may not have been the only, or even the primary, reason for August's move to the city, for 1884 was also the year that he married a young woman who had also come to Chicago seeking her fortune, Rose Whiteneck.

Because of their waterborne wanderings, sailors could live in one place while having a sense of community that incorporated people and places hundreds of miles away. For a landsman a town on the other side of Lake Michigan was remote, and a community on one of the islands or bays at the northern end of the lake might just as well be a foreign land. But a sailor could date his sweetheart in Michigan, visit his hometown in Wisconsin, and load or unload a cargo in Illinois all within the course of a week. This was no doubt the case with August Schuenemann. While he had his residence in Chicago, he was still very much tied to Ahnapee and other communities around the lakes and very much a part of the fraternity of sailors among whom he had learned his trade. His mailing address was 449 West

Twelfth Street, but for long stretches of time his abode was one or another sailing vessel found somewhere between Chicago and any one of a number of ports around the lakeshore. Thus, in some ways, the move to Chicago did not change August's lifestyle. He continued to earn his living on small sailing vessels, carrying the humble raw materials that he had been carrying right along—stone, wood, shingles, and so on. But he also got to know the wants and needs of a new market, an urban market, and even more specifically a German American urban market. No doubt this had everything to do with the fact that 1884 was also the first year that there is a contemporaneous source showing that Captain August Schuenemann brought a shipload of Christmas trees to Chicago, making him the first "Christmas tree Schuenemann."[7]

August and Herman had a head start over many of the Germans in Chicago who were new arrivals to the United States. Not only did they have command of both German and English, but they also had business connections to build on. In addition, they had been raised in a family where education, political involvement, and social involvement were all valued. Yes, their father was poor once he returned from the Civil War as a disabled veteran, and indeed his disability deprived him of the chance to be a farmer-landowner. Nonetheless, Frederick Schuenemann played an active role in his community. Before the war he had been one of the founding members of his church, the Erste deutsche Evangelische Lutherische St. Pauls Gemeinde (the First German Evangelical Lutheran Church of St. Paul) in Ahnapee. He, along with seventeen other men, signed the church's constitution and paid 91¢ each into the church's treasury.[8] After the war, even in the grips of his blinding illness, Frederick continued to show an active interest in the community. (One year he was a write-in candidate for alderman of the German ward in town.)[9] Frederick did not passively fit into the societal slot where the racist, classist, sexist, nativist members of the village oligarchy like Charles Griswold Boalt or Edward Decker wanted to put him. He did not see himself as the indebted and subservient recipient of some largesse that those who were born in the United States bestowed on him purely out of the kindness of their hearts. Frederick surely bristled to hear Judge Boalt patronize him as "one of *our* Germans." He knew that he was as much a builder of the community as any blue blood from Ohio, and he would remind his sons and daughters that they were too. So, the Schuenemann boys came to Chicago already having the language, social skills, and self-image as Americans to assert themselves as worthy of a place within this city to which everyone came for the same reason—to make money. For its part, Chicago provided a ready-made, diverse, and dynamic community within which to find one's place. August and Herman were ready, willing, and able to "go for the brass ring"—a place in the ranks of the new urban middle class.

No doubt August, and later Herman, first saw the city from the water, coming down from the north, coasting a safe distance offshore. The first sign that they were nearing the metropolis would have been the thick haze hugging the horizon. Then the congestion of boats converging and diverging as they approached and departed from the harbor. Then the belching smokestacks of factories and Illinois Central steam engines coexisting with the commercial buildings that crowded the lakefront and riverfront. Next the foul smell of a river transformed into a sewer. Then the whistles and bells of the tugs and the curses of tug captains and bridge tenders all up and down the narrow channel that pierced the heart of the city. And finally, the clanging bells of the cable cars; the rumble of heavily loaded wagons; the clamor of newsboys and street vendors; and the babel of languages— English, German, Gaelic, Italian, French, Polish, and Slovak.

Going to the city offered relief from the heartache of the beleaguered family as well as hope for a new economic security. At home in Ahnapee the Schuenemanns had been forced to accept charity when struck with the double whammy of a national recession and the harsh winter of 1875.[10] The patriarch of the family was frustrated in having to make multiple applications to Washington, DC, to get the soldier's pension that was due him.[11] His failing eyesight, which had already forced him to give up his dream of independence as a farmer, along with the first of several strokes, made it necessary for Frederick to go to the Soldier's Home in Milwaukee for an extended stay.[12] Tragically, the family was pulled down even further when one of the Schuenemann daughters, who had married and given birth to several children of her own, had a psychotic breakdown and was taken by the sheriff to the insane asylum at Oshkosh.[13] The family had reached its lowest point, and the able bodied and spirited had to seek work and security elsewhere.

August had already worked under the tutelage of Johnny Doak and had established himself among the "merry band" of sailors that inhabited Ahnapee by investing in the old and shabby schooner *William H. Hinsdale*. His ability was recognized when, at the age of twenty-six, he was entrusted with his first command as the master of the scow-schooner *Sea Star*. His brother Herman, on the other hand, was still wet behind the ears and in his late teens in 1884. It was not until 1892 that Herman was listed in *The Lakeside Annual Directory of the City of Chicago,* but the records of the St. Paul's Evangelical and Reformed Church in Chicago indicate that Herman was married there in 1891 and was living in Chicago at 170 LaSalle Street. The boys' father finally had succumbed to death in 1889, and gradually the family members left Ahnapee for the city of Chicago. Their mother, Louisa, first appears in the directory in 1892. Later her youngest children, twin boys, Louis and Frederick, are listed as living with their widowed mother.[14]

Unfortunately, the Schuenemann family left no biographical materials behind, and so what can be learned about them comes from fragments such as city directories, court papers, church records, municipal records, wills, newspaper announcements, newspaper stories, and a precious few photographs. The conglomerate of these leaves a picture of a family that came out of poverty and tragedy and built a new life in Chicago that would eventually be shaken, but not destroyed, by yet more tragic events.

The two brothers August and Herman, along with their wives, provided the economic anchor. It took teamwork and a business plan that helped them take advantage of Chicago's growth leading up to the Columbian Exposition. The essence of their success was to make sailing a means to an end, rather than an end in itself, and they did this by combining sailing with merchandising.

In 1889 August and Herman owned and operated the schooner *Josephine Dresden*. It was a substantial craft with sleeker and prettier

Historical Collections of the Great Lakes
Bowling Green State University

The schooner *Josephine Dresden* sits very low in the water with a full cargo of wood. (Historical Collections of the Great Lakes, Bowling Green State University, Bowling Green, Ohio.)

lines than the scow-schooners they had been sailing on. The vessel had two masts, was 95.2 feet from stem to stern, 21.2 feet at its widest point, and 6.2 feet from keel to deck. The schooner's attractive appearance, which included a "cutwater figurehead," belied the vessel's age of thirty-seven years. At a cost of $1,400 it was the most expensive piece of marine property that either of the brothers ever owned, and apparently it earned its keep.[15] The enrollment of 1889 lists Herman as the owner/manager and August as the master of the vessel, suggesting a division of labor that became a pattern. Perhaps more comfortable dealing with people, and with a better head for business, Herman took charge of the parts of their enterprise that would tend to keep him closer to home. August, on the other hand, was more comfortable dealing with the vagaries of weather, the mechanics of sailing, and the upkeep of a vessel that would have needed lots of care. For the next three years the *Josephine Dresden* made regular trips between Chicago and their hometown, Ahnapee, carrying the typical cargo for a small schooner of the day—railroad ties, posts, cordwood, and so on. Meanwhile, other members of the family broke into the coal business, not on a large scale as importers or wholesalers of bulk quantities, but in a much smaller and more limited fashion as distributors for the local neighborhood. The Schuenemanns had entrepreneurial spirit and drive.

Chicago was proving itself a city of national and even international significance. Its population surpassed a million, and its economic reach spanned the continent. The confirmation that it was a world-class city came when it beat out New York City for the opportunity to host the Columbian Exposition in celebration of Christopher Columbus's "discovery" of the "New World." Chicago was to play host to the world, and attendees were to discover that the United States was not just two coasts with a cultural wasteland in between. But making the kind of impression that was desired meant creating something from nothing. The organizers wanted to begin with a blank slate, and so they selected a site south of the city that had never been developed before. The sculpting of the grounds out of sand dunes and wetlands, and the design and construction of some of the largest buildings yet built in North America, brought architects, engineers, and designers from all over the country. Translating the grandiose vision of what would come to be called the White City (because of the uniform white color of the exhibition halls) brought an army of workers to the lakeshore, while putting roofs over their heads, food on their tables, and clothes on their backs created work for still more. And then there was the infrastructure needed to enable the masses of visitors to get to the exposition grounds and find hotels and restaurants for room and board. The enterprise was so gigantic that it created a bubble of prosperity around Chicago that protected the city from the economic depression that was hitting the rest of the nation. When the exposition was over, however, the people of Chicago were in for a rude awakening. The protective bubble popped. Thousands of people woke up one day without jobs, and their plight went unnoticed as the attention of the world was drawn to other things. The Schuenemann family, however, carried on and, it seems, even improved their position in the city through the 1890s.

In the years leading up to the Columbian Exposition, the Schuenemanns were making progress. Not only did they own and operate a vessel on the lake, but the business interests of the family began to spread out. Herman led the way, taking on a partnership in the grocery business and later planning to go into partnership in a saloon (which never actually opened). August, meanwhile, kept his attention on sailing. When they sold the *Josephine Dresden* in 1893, they bought the schooner *Thomas C. Wilson,* another old wooden vessel. The price was $900, and notably the owner listed on the enrollment papers was not Herman, or even August, but Rose Schuenemann, August's wife. (Sailors may have wanted their wives to be the legal owners of their vessels so that if they were libeled and sued, their vessel could not be seized as an asset belonging to them.)

The first business enterprise that Herman partnered in was a grocery business listed in the directory of 1894 as Schuenemann and Webb. (The directory also gives August's profession that year as "grocer.") The address of the business is most intriguing—146 South Water Street—which, it turns out, was at the corner of South Water and Clark Street, at the southern end of the Clark Street bridge, the very same spot where the schooner *Rouse Simmons,* Chicago's renowned Christmas Tree Ship (and its predecessors) would later tie up. The address is worth noting, too, because of the distinctive role that South Water Street (along with Market Street and North Water Street) played in late-nineteenth-century Chicago. Both sides of the street from end to end were occupied almost exclusively by wholesale businesses that supplied the restaurants, groceries, and neighborhood stores all over the metropolis. Every day huge quantities of fresh foodstuffs exchanged hands in the final step that brought these goods from the farm to the table. Pictures of South Water Street show it as lined with shops having large canvas awnings out front under which goods were kept temporarily while veritable hordes of wagons pulled by brawny teams of horses lined the street to carry the goods to hundreds, if not thousands, of retail establishments. Building after building stood cheek by jowl with their front doors opening onto the street and their back doors opening onto a narrow wooden dock that ran parallel to the Chicago River. Produce that came into the city on boats could enter the buildings in the very early hours of the day from the river side and be sorted, priced, and sold out the front doors just hours later. In the morning the street was the scene of organized chaos as buyers competed with each other to get the freshest, plumpest, crispest, juiciest produce at the lowest possible price. A visitor's guide to Chicago published in 1891 warned those who would take a walking tour of the wholesale district: "It would be all your life is worth to venture down the middle of it [South Water Street], and you can only pass along the sidewalks by climbing over fruit boxes, chicken crates and barrels. There is a mixed odor here of onions, strawberries, California grapes, Florida oranges, pickles, saur kraut [*sic*], hay, wet straw, fresh fish and eggs of uncertain age." It was a place that assaulted all the senses and more than likely was the busiest place in Chicago with the possible exception of the floor of the Board of Trade.[16]

Nearby were the great wholesale houses and warehouse facilities of companies like Marshall Fields and Reid & Murdock, but along South Water Street there was space for the entrepreneurial enterprises that operated on a much smaller scale and, perhaps too often, had a much shorter life span among the fierce competition of the street. Perhaps it was the competition that accounts for the fact that Schuenemann and Webb appears in the *Lakeside Directory* for only one year. But, even if that business did fail, it was not the only enterprise in which Herman Schuenemann invested. The next year he was listed as partner in a retail grocery business on Lincoln Avenue, three blocks south of Belmont.[17] The name of the business, Miller & Schuenemann, suggests that Herman may have been the junior partner in this endeavor, but it is the address that has the most to say about the family's life in the busy urban environment. The Schuenemanns had moved north, away from the working-class neighborhood south of the Loop to a newer neighborhood that was in the heart of the district most densely populated by German American Chicagoans. As a second generation German American, Herman could easily move back and forth between the culture of America and the culture that new immigrants brought with them from the old country. The Schuenemanns drew their economic strength from the German-speaking community of Chicago, while simultaneously they helped that community secure its place within this most American of cities.

One more tantalizing, though frustratingly spare, fact that is known about Herman's business life is that in 1903 he and a partner named Charles Wolfskee initiated a deal to be the proprietors of a saloon. The deal collapsed, and Herman got his money back after some litigation, so it seems that he never actually ran this saloon. His ambition to do so, however, says a lot about his own perception of his place in the community. The saloon of that day, especially among Germans, was not the vile den of iniquity that has often been portrayed. Instead, it was an institution that tended to add to the cohesiveness of the neighborhood. "The working-class saloon," observed Donald L. Miller, "was a neighborhood institution second in importance only to the family and the parish church." The same place that one went for a draft or a bucket of beer was also a center for social life, political debate, advice on matters of health and employment, and assistance with literacy skills for residents who lacked them. The saloonkeeper was, therefore, a respected and valued member of the community. In German neighborhoods, saloons were not seen as a place for men alone to congregate. They welcomed families for meals, and, in spite of what many temperance advocates believed, the decorum of patrons made saloons comfortable places to bring children. Finally, operating a saloon was one business that a man could get into without having to have a lot of capital. For the fledgling businessman it was "a way to move up in the world."[18]

Theodore Charrney heard from the next generation of Schuenemanns that, in 1902, Herman also managed a beer garden (or "picnic grove") in Forest Park, one of the new suburbs of Chicago, which was accessible by the interurban rail system and was a popular place for Chicago's Germans to congregate. "From May to September, he dispensed beer, soft drinks, candies, ice cream, popcorn and food to the lively accompaniment of the German bands playing music for the devotees of the dance." Later he operated a beer garden near one of the small amusement parks that were popular around the city after the Columbian Exposition.[19] These enterprises must have reminded Herman of the *Wilhelmshoehe,* the German tavern and sports club that was the meeting place for so many of his neighbors when he was a youth in Ahnapee. It was a comfortable atmosphere that united his personal past and present as well as the past and present of so many of his Chicago neighbors who were newer to the United States.

The house where Herman; his wife, Barbara; and their three children lived for the longest time is also indicative of their place in the community. It was on the west side of North Clark Street between North Avenue (once referred to as "the German Broadway") and Eugenia Street (directly across from where the Chicago History Museum now stands). Built of brick and stone, with bay windows facing east toward the lake, the house was a multifamily residence where the Schuenemanns were renters. Immediately across the street was the southern end of Lincoln Park, where the Lincoln statue was located. A block to the south was the home of the Germania Club, a social center for some of Chicago's most prominent German citizens. To the south and east were the turreted lakeshore homes of some of Chicago's most wealthy and influential families (the mansions of Potter Palmer, Cyrus McCormick, and Perry H. Smith). To the west was a large German working-class neighborhood that yielded to the buildings of some of Chicago's most vibrant industries located along the north branch of the Chicago River. Clark Street was "the buffer" between the residential and commercial sections of the near north side, as close to the homes of Chicago's sentinel citizens as one could get without being one of them.[20] And it was on this street that Herman and his family resided for the last twelve years of his life. Herman could have walked down Clark Street (or have ridden on one of Charles Yerkes's cable cars) between South Water Street and his home a thousand times or more. Perhaps he stopped in Washington Park to watch the building of the Newberry Library or stood on the front steps of his house and gazed over to the lakeshore.

Even with all these inferences of achievement of middle-class status, it would be a mistake to think that the Schuenemanns ever felt secure. Their grip on prosperity was precarious, and the risk of falling back into the underclass of laborers from which they had come was never far below consciousness. Any serious setback—a debilitating illness, a crippling accident, a house fire, or a poorly chosen investment— could bring their fragile semblance of achievement crashing down. And disaster was no less a stranger to August and Herman in their adult years than it had been in their youth. It would strike them in a personal, profound, and painful way.

In the fall of 1898, Captain August Schuenemann went to Sturgeon Bay for his last cargo of the year. In contrast with other years, though, he arrived without a vessel. (The record is silent about the end of his previous command.) In any case, he needed both the cargo and the boat to take his cargo home in, and apparently this had to be done as cheaply as possible, because the vessel that August purchased cost him only $200. Yet even then he had to borrow $100 from a local merchant in order to have enough capital to purchase his cargo—a load of Christmas trees for Chicago. Two hundred dollars did not go very far. The vessel that he found for that amount was a little "flat-bottomed schooner" (fifty-five tons gross), the *S. Thal,* which had been built at Oshkosh, Wisconsin, thirty-one years earlier for use on Lake Winnebago.[21] A few years earlier the *Thal* was brought to Green Bay, where it was being used for local cargoes, but its original reason for being no longer existed. The vessel was living on borrowed time, and its condition likely reflected its failing fortunes.[22] But August had made many late season voyages from north to south on Lake Michigan, and the *S. Thal* was but the latest of a series of vessels he commanded that was in ill repair and ill equipped. The *Thal,* however, was destined to be his last command and his voyage from Sturgeon Bay to Chicago his last voyage.

They made it as far as Glencoe, Illinois, where a prominence of land projected out into the lake. Here the water was shallower because of a sandbar spitting out even further offshore. With shallow water and an onshore wind the waves were breaking violently as the *Thal* approached late in the day on November 9, 1898. A casual observer saw a small two-masted schooner offshore. He couldn't make out its name. It appeared to be in too close to the beach, and it was trying valiantly to claw its way out into deeper water as it was being pummeled by waves. The next morning it was gone. Debris on the beach told of the tragedy that had occurred under the darkness of night. It was all the evidence there was to identify the vessel as the *S. Thal.* August Schuenemann and two anonymous crew members (the only three people on board) lost their lives in the surf.[23]

In 1898 the Schuenemann Christmas Tree Ship was not yet the icon in Chicago that it was fourteen years later when the *Rouse Simmons* was lost. The loss of the *S. Thal* was a story for a day. The fact that it was carrying Christmas trees and was captained by one of the Schuenemann brothers was mentioned with no special flourish of attention. But the loss of August must have rocked the family at its deepest level. Years later, when Herman was lost, it was reported that Herman and Barbara's twin daughters (Hazel and Pearl), who were born a month prior to August's death, always insisted that their father call them on their birthday if he was away from home. The thought that something dreadful could happen to him was apparently on their minds even from an early age.

But this tragedy did not stop Herman from pursuing the business of selling Christmas trees. In fact, Herman would take the maritime Christmas tree trade to a whole new level unrivaled anywhere else.

THIRTEEN

HERMAN SCHUENEMANN
BECOMES CAPTAIN SANTA

Oh, Papa, come look! Oh, Mama, can you see?
I've been waiting for so long for this to come to be.
Oh, Papa, come look! Oh, Mama, can't you see?
Here comes the Christmas Ship with all the Christmas trees.

—Lee Murdock,
"The Christmas Tree Ship"

*W*hat made Herman's career so noteworthy, especially after the death of August, were his grand vision and stalwart efforts, which transformed a small family business into a large business that dominated the Christmas tree trade in the metropolis of Chicago. Herman Schuenemann changed the face of Christmas in the upper Midwest by making it possible for residents of an industrialized city to recapture an old and cherished tradition from an agrarian age. Just as he had a foot in two different ethnic camps (German and American), he also had one foot in the past with its antiquated, but lamented, ways and the other foot in the future with its possibilities for new and progressive accomplishments. He achieved success not by abandoning his heritage but by applying what it had given him to the creation of something new.

Christmas is much more spectacular as a secular holiday than it is as a sacred holiday. The sending of cards, giving of gifts, ornamentation of the home, and traditions connected with Santa Claus are only nominally connected with the religious significance of the season. Even the Christmas tree tradition is a Johnny-come-lately that was retrofitted to the occasion. As cold; rigid; stuffy; and, well, plain old "puritanical" as the Puritans were, they were correct: in its most popular manifestations, the holiday is more of a secular than a sacred occasion. Along with the inevitable symbolism of light overcoming the darkness that comes with the winter solstice, secular Christmas is about the balance of light and darkness in the *human* character. It is a time when people who have prospered beyond the fulfillment of their basic needs for food and shelter can luxuriate in their prosperity. The indulgence of excess is not only sanctioned, it is promoted, as long as there is an altruistic aim. Extravagance in giving is the norm, and purchasing gifts is the central activity. This in turn makes Christmas an engine of commerce to which the theological message of the season adds a kind of blessing as it frames the birth of Jesus as being God's gift to humankind.

With urbanization and industrialization came ready access to abundant amounts of products that could serve as gifts. This abundance provided the fuel for the kind of consumption craze that was ignited by the holiday with its emphasis on generosity, kindness, and charity. Thus, the end of the nineteenth century and the beginning of the twentieth century in the United States were a period when Christmas was a growth industry. Electric lights replaced candles on the tree. Artistically painted glass balls replaced ornaments handmade from materials found around the house or in the barn. Store windows became elaborate stage sets where mechanized puppets played out dramas before the eyes of dazzled children and adults.[1]

Still another dimension of Christmas that would have been particularly felt and appreciated by German Americans was the holiday's evocation of old-world sentiments and traditions. The 1880s saw a new peak in the rate of immigration from northern Europe (primarily German states) to the United States. In 1892 the Chicago *Abendpost* reported that there were almost 395,000 Germans living in the city.[2] As much as immigrants came seeking new opportunities, they did not leave behind their cultural identity. In fact, that cultural identity became all the more important as it gave them a ready-made community to which to attach themselves—the community of those who had arrived before them from their native land. And, because there was a relatively large proportion of skilled workers and educated individuals among the German immigrants, they often had greater purchasing power than other immigrant groups. Thus, Christmas was bound to become a meaningful and important occasion in the German American community.

Merchants, politicians, and other influence seekers were awakening to the opportunity that Christmas presented, too. In the first decade of the twentieth century newspapers were already carrying prognostications about the economic health of the nation based on the amount of commercial sales that occurred on the day after Thanksgiving. Weeks before the holiday itself the front page of the paper posted with each edition the number of shopping days left before Christmas. Large spreads of advertising lured consumers into the department stores, which were every bit as modern and spectacular for their day as were the huge suburban malls in the last quarter of the twentieth century. Escalators were a new invention that alone, for some, was worth the trip to a State Street store in Chicago. Opulent displays of decorations stimulated the senses and encouraged potential customers to loosen their grips on their wallets. Some stores ran large German-language advertisements, making it absolutely clear that German customers were welcomed and would feel at home while shopping.

Meanwhile, all around the city the "haves" were finding ways to give to the "have-nots." Everyone wanted to be the reformed Scrooge heaping kindnesses on the Cratchit family.

Inextricably connected with gift giving was the Christmas tree. For over a half a century the tree had traditionally been decorated with the gifts to be given. Small presents such as dolls, toy soldiers, fruits, nuts, candies, ribbons and bows, woolen socks or mittens, were tied to the branches of the tree, and, when it was time for the distribution of gifts, the tree was stripped bare. As time went on and prosperity increased, the size of the gifts became larger and larger so that they could no longer be hung on the tree. Instead, they were placed nearby, unwrapped. The tree was decorated with other ornaments along with candles or, later, electric lights. When all was ready, the tableau of tree and gifts was hidden from the children until the magic moment arrived and then dramatically presented to call forth the greatest expressions of delight and surprise.

As a secular and commercial phenomenon, Christmas became the ultimate middle-class holiday. There was no surer sign that one had arrived in that coveted class than to be able to afford the costly customs of Christmas. And the Schuenemanns, who had so recently become part of that middle class through their own hard work and enterprising ideas, became increasingly more flamboyant and successful as promoters of the holiday.

The year before August died in the loss of the schooner *S. Thal* Herman had bought the largest vessel that either of them ever owned. It was the schooner *Mary Collins,* which had been measured as having a carrying capacity of 231 gross tons. The vessel was four times larger in hull capacity than the *S. Thal,* and it just edged out the *Rouse Simmons* in size, being three feet longer, almost a foot deeper, and one foot narrower on the beam. Reports consistently placed its carrying capacity at ten thousand (or more) Christmas trees and several tons of lycopodium for the making of wreaths and garlands. The vessels that August is known to have used for Christmas trees were all under 100 gross tons except for one, while all the schooners used by Herman, except one, had over 200 tons carrying capacity. To afford such large vessels Herman bought hulls that were older. As a whole, the vessels that the Schuenemann brothers used were significantly older than those used by other lake mariners in the same trade. The median age of a Schuenemann tree ship was 36.5 years at the time of use, while the median age of all other tree vessels was 28 years at the time of use. Additionally, all of Herman's vessels were older than August's except in one instance, and, at least in some cases, this also meant that Herman's were riskier to use.[3]

Another difference between August's Christmas tree voyages and those of Herman was that the older brother restricted his range to the Kewaunee and Door County region of Wisconsin—"the Christmas Tree Coast." As soon as Herman acquired the *Mary Collins,* however, his voyages consistently took him beyond Wisconsin to the Upper Peninsula of Michigan in the area around Manistique where Thompson's Pier was located. There he developed some close business ties with local residents, and, if his own publicity is to be trusted (for he was known to add color to his stories),[4] with the Chippewa.

Herman was taking the business of bringing trees to Chicago in a new direction. He was operating on a much larger scale than his older brother had, and, as a good businessman would, he added other product lines to his offerings as the business expanded. Those other products were wreaths and garlands produced in abundance on board the ship as it was docked in the river and perhaps also made by local residents of the Manistique area and shipped ready made. It is difficult to say how extensive the wreath making was, but it must have been a substantial sideline. While his wife and daughters are frequently mentioned as toiling at shaping the pine boughs into the correct forms, other women were hired to assist in the production. In his research Theodore Charrney was able to solicit some firsthand accounts of the women working under the protection of a temporary housing that Herman built over the deck and heated with a stove, because the vessel's cabin was not big enough to accommodate all the workers.[5] A photograph of two tree ships side by side in the Chicago River bears this out. One of the vessels, easily identified as the *George L. Wrenn,* has a housing built over its deck between the mainmast and mizzenmast. Lying beside it and immediately adjacent to the dock is the schooner *John Mee.* The *Mee*'s deck is left open, allowing space for customers to come on board and make their purchases, while the *Wrenn* offers protection to the work crew. A newspaper article from 1898 describes "a score of girls and women" busily employed in the garland "factory" under a temporary deck housing. "The girls on the one side—on the starboard, to be nautical—make endless strings of green for decoration, weaving the lycopodium sprigs together with fine soft wire. They get for this 1 cent a yard and a good worker will make 200 to 250 yards a day. On the other side of the table—the port watch so to speak—the girls are making the round rings of evergreen so common this time of the year. These are built up about a willow wreath and are more difficult to make, one not making more than five or six dozen a day. For this they get 2 cents a wreath."[6] At least

The Christmas tree schooners *George L. Wrenn* and *John Mee* in the Chicago River. The *Wrenn* has a makeshift shelter covering its deck in front of the cabin. (Historical Collections of the Great Lakes, Bowling Green State University, Bowling Green, Ohio.)

one newspaper article suggests that space in a nearby building on South Water Street was also commandeered for the weaving of the greens.[7]

The idea of locating the schooner in a central location such as at the Clark Street bridge and selling trees directly off the deck of the boat was very likely another Herman Schuenemann innovation. At least there is no known mention of this venue for sales prior to Herman's appearance on the scene.

All of this activity could not have been supported if there was not an enterprising person with a business strategy behind the operation. The market for trees would naturally have been a good one in Chicago, but capturing the lion's share of that market would have taken energy, imagination, and hard work, especially when there was competition from other tree dealers—some of whom shipped by boat and some of whom shipped by railroad. Establishing a strong presence in this market was the genius of Captain Herman Schuenemann, and one of the ways he accomplished this was by transforming himself into Captain Santa.

The American image of Santa Claus has evolved over centuries from the earliest portrayals of Kris Kringle in Dutch Manhattan to the cinematic depictions of today. Powerful influences prior to the early 1900s had begun to shape a popular picture. (Who could forget the poem "A Visit from Saint Nicholas," with its familiar first line, "'Twas the night before Christmas and all through the house . . ."?) Although no one image of Santa Claus dominated at the time that Herman Schuenemann was in business, some general qualities were widely evoked. He was of short stature, had a big belly, and smoked a pipe; he loved children and delighted in pleasing them; and, perhaps most important of all, he was jolly. Oh, yes, and he arrived from the north in an unorthodox, magical way that spoke of a day gone by— a day before the modern inventions of steam engines, electricity, and internal combustion.[8]

Herman Schuenemann welcomed the publicity that associated him with Santa Claus—it was, after all, good for business—but it is doubtful that he set out to make himself a characterization of Santa per se. He did not dress up in a costume, don a white beard, or give away toys. His appearance did not reflect some of the common features associated with Santa. He was not especially short. He did not have a big belly. He did not look like an old man. Instead, he suggested Santa simply by the nature of who he was as a person. He was jovial, personable, and outgoing. He dominated the scene without being boisterous or insincere. He enjoyed what he did, and he enjoyed the people who came to see him, young and old alike. These are the very same characteristics that would have attracted him to the beer garden or saloon business and that would have made him successful in that realm. In a manner of speaking, Herman was an entertainer; he created atmospheres in which people felt welcomed and had fun. The kind of energy that it would take to gain notoriety in Chicago in these kinds of businesses suggests that he loved doing what he did and that his enthusiasm was contagious.

Another "Santa-like" characteristic of Herman's business was the means he had of transporting his trees. If that is taken literally, it is quite a leap from Saint Nicholas's sleigh pulled by eight tiny reindeer landing on a roof to a three-masted schooner sailing into a harbor. But as symbols, both have some of the same suggestive powers. The sleigh and the schooner are both throwbacks to an earlier and (through the lens of nostalgia) simpler time. Both involve a means of conveyance that has the quality of the fantastic. Both are associated with coming down from the remote, pristine, and wide-open north-lands to the all-too-familiar, sullied, and congested lands where humans struggle with the ambiguities of life.

But the greatest influence forging the association between Herman and Santa Claus was his relationship with the popular press. There he became "Captain Santa."

As the decade of the 1890s ended and the new century began, Herman became a darling of the newspapers. At a time of year when human interest and sentimentality sold newspapers, Herman provided fodder for the pen. While it would be hard to prove that he was intentional in shaping the stories that were told about him, it is highly likely that he perpetuated "enhancements" (some might say untruths) to make his image even more mythic in quality. For instance, the papers tended to blur his voyages together so that the public perception might be that not only had the captain been making tree voyages for many years (which he had, of course) but that he had used the same old faithful vessel throughout that whole time. Even more than preserving a tradition, the idea of using the same vessel for decade upon decade heightened the magical quality of the annual trip through the snow and ice and raging seas. The old ship was as stalwart as the old captain.[9] There may also have been some encouragement given to the press to exaggerate the actual number of trees that were carried or to avoid mentioning that many of the trees were brought to Chicago by railroad car. Another exaggeration may have been in the relationship between Captain Santa and the Chippewa at a time when urban dwellers (who had no memory of the frontier days) would associate the Chippewa with an image of exotic aboriginals.

The stories became more and more dramatic as the years went on.

In 1910 a press release quoted Captain Schuenemann as saying that he had to go deeper each year into the wilderness surrounding Lake Superior (rather than Lake Michigan, his true destination) to get his trees and that he was seven weeks (!) in making his six hundred mile (!) voyage back to Chicago from the remote north. (One can only imagine what shape a cargo of cut evergreens would have been in after such a long voyage!)[10] Eventually, his daughters began to take a role in the mythic tale. ("The captain takes his three daughters—Elsie, Hazel and Pearl—with him on his tree gathering trips. . . . and they feel that the responsibility of a happy Christmas for thousands of Chicago children rests with them.")[11] All of these things evoked an aura of the captain being larger than life, just as a similar aura was associated with Santa, who traveled by ageless reindeer in an equally ageless sleigh filled with enough toys for every child on the planet, from a faraway land of ice and snow, where he lived with a race of elves in primeval surroundings.

An excerpt from another early newspaper depiction will show the literary devices that brightened the happy holiday scene. (Italics have been added to emphasize the evocative and picturesque language.)

"The schooner *Mollie* [*sic*] *Collins,* that [*sic*] was towed down the river to her docks some days ago loaded with greens from the *primeval forests* of Michigan at the foot of Lake Michigan, has *for years* taken on a load of these *verdant decorations.* . . . On October 16 this vessel tied up at a *little port* where lumber is loaded. The crew of seven men under Oscar Armstrong, who has *sailed under Capt. Ed. Schenniman* [*sic*] for *eighteen years,* took the *big mainsail for a tent,* the *tiny* stove from the foc'sle and some tools and provisions and *rattled* into the heart of the woods on a logging train. There for twenty-nine days, the men camped, *miles from anywhere,* cutting the trees and picking ground pine for their cargo.

"The *snow fell* so early this year in the northern woods that it made the work of getting greens harder than common. The woods are *gradually being robbed* of the young trees suitable for *the Santa Claus treasures* and each year the task of procuring them becomes harder."[12]

The use of hyperbole increased over the years that Herman was the moving force behind the business. Some of it was straightforward misstatement of facts. For example, this: "The *Mary Collins* is

Chicago's first Christmas schooner."[13] But much of it might better be called poetic license. "At the gangway stands the skipper, *a short, rosy-faced man with a pipe* which he puffs while musing over his *treasure load. Every winter* for the last twenty-eight years he has converted his lumber barge into *a festive ship* at this season, sailing to *the north seas,* where he gathers his *precious cargo*" (emphasis added).[14] The next year this Santa-like figure speaks: "I guess the kids are gladdest [*sic*] of anybody to see us come pulling into the river every December. . . . There's generally a little crowd of them on the rail of the bridge when she swings open for us, and they wave their hands and cheer, and we cheer back. *Some of them think we are actually coming from the north pole*" (emphasis added).[15] He may refer to the children's naiveté with a wink and a nod, but the image that was put out for the children was skillfully cultivated.

Captain Santa was not only popular among the children, however. There is a clear impression created in the depiction of the business that Herman Schuenemann's Christmas tree voyages were also a gift to adults. Beyond making it possible for them to bring home a valued symbol of the season, it also helped by putting a few extra dollars into the pockets of young women and mothers who worked as wreath makers. "'Hooray for Captain Schuenemann!' shouted some of the women [who had been working on wreaths in the cabin of his schooner] as they waved their handkerchiefs at the jolly old skipper, who resembles Santa Claus."[16]

Once photographs began to appear in the Chicago newspapers, the image of Captain Santa received another boost. On November 30, 1910 the *Inter Ocean* featured him on page three with three large photographs and a lengthy story. Top center is a head and shoulders shot of the captain. His face, round and full, smiles warmly, with welcoming eyes and a bushy mustache. The captain is wearing a sailor's traditional rain gear, the familiar oilcloth hat with the broad brim designed to shed water down the back and the matching coat. In the corner of the picture is part of a Christmas tree that the captain is hefting as he unloads his precious cargo. The author of the article casts Captain Schuenemann as the man who has saved Christmas once again, bringing joy into the lives of a beleaguered public:

"Chicago will not suffer a dearth in the Christmas tree market this year. Whatever may happen to beefsteaks and butter, this one necessity of life will remain within reach of the average man's purse."

This particular photograph is a prime example of how Herman cultivated his image. The oilcloth rain gear is obviously part of a stage set. Not only is it not storming, but other men pictured with the captain in the other two photographs are dressed with no concern for precipitation. The schooner's sails have been stripped from the spars, and the boat has quite plainly been safely in the harbor for some time. A close examination of one of the subsequent pictures shows that the captain is wearing dress pants and shoes under his rain slicker, giving all the confirmation that is needed that his clothing is more costume than uniform and that Herman had a genius for capturing the attention of the newspapers and the public by giving them a story that appealed to the hearts of many. Indeed, it is remarkable to think that of all the Christmas tree ships that served Chicago over the years, Captain Schuenemann's was the only one to be featured with detailed articles and photographs year after year. In promoting his business Herman was inevitably playing a vital role in making Christmas the celebratory event that it has become—a time to put up a tree even if there are no beefsteak and butter to put on the table.

Whether these reports were merely inspired by Herman Schuenemann or were consciously planted by him, they had the effect of creating an enduring public persona and making him a prominent feature on the holiday scene in Chicago year after year. His brother August had been popular around the docks among seamen, merchants, and farmers with whom he did business, and this popularity won him the moniker "Christmas Tree Schuenemann." But Herman went much further. His image extended well beyond the docks and was meant to catch the eye of a much broader public. Herman entered the realm of fantasy as "Captain Santa Claus."

The cost of being Captain Santa was steep. It was hard work jammed into a narrow time frame. But most of all it was dangerous. In 1900 Herman Schuenemann headed north in the schooner *Mary Collins*. It was his third year using this vessel. But before he could reach his destination the *Mary Collins* went ashore near Point aux Barque at the foot (north end) of Lake Michigan. Gale-force wind, fog, and a faulty compass were all mentioned as possible causes, but the wreck may also have been the result of human error. No one was injured or killed, but, after a vigorous attempt to rescue the boat, Captain Schuenemann had to abandon the *Mary Collins*.[17] That year he convinced his friend Captain Nelson to bring the schooner *Ida* to the Upper Peninsula so that he could still bring trees to Chicago.[18] After that Herman used the *Bertha Barnes* and *Truman Moss* for one year each before he and Barbara bought the schooner with which they had their longest association, the *George L. Wrenn*.

Herman used the *Wrenn* for eight years, 1901 to 1909. Before him, the vessel had been owned by a group of investors who were going to send it on a circumnavigation of the globe with the mission of collecting artifacts of the world's cultures to be used for scientific study and museum display.[19] The trip never happened, but it explains a feature of the *Wrenn* that was seen on very few lake boats. The main cabin stretched the entire width of the boat, from gunwale to gunwale, making it substantially larger than others. (Normally, cabins were narrow enough to allow a walkway down each side of the ship on the level of the quarterdeck.)

From reading the newspaper coverage of Captain Santa's tree voyages in the first decade of the twentieth century it might be concluded that the business was profitable and expanding. The choice and condition of the vessels used, however, seem to support an opposite conclusion. Of course, there were other factors that would play a role in the solvency of the business. Herman's other business ventures (this was the time that he was managing a warm weather beer garden first in Forest Park and then on the north side of Chicago) may have drained capital if they were not successful. Also, other business deals (perhaps real estate investment) may have resulted in losses that had to be made up elsewhere. At any rate, it is indisputable that Herman either did not have the will or the means to maintain his tree ships adequately.

Recurrent need for essential repair jobs makes it evident that his vessels placed him repeatedly in grave danger. During the period that Herman used the *George Wrenn* it was hauled out for caulking and repair at least three times.[20] By 1906 the vessel was no longer being used to carry freight during the sailing season. Instead, it remained docked in the Chicago River all year with the exception of the annual Christmas tree voyage. People in Manistique, Michigan, where the *Wrenn* had been a frequent visitor, found it a "sorry sight" when Captain Schuenemann brought it north that year.[21] Two years later the Christmas tree voyage had to be interrupted to allow time for the *Wrenn* to be pulled out and caulked. Something scary must have happened on that voyage because the next year Captain Schuenemann used the *Bertha Barnes* for his tree ship and was quoted in Chicago as saying that he had been forced to stop using the *Wrenn* because "last year" it nearly "chucked" the captain and his crew into "Davy Jones' Locker."[22]

The *Rouse Simmons,* which Captain Santa used for the first time in 1910, was also a marginally safe vessel to be out on the lake. Its home port was St. James on Beaver Island in Lake Michigan but far to the north and east of Chicago. The vessel's primary owner, Mannes Bonner, acquired it after it had suffered a severe pounding on the shore of Grand Traverse Bay and needed major repairs.[23] He used it locally for shipping wood and bark from the island, but as year followed year, the *Rouse Simmons* spent more and more time inactive and at anchor, a situation that can lead to a dangerous degree of neglect. The second year that Herman used the *Simmons* they had to interrupt their voyage north to Thompson's Pier long enough to pull it out and have its bottom recaulked.[24]

In the end, Captain Schuenemann asked more of his schooner than it could provide. Ultimately, his mistake cost him his life.

Herman Schuenemann died in the cold and storm-tossed waters of Lake Michigan trying to save an image . . . not just his own image as Captain Santa but the more complete image that embodied the myth and magic of secular Christmas. He might have given up using schooners to bring trees to Chicago years before. There were certainly enough indications along the way to demonstrate to any reasonable man what the dangers were. He could have done what his wife and children were ultimately forced to do—bring Christmas trees to Chicago on railroad cars and use an old retired schooner as a stage to sell them from. With his experience in other businesses he might have invested more of his efforts as the owner of a beer garden, saloon, grocery store, or real estate. But he chose to stick with the maritime Christmas tree trade. Even with debt piling up and an increasing liability with each voyage he made, Captain Schuenemann kept going back. His choice, however, was not based purely on such objective measures as the age of a schooner, the kind of weather conditions, or the amount of financial and moral liability he was accepting. Herman had "his public." How could he let them down? What may have been a marketing gambit to some was an enduring truth to others. Captain Santa really did work his magic every year. Was Herman intoxicated by his image, or was he codependent to an intoxicated press and public? No matter. He was not ready to let the image go, and it cost him and his shipmates their lives. The only consolation is that, because of the tragic ending, the image has been burned into our collective history. Some treat it as history and others as legend, and both are right.

FOURTEEN

LIES, MISTAKES,
AND HOAX

Ask me no questions and I'll tell you no lies.
—Oliver Goldsmith (1728–74)

*S*o, the disappearance of the *Rouse Simmons* was a story that already had roots in the newspapers of Chicago and in the minds of an incalculable number of Chicagoans, young and old. Christmas tree ships had been a regular part of the holiday season in the city at least as far back as 1876, when Captain McDonald from Ahnapee brought a cargo of trees on the scow-schooner *Lady Ellen*. But in the past decade the scale of the operation and the visibility to the public had grown tremendously due to the synergy between Captain Santa (Herman Schuenemann) and the Chicago press. As a result, when the final voyage ended in tragedy, the press was primed for making it a really big story . . . not a really accurate story, not even a really truthful story . . . just a really BIG story.

The story that first broke in Chicago was that wreckage from the *Rouse Simmons* had been found across Lake Michigan at Pentwater— the town where the fishing fleet had been caught in the gale of November 23, resulting in the wreck of the tug *Two Brothers* with the loss of the three men on board. No claim was made that a name was found on any of the debris, but the *Daily News* stated that "many Christmas trees" were on the beach, while the *American* quoted Captain M. R. Ewald of the Pentwater Life Saving Station at length. "I have no doubt but that the *Rouse Simmons* went down in mid-lake, probably Sunday night when the big nor'wester was on. The first wreckage of the ship came in last Wednesday [November 27] when a Christmas tree, plainly cut for that purpose, squared off at the base, floated ashore and was found by the patrol. After that an old-fashioned hatch like the type on the old vessels came in. The next of the wreckage was bits of deckhousing with evergreen sticking to the splinters. The stuff is still being tossed upon the beaches."[1]

In contrast to such seemingly sure evidence of the disaster, the newspapers on the east shore of the lake—nearer to Pentwater—reported nothing about Christmas trees being found, except when they were quoting the press releases from Chicago. In fact, the findings there were quite the opposite! The *Muskegon News Chronicle* said, "Wreckage which has been floating ashore here, consists largely of lumber, a proof that it is not from the *Rouse Simmons* as at first thought, as the *Simmons* was carrying a cargo of Christmas trees." If we believe the Muskegon paper, there is no way to explain the clear and definitive evidence from Captain Ewald other than as a fabrication of the newspaper.[2]

On Friday, December 6, almost two weeks after the strange disappearance between Kewaunee and Two Rivers 150 miles to the north, several Chicago papers proclaimed that the body of the first mate of the *Simmons,* Steven Nelson, had been found on the beach at Pentwater—a story that has been frequently repeated. "FIND BODY OF MAN BELIEVED VICTIM OF ROUSE SIMMONS" and "CHRISTMAS SHIP DEAD WASHED ASHORE," read the tenth edition of the Chicago *American*. Again sources were quoted, including Thomas Hanson, treasurer of the Lake Seamen's Union; and Elsie Schuenemann, daughter of the captain of the *Simmons*. However, the fact of the matter is very different. The body was most definitely not sailor Nelson at all! It was that of Tony Johnson, the helper on board the fishing tug *Two Brothers,* whom eyewitnesses had seen jumping off the stern of the boat in the moments when it had hung precariously on the breakwater back on November 23. The next day the *American* acknowledged its mistake but in a most inconspicuous manner that few were likely to see.[3]

In spite of the attention given to events at Pentwater in the press, it would appear that officials of the Life Saving and Revenue Cutter Services gave little or no credibility to these reports. Instead, the attention of officials was directed to the stretch of lake between Kewaunee and Two Rivers, Wisconsin. Even as Chicagoans were first learning of the potential disaster, the Milwaukee-based revenue cutter *Tuscarora* was preparing to sail in search of the *Rouse Simmons*. Their orders were not to cross the lake toward Pentwater but to head north along the Wisconsin shore. But, at the last moment, the captain of the *Tuscarora* changed his course 180 degrees and headed south.

A thick fog hung over Lake Michigan on December 4 as the revenue cutter steamed out into the lake. As the *Tuscarora* cleared the harbor it passed an incoming freighter, the *George W. Orr*, and officers on the two vessels spoke briefly. Captain Berry of the *Tuscarora* was led to believe that Captain Herman Jaenke of the steamer *Orr* had located the *Rouse Simmons* by the sound of its fog bell. Jaenke placed the bell three miles due east of the Milwaukee piers. Apparently he made no claim of a visual sighting. Based on this seemingly shaky evidence received in a chance meeting, and in direct contradiction of credible witnesses from the Life Saving Service in Kewaunee and Two Rivers, Captain Berry decided to retrace the course of the *Orr*, which had come from the south. So the *Tuscarora* felt its way tentatively through the fog past Racine and Kenosha to Waukegan, Illinois. Of course, no evidence of the *Rouse Simmons* was found.[4]

But Captain Jaenke was wrong. Earlier that November, the city of Milwaukee had taken delivery of a new lightship, the largest on the lakes at the time. *Lightship 95* had been stationed for permanent duty exactly three miles out in the lake due east of the Milwaukee pier head. The lightship was equipped with a beacon for use in clear weather, a fog whistle for days like December 4 when visibility was poor, and a fog bell for the times when the whistle failed.[5] The Chicago *Daily News* later quoted the captain of the freighter *George W. Orr:* "I did not actually see the vessel, but I heard the ringing of a

The revenue cutter *Tuscarora* presented an impressive profile. (Historical Collections of the Great Lakes, Bowling Green State University, Bowling Green, Ohio.)

bell and knowing that the schooner *Rouse Simmons* had a bell I thought at first that the fog signal was that of the . . . boat. The vessel was about three miles off shore." Then came the clincher: "Now that I have learned that the government lightship is anchored about three miles off one of the piers at Milwaukee, and also possesses a bell, in addition to a fog whistle, I am quite positive that I was mistaken in thinking the boat was the *Rouse Simmons*. The lake was so foggy I couldn't see the boat, and that accounts for my error."[6]

It is not hard to understand the mistake that Captain Jaenke made in thinking that it was a schooner's bell that he had heard. But why would he assume it was the bell of the *Rouse Simmons*? Bells were not uncommon. Even more inexplicable was the behavior of Captain Berry of the revenue cutter *Tuscarora*. Surely he knew that a new lightship had been placed out in the lake precisely where the sound was reported. Surely he knew that the sound of a bell was no real evidence of what vessel was lurking out in the fog. And surely he did not think that his own perfunctory cruise to Waukegan and back with that same fog preventing clear observations was an adequate attempt to find the *Rouse Simmons*.

Undoubtedly, the original search area was chosen because of the reports of the lifesavers who saw the three-masted schooner in distress and who had searched in vain for it during the storm of November 23. Captain Berry seems to have abandoned a rational and premeditated plan of search and rescue to follow a whim in a fog that rendered the whole voyage purposeless.

The logbook of the *Tuscarora* shows that the revenue cutter then spent twenty-three hours sitting in Waukegan while the crew did several token inspections of local vessels. Only then did Captain Berry take his vessel back out into the lake to sail back north. Rather than returning to his home base, he continued on past Milwaukee and finally carried out the search that was first intended. But, again, his actions might leave some scratching their heads and wondering about how seriously he was taking his mission. The *Tuscarora* passed Milwaukee at about midnight on December 6. At 2:00 a.m. Sheboygan was abeam on the port side. A couple of hours later they passed Two Rivers. Now they were in the target area—the region where the three-masted schooner, similar in every way to the *Rouse Simmons,* disappeared. The log does not record how far north the cutter proceeded before altering course to sail back south, but by 8:40 a.m. it had already reached its furthest point and had retreated as far as Two Rivers on its way home to Milwaukee. In other words, during the most crucial hours of the search it was night, the wind was WSW and blowing at gale force, the temperature was falling to below freezing, the sky was overcast, and the moon was only a sliver (thirty-six hours short of being a new moon). The search for the *Rouse Simmons* was carried out in pitch darkness and without any consultation with people onshore. The more that is known about the actions of Captain Berry, the more questionable they become. And this will not be the last opportunity to question the man's judgments or motives.[7]

The flimsy report of Captain Jaenke of the freighter *Orr* was jumped on by the Chicago *American* in the banner headline that appeared the following day: "SANTA CLAUS SHIP MAY BE SAFE." However, hope for a happy outcome lasted only hours. Later that same day, even before the *Tuscarora*'s captain was able to report the results of his futile search, newsboys who hawked the papers on crowded street corners were shouting out gloom and doom once more: "LOSE HOPE FOR SHIP—SANTA CLAUS SHIP LOST."[8]

In crisis and turmoil, misinformation, misinterpretation, and mistakes are understandable. When people are desperate and there is no credible information, any information will do. But the information that was being spread in public was not simply full of mistakes, it was full of lies. On the official level, more credible information was available within the Life Saving Service, but it was being used in a careless and irresponsible way by people who were not invested in solving the mystery of the disappearing schooner.

On Thursday, December 5, Chicago papers gave brief mention to bits of evergreen trees being found in the nets of fishermen near Two Rivers. The following day a full-blown narrative appeared in the *Daily News* about how "Lake Michigan hurled hundreds of Christmas trees on the bleak shore near Sturgeon Bay." The scene was described from the vantage point of A. S. Putnam, a shipbuilder and livery owner from Sturgeon Bay who, allegedly, had been interviewed over the telephone by a reporter from the *News*. The picture is full of action and vivid with detail. Putnam (if he is, indeed, responsible for these words) describes a people hypervigilant in their hopes of spotting the *Rouse Simmons* and hyperactive in their attempts to find remains.

> Night and day we have watched the lake for a sight of the missing boat. The men established a beach patrol in order that they might send immediate help to the missing vessel if it appeared near our town in distress. Not only did the men take part in the search, but also wives, mothers and sisters, eager to administer aid if it became necessary. Daily the waters rose and fell on the shores but nothing appeared. Late yesterday afternoon the *Sylvia,* a fishing boat, while making its way to a pier plunged

into a floating forest of Christmas trees a mile from shore. All about the fishermen lay the greens like seaweed. The other boats reported the same experience. . . .

At dawn men, women and children braved the cold to hurry to the lake. There, piled high on the sand, were Christmas trees, broken and torn. The water dyed a dark green by the torn branches and trees that still lay in the waves, which even tossed their tops above the surface as they lashed each other.

There were hundreds of them. The biting wind was forgotten and mothers and daughters mingled with fishermen in searching among the greens for timber and bodies of those we believe went down with the boat. Some even went into the icy surf to search.

The noise of the crashing breakers and their size did not daunt some of the boldest and they even ventured to launch a boat to search the waters. The fate of those who probably succumbed with the *Rouse Simmons* might have been theirs had they been successful in getting far offshore. They realized the impossible task and decided to wait until the timber drifted ashore.

. . . We are on the watch night and day and I feel pretty sure that sooner or later bodies will appear. We are only waiting for an east wind, which will bring everything to our coast, and then the mystery of the wreck will be clear.[9]

Water "dyed a dark green" by broken and torn evergreens! Mothers and daughters mingling with fishermen searching for timber and bodies among the trees! Such drama! Such fiction! Such lies! There was not a word of truth in the story. The possibility that the answers to surviving family members' questions might be found in Sturgeon Bay prompted the Chicago police to investigate. The results of that investigation were never reported in the *Daily News*. Instead the *Inter Ocean,* a paper not given to printing sensational stories, told what detective John J. Halpin had discovered: "Reports of wreckage and Christmas trees floating ashore in Sturgeon Bay or that vicinity were false. The greens picked up there were not of the kind carried on the *Rouse Simmons*."[10]

Meanwhile, the newspaper in Sturgeon Bay (which, by the way, is not on the Lake Michigan shore but rather is across the peninsula that divides Lake Michigan from Green Bay) reported no such activities. Indeed, a week later the hometown *Advocate* called the Chicago papers "sensational dailies" and described the report of trees coming ashore at Sturgeon Bay by the hundreds as "the most ridiculous lot of trash that could originate in the imaginative mind of a human being." The Sturgeon Bay boatbuilder and livery owner A. S. Putnam was exonerated. Someone had seen brush thrown into the water of the Sturgeon Bay Lake Michigan Ship Canal, and Putnam had merely telegraphed Mrs. Barbara Schuenemann in Chicago to say that if it proved true that trees were coming ashore, he would have them collected and shipped to her so that she might recoup some of her loss.[11]

The histrionics of the Chicago reporting were immediately recognized for what they were by the sober minded Captain Sogge of the Two Rivers Life Saving Station. Nonetheless, duty dictated that he be diligent in his investigation, and so on December 6 he made another sweep of the shoreline between Two Rivers and Kewaunee, the area where the three-masted schooner in distress was seen on November 23. His notation from that morning's voyage on an icy cold Lake Michigan reads: "8 A.M. launched power Lifeboat. Made a true search allong [*sic*] the Shore N. to the point, and beyond the point in the bay to sandy bay point, a distance 18 mile N., to satisfy myself of any wreckage been showed up after the South East and South blow of yesterday, but not a particle was to be seen. Returned at the station 12:15 p.m. considerable iced down."[12] Not a particle seen! Captain Sogge might not have known for sure what happened to the *Rouse Simmons,* but he knew that the truth was not going to be found in the newspaper.

As Chicagoans were reading about the so-called proofs that the *Rouse Simmons* was lost forever, they were getting some firsthand evidence of what punishment the weather and the lake could inflict.

When the fog of Wednesday lifted it was pursued by a wind that grew in intensity until it reached its full fury on Friday, December 6. In the city, a gale of fifty miles an hour was reported. As before, the temperatures dropped as the storm strengthened until it was well below freezing. On Lincoln Avenue passengers were said to have fled when a Chicago trolley car was almost hit by a sign, fifty feet long, blown down by the wind. Windows at a variety of locations were reported to have been blown out, and roofs were damaged. For awhile attention shifted away from the *Rouse Simmons* as newspapers began to pick up the anxiety felt for other ships that were still out of port. Rescue missions were needed on Lakes Superior, Huron, and Erie, and there was concern for several old vessels that were known to be out on Lake Michigan but had not been heard from.

Of particular importance were the *Minerva, George A. Marsh, J. V. Taylor, Edward S. Skeele, Cora A. Hossack,* and *Butcher Boy* (all schooners); the *Alabama* (a passenger steamer); and the *Arizona* (a steam freighter). As each was finally heard from, some argued that the *Simmons* might likewise appear, while others were convinced that it could not have survived the horrors that were described by the disembarking crews.[13]

When the *Minerva* arrived in Chicago, the *Daily News* ran a picture of it, an ice enshrouded hulk, with the caption "Schooner *Minerva* in port after hard battle with waves that sank the *Rouse Simmons*." The next day, two schooners, the *George A. Marsh* and *Cora A. Hossack,* arrived. They had left Sturgeon Bay together and sailed at a distance of several miles from each other, keeping watch all the way for any evidence of the *Rouse Simmons*. "A few pieces of water soaked pine trees, believed to be part of the *Simmons* cargo, were seen south of Waukegan, but no wreckage or bodies were found," said the *Inter Ocean*. (There is, of course, even less credibility to a report of Christmas trees being found as far south as Waukegan than there was to the sighting of trees at Sturgeon Bay.) By Monday December 9, the remaining three survivors were reported to have limped into the harbor of Chicago—the *J. V. Taylor,* the *Edward S. Skeele,* and the *Cora A. Hossack*.[14]

Captain Bernsten of the *Skeele* brought news of having spoken to the captain of the car ferry *Ann Arbor No. 5,* whom he had met at Manitowoc. This was the first time that the news media in Chicago had heard of the steamer's sighting of a schooner badly heeled over and laboring under shortened sail north of Kewaunee on the same day and only a short time before lifesavers had spotted a similarly rigged boat out in the lake flying a signal of distress. It did not take a lot of imagination to create a scandal out of the report. Under the headline "CHRISTMAS SHIP AID REFUSED" the *Chicago American* ran a story that began "Reports indicating that a steam vessel refused aid to the schooner *Rouse Simmons,* a few hours before the old three-master was lost with eighteen men on board, reached Chicago today."[15]

Refusing would have been scandalous, to be sure, and the *American* suggested that some were eager for a federal investigation of the car ferry's actions. But when the facts were fully known, no one (including Captain Bernsten of the schooner *Skeele*) was willing to point the finger of blame at the captain of the *Ann Arbor No. 5.* It was not hard to accept that the *Simmons,* if it was indeed the *Simmons,* was not signaling distress when seen by the car ferry. The steamer's captain had done all that was required of him by yielding way to it. True, he did not go to the aid of the schooner, but he most certainly did not refuse aid. The *Sturgeon Bay Advocate* would later quote Captain Bernsten: "Having had a talk with the captain of the *Ann Arbor No. 5* about the fate of the schooner *Rouse Simmons . . .* She was flying no signals of distress as far as they could see, although she was about half a mile from them at the time. The vessel appeared to be listed badly and they thought something was wrong but as there were no signals visible they did not deem it necessary to go to her, never thinking but what she would make harbor in safety."[16]

Still, one more schooner remained to be heard from. That vessel was the *Butcher Boy.* Coincidentally, it had been arriving at Manistique, Michigan, on the same day that the *Rouse Simmons* had departed from nearby Thompson's Pier. But the master of the *Butcher Boy,* Captain Gustave Hansen, had not set sail from Manistique until after the gale of December 6 had passed. Even then, he was forced to seek shelter behind Plum Island, just north of the Door County Peninsula. There the *Butcher Boy* lay to until Wednesday, December 11, when a shift of the wind to the north made it possible to sail, even though the cold air ensured that the boat would ice up badly.[17]

Although it was unknown at the time to the captain and crew of the *Butcher Boy,* the schooner created quite a stir as it passed within sight of the Sturgeon Bay Canal. The *Advocate* reported that there was "considerable excitement" at the canal when a report reached town from further north along the coastline that a schooner "with canvas that looked like the *Rouse Simmons*" was heading south. Word had been received from Chicago that all of the schooners missing from that port during the storm of December 6 had arrived safely. Could this lone and last vessel from the north be the long awaited *Simmons*?

The word that had been passed by telephone or telegraph inspired a scheme in Sturgeon Bay to obtain positive identification of the unknown schooner. The car ferry was in port and about to head out through the canal for its eastward crossing of the lake. Locals asked its captain to run in close to the coasting schooner to learn its name and, if it was the *Rouse Simmons,* to hoist a flag. The captain obliged, but no signal flag was raised. The *Ann Arbor* reconnoitered and passed by the schooner *Butcher Boy,* adding nothing to help solve the mystery. It isn't hard to imagine the deflation of emotions on shore. The last real hope of a miracle had been quashed.[18]

When the *Butcher Boy* finally reached Chicago, its captain was widely quoted for his comments about his last sighting of the *Rouse Simmons* as the schooner was leaving Thompson's Pier. "When I saw the *Rouse Simmons* beating out, I said to the others: 'Captain Schuenemann must be in a terrible hurry to get those trees to market. I wouldn't go out in this storm for all the trees the *Mauretania* could carry. Those boys will be lucky if they don't go to the bottom.'"[19]

In the Chicago press and in the minds of readers all up and down the Lake Michigan shoreline the November 23 storm and the storm of December 6 were becoming merged. With the *Butcher Boy* not reaching Chicago until December 13, it would have been natural to assume that its captain's sighting of the *Simmons* at the northern extremity of Lake Michigan had occurred as the latter of the two storms was building. In fact, the idea had already been established as a fact by the *Chicago American*'s report on December 6 that the "Santa Ship" had been "doomed" by the "big gale" that began on December 5. And so the stage was set for what became the most enduring, and some might say endearing, story to come out of the events surrounding the loss of the Christmas Tree Ship. But the mistaken assumptions about which storm it was that "doomed" the *Rouse Simmons* also prove that this oft repeated story was the biggest and most cruel lie of them all.

On Friday, December 13, the Chicago papers broke the new story. "Word from death ship," the *Chicago American* called it. "Positive proof of the sinking of the *Rouse Simmons*" was the lead from the *Daily Journal*. Allegedly, a bottle had been found near Sheboygan containing a farewell note from the sinking ship's captain, Herman Schuenemann.

But, as with other falsehoods, the story was radically different elsewhere. In Manitowoc the story was branded "a fake." In Sturgeon Bay it was attributed to "the fertile imagination of the Chicago papers." In Sheboygan, the town where the note was supposedly found, the *Press* reported that "no such letter was found here" and that the fisherman who was said to have found the note in a bottle bobbing on the surface of the lake was "unknown among fishermen here."[20]

The detailed description given by the two Chicago papers that reported the note-in-the-bottle story made it seem authentic enough. The bottle was black and "sealed with a whittled stopper, cut evidently from a limb of a Christmas tree," while the words were "written in pencil with a faltering hand," said the *American*. It contained the last words of a man who knew that he was doomed to death and "was written on a page of the ship's log," reported the *Daily Journal*. Both agreed on the wording, if not a few of the details: "Friday—Everybody good-by. I guess we are all through. Sea washed off our deck load on Thursday. During the night the small boat was washed off. Leaking badly. Engwald and Steve fell overboard Thursday. God help us. HERMAN SCHUENEMANN."[21]

Here the confusion between the storm of Friday, December 6, and the gale of Saturday, November 23, becomes a detail of critical importance. The *American* was sure that the Friday mentioned in the note must have been December 6, the day on which Chicago had tasted the blast of the wintry storm and a day that other shipmasters had described as one of the worst they had ever spent on Lake Michigan. The *Daily Journal*, on the other hand, was equally convinced that it must have been Friday, November 29, perhaps recollecting that it was just about Thanksgiving Day (November 28) when the word had begun to spread that the *Rouse Simmons* was missing.

Of course, both papers were wrong. The details of the note were based upon information that had not been publicly discredited but that examination easily proves false. "Sea washed off our deck load on Thursday," said the note, but reports of a deck load of trees being found had been debunked. "During the night the small boat was washed off," said the note, but the sighting of a yawl on the open water was never substantiated with any physical evidence. "Engwald and Steve fell overboard Thursday," said the note, but the body at Pentwater was not from the *Simmons,* and no other had been found anywhere around the shore of the lake. But, most telling of all, the days named in the note contradict everything to which reliable first-hand witnesses had testified. Unless we discredit the Kewaunee life-savers; the Two Rivers lifesavers; the captain of the *Ann Arbor No. 5;* and the captain of the schooner *Butcher Boy;* not to mention the people of Thompson, Michigan, all of whom give witness to the *Simmons* having departed from Thompson's Pier on Friday, November 22, and having foundered late in the day on Saturday between Kewaunee and Two Rivers, the note must be a hoax, plain and simple. The *Rouse Simmons* was not on the lake on Thursday during its last voyage.

A letter was received by the Sheboygan Police Department requesting a copy of the farewell note that had been found by the fisherman of that city. The plea had come from Mrs. Frank Bausewein, a Chicago woman, the grieving mother of a young member of Captain Schuenemann's crew, a young man who was engaged to be married and who had sailed to earn extra money to launch him on his dreams. The article in the *Press* on Friday, December 20, ended on this sad note: "The Police Department returned an answer saying that the report was false, no such letter having been found here." Now the survivors of the crew of the *Rouse Simmons* had themselves become victims, not of nature's fury but of a prankster's thoughtlessness.

It would be fascinating to know how the note-in-the-bottle story came to be. The easiest explanation would be to say that it was a pure fiction invented by the Chicago papers to sell another edition. Such a thing is not beyond the realm of possibility. Those who enjoy speculation, however, might consider another scenario that is suggested by the connection of the note to federal officials in Milwaukee. According to the *Chicago American,* the man who found the bottle "turned it over to authorities [and] United States marine officials at Milwaukee, who were communicated with today, sent the news to Chicago."[22] Milwaukee, of course, was home base for the revenue cutter *Tuscarora* and the negligent Captain Berry.

The certainty of the loss of the *Simmons,* felt in Milwaukee[23] and elsewhere, was not shared by key figures in Chicago. A movement was afoot to launch yet another search. Inspired by stories of how the schooners *Minerva, George A. Marsh, Cora A. Hossack, Edward S. Skeele, J. V. Taylor,* and *Butcher Boy* had survived the wintry fury of December 6 by seeking shelter at places like Manistique, Bailey's Harbor, Sturgeon Bay, and Manitowoc, family and friends of the crew of the *Rouse Simmons* could not rule out the possibility that the *Rouse Simmons,* too, had sought shelter. But where? All of the obvious places had been checked. Perhaps the schooner was in a more out-of-the-way place—one of the small islands in the Fox or Beaver Island chains at the northern end of the lake. Maybe it was grounded on a reef or beach and unable to get off. Maybe it was trapped in the ice of a shallow bay. Perhaps the crew was surviving on the meager rations that were meant to last only for a voyage of a couple of days, huddled against the cold winds and crested waves of Lake Michigan, burning whatever dry wood they could find to keep warm until they were discovered. Perhaps! Maybe! Just maybe!

In Washington, DC, the voice of the friends of the crew of the *Rouse Simmons* was heard. Officially, the *Tuscarora* was ordered back out on the lake to search the northerly islands. But what was Captain Berry to do? Immediately after he had returned from his cruise of December 6 and 7, he had decommissioned his boat. Its boilers were cold, its galley emptied, its equipment mothballed, and its crew dispersed to their homes. Besides, argued the captain, the *Tuscarora* was not a vessel built to withstand the ice that it might encounter on such a voyage. After several days with no action on the part of Captain Berry and the *Tuscarora,* the orders were rescinded by the secretary of the treasury. Instead, the *Mackinac,* a revenue cutter based at Sault Ste. Marie, built to cope with ice and still in commission, was assigned to search for the Christmas Tree Ship among the islands.[24]

On its voyage the *Mackinac* stopped at St. James, Michigan, on Beaver Island to pick up the man who actually owned the controlling interest in the *Rouse Simmons,* Captain Mannes J. Bonner. The report that Lieutenant Wheeler of the Revenue Cutter Service later filed shows that the skepticism about finding the *Simmons* was not particular to the government officials.

> Going over the charts carefully with Capt. Bonner and others I was convincingly informed that with the single exception of Gull Island, all of the northern islands had been repeatedly visited since the disappearance of the *Simmons;* that it was impossible for the *Simmons* or any great quantity of wreckage to have reached any of these islands without being discovered and reported.
>
> Capt. Bonner was very appreciative of the service thus attempted by the cutter, and was most anxious to locate the vessel, but he honestly said that he did not wish to advise doing work for no purpose at this season.[25]

Indeed, the season was late. All navigational aids had already been removed. All but a few lighthouses in the north had been closed for the winter. Ice and snow were daily dangers. Still, the *Mackinac* discharged its duty—even going so far as to put a landing party ashore on one of the islands to search for remains—and returned, with difficulty, to its home base at Sault Ste. Marie. Unfortunately, the revenue cutter's cruise only served to validate the skeptics' opinions.[26]

Having found nothing to witness to the fate of the *Simmons,* Lieutenant Wheeler of the *Mackinac* could hardly pronounce a verdict. Officially, the vessel's disappearance remained an unsolved mystery. But that did not prevent an unofficial verdict from being declared. The *Simmons* was no longer news. Just as swiftly as it had disappeared from the face of Lake Michigan, it disappeared from the front pages of the Chicago papers. The papers ignored the results of the late December search by the Revenue Cutter Service. Only those closer to the scene reported the verdict reached by the Revenue Cutter Service. From Sault Ste. Marie: "When no trace of the boat was discovered the search was given up for good, all unqualifiedly declaring she had become waterlogged and sunk with all on board."[27]

To many, of course, this verdict was no surprise. They had no trouble accepting that the *Rouse Simmons* was an old workhorse that simply could not do what was being asked of it. Some in the maritime community would recall that the year before the schooner had been forced to stop in Sturgeon Bay on its way north to have its bottom caulked because it was taking on so much water. On the Michigan side of the lake others would recall that a few years earlier the vessel had been found waterlogged in midlake by the car ferry *Grand Haven,* which took it in tow and brought it safely into Milwaukee. And at the northern end of the lake mariners would know that nine years before it disappeared the *Rouse Simmons* was described as "badly broken up" when it grounded in Traverse Bay near Torch Lake.[28] By 1912 the *Rouse Simmons* was forty-four years old. Its career as part of the lumber fleet running between Muskegon and Chicago had ended decades before, and since then the vessel had been maintained in a haphazard manner, unable to earn enough in freight charges to buy a berth in a dry dock where it could be properly refitted. But, to those who knew it when, and especially to those who knew its crew, the verdict was not so easy to accept.

The last word on the fate of the *Rouse Simmons* may not have been heard, however. During the summer of 2006 an underwater archaeological research team from the Wisconsin Historical Society investigated the site. Although the investigation is not complete and the report has not yet been published, there is intriguing news from the site. The wreck is found in 170 feet of water with its bow pointing northwest, about 180 degrees off the course that it was on when last sighted. According to Keith Meverden, the director of the project, the schooner was still able to steer up to its final minutes and had apparently come about in an attempt to ride out the storm with its bow into the wind. Further research will hopefully shed more light on other measures that the crew was taking to avert disaster.[29]

FIFTEEN

UNSEAWORTHY

They seldom stayed in port on account of bad weather. In late November and early December, when rates and wages and risks were high, they kept going as long as they could get a cargo and vessel insurance, and some skippers would take chances without [insurance] and continue until near Christmastime. . . . Whenever a vessel got caught in a hard blow from the north in late season, it would ice up and sink lower and lower in the water under tons of added weight. Some vessels disappeared with all hands.

—Richard J. Edmonds, sailor

*I*n the blizzard of words that was generated about the missing schooner its unseaworthiness was not overlooked, and accusations of negligence surfaced almost from the start. There would certainly have been even more rancor if the men who died (other than Captains Nelson and Schuenemann) were not common laborers whose families possessed limited influence within the community. There was no recorded crew list to say exactly who the victims were, and the contradictory reports in the newspapers added to the impression that they were nameless and insignificant folk. But it would be a mistake to think that these men could drown and not be painfully missed. There were no expendable lives here. Still, the exact names of the crew and the number of sailors on board will never be known.

The German-language newspaper *Die Illinois Staats-Zeitung* did not get caught up in the hype of the English-language papers. Instead, it reported the tragedy only once, on December 6; did not include any of the false sightings of wreckage; and accurately identified the place where the *Rouse Simmons* went down as near Two Rivers, Wisconsin. As part of the German-speaking community *Die Staats-Zeitung* may have had more investment in not distorting the truth and more access to people who actually knew men on board the Christmas Tree Ship. Among the souls lost on board the paper named eleven: Captain Charles Nelson, who is identified as the owner and commander of the annual venture, and Captain Nelson's wife; Captain Herman Schueneman [*sic*], the "former commander" and owner of the cargo of Christmas trees; Steve Nelson, a seaman; Albert Curta, the ship's cook and resident of 418 North Desplaines Street, Chicago; sailors Charles Nelson, Frank Carlson, Engwald Newhouse, and Philipp (in other accounts the spelling is *Philip*) Larson; sailor Gilbert Swanson, son of Captain Swanson; and steward Philipp (in other accounts the spelling is *Philip*) Bausewein. Of these one can be removed from the list because Captain Nelson was a widower.

Historian Theodore Charrney, who researched the subject exhaustively and had the opportunity to interview people who were personally connected to the event (including members of the Schuenemann family and one of the crew's family), came up with a list of twelve victims. His list bears a noteworthy similarity to the *Illinois Staats-Zeitung* list: Captain Charles Nelson; Captain Herman Schuenemann; Steve E. Nelson, mate; Charles Nelson, sailor; Frank "the Liar" Carlson, sailor; Albert Lykstad, cook; Ingvald Nyhouse, also known as Engwald Newhouse, sailor; William Oberg, lumber shover; Sven Inglehart, lumber shover; Jacob "Pink Jack" Johnson, alias Jack Pitt, lumber shover; Andrew "Big Andy" Danielson, sometimes called Anderson, lumber shover; Philip Bausewein, who Charrney believes is sometimes erroneously listed as Philip Larson, woodcutter.[1] These lists lend credence to each other when it is noted that there are six names in common and seven if Philip Larson is not an error. Interestingly, the names of the lumber shovers, common laborers who could have been hired by Captain Schuenemann to cut Christmas trees and help load the schooner, were the names that did not find their way into the newspaper report. These individuals were the nameless, faceless ones except to a few who preserved their memories halfway through the twentieth century. So it is not accurate to say that the men who lost their lives were just a group of tramps or nobodies. There is still the possibility that there were others on board who indeed were forgotten, but at least the majority were missed and grieved in their deaths.

Philip Bausewein (often spelled *Brauswein* in the newspaper reports), identified in the English press as a Chicago teamster, was one of the more high profile victims. His name survives because he left behind a fiancée and a mother who were loud enough and articulate enough to catch the attention of the press and, perhaps, a few local politicians. Bausewein's name also appears in Captain Schuenemann's Last Will and Testament as one of only two employees on that last venture who made a claim against the estate.[2]

Then there was the survivor, Hogan Hoganson. (William "Big Bill" Sullivan also claimed to be a surviving crew member, but his story, as quoted in the Chicago *Tribune,* was not congruent with what actually occurred.)[3] Hoganson's employment, like Bausewein's, is testified to by Captain Schuenemann's will. Hoganson was the only member of the crew who lived to make a claim. He survived because he had opted to return to Chicago by train rather than on board the doomed schooner. Once he reached the city, he was vociferous in his claim that he jumped ship because the *Simmons* was obviously unseaworthy. Of course, his story raised him instantly, though briefly, to celebrity status in the Chicago papers. "Before we had left the [Chicago] harbor I complained to Steve Nelson, the mate," Hoganson told the papers, "that the foc'sle wasn't fit for a human being to sleep in and he promised to have it looked after. He never did, and perhaps that had something to do with the way my forebodings stayed with me. Gloomy thoughts are easy to entertain in gloomy surroundings, you know."[4] Hoganson's words made the headlines when he claimed that he should have known better than to sail on the *Rouse Simmons* in the first place because the rats had deserted the ship before it ever left the Chicago harbor. In another venue Hoganson was the source for a report of how the schooner was loaded before it left the Upper Peninsula of Michigan. "She carried no ballast," he said, "other than the trees piled in the hold. The rest was deck load. Captain Schuenemann constructed a deck house running from the foremast to the cabin using between 15,000 and 20,000 feet of green lumber. It was eleven feet high and would offer great resistance in a gale." Reportedly, Hoganson voiced his concerns about the vessel being top heavy and unseaworthy to Captain Schuenemann, but his concerns were dismissed, and he along with two others was allegedly discharged from the crew in Manistique, Michigan, with the threat that he would not be paid because he was not making the homeward voyage.[5]

Finally, the question of who was actually in command of the Christmas Tree Ship. Both Captain Schuenemann and Captain Nelson were on board on the last voyage. Captain Nelson had been a professional sailor all of his adult life. Born in Denmark, he had sailed on the oceans before coming to the Great Lakes, and in the waning days of the nineteenth century he was the master of the lumber schooner *Ida,* a vessel of the same type and vintage as the *Rouse Simmons.* In comparison to Captain Nelson, Herman Schuenemann was definitely less the seaman. He had owned and captained vessels before, true enough, but his main occupation was as a businessman who used vessels to support his merchandising operations. Thus, it is very possible that while Captain Schuenemann is said to have been the master of the vessel, Captain Nelson, as the more experienced mariner on board, was actually in command of the *Simmons* while Schuenemann's role on board was more that of a supercargo. Support for this conclusion is found in the reporting of the newspaper that has the most credibility as a source for maritime news, the *Sturgeon Bay Advocate.* In 1911 both Captains Nelson and Schuenemann were on board the *Rouse Simmons* as it made its voyage to Manistique and returned to Chicago with Christmas trees. In reporting this voyage, the *Advocate*'s marine editor, who would have known the men personally, explicitly identified Captain Nelson as the master of the vessel, while Captain Schuenemann was said to be "accompanying" the vessel because he had a material interest in the schooner and its cargo.[6]

Of course sailor Hogan Hoganson knew Captain Nelson, and he referred to the captain when discussing the unseaworthiness of the *Simmons*. According to Hoganson, Captain Nelson had reported to the harbormaster at Chicago before they sailed that the rats had deserted the ship.[7] But the reservations of Captain Nelson become even more believable in the stories that originated with his daughter Alvinda. The *Chicago Daily News* of December 5 quoted Alvinda at length: "My father didn't want to take this cruise. Capt. Schuene- mann came to father and begged him to take charge of the boat. We—my husband and myself—had begged him to give up the lakes and he had consented. Then, to please Schuenemann, he said he would take one more cruise. Before he left he shook his head regard- ing the *Rouse Simmons*. He said that it needed a general overhauling and had asked that it be done. However he said it was not done and things were left as they were."

Captain Nelson had been in charge when the *Rouse Simmons* went into Sturgeon Bay the year before for caulking. But in 1912, there was no mention of maintenance or repair. Theodore Charrney inter- viewed some old-timers in Upper Michigan who said that before the *Simmons* left the dock at Thompson's Pier Captain Nelson and Cap- tain Schuenemann had an argument about whether they should sail or not. Needless to say, Captain Nelson argued in the negative. Some drew attention to the height of the deck load of trees and its influence in making the boat top heavy. Others reported that there was no bal- last in the hold of the boat to counteract the tendency to roll.[8] Thus, there is a growing amount of circumstantial evidence suggesting that the Christmas Tree Ship was unseaworthy, that its condition was widely recognized as such, and that Captain Herman Schuenemann chose to both ignore the fact and challenge his boat further by load- ing it in a dangerous fashion.

Although they were not provided with a platform to make their voices heard, there were most certainly some in Chicago who were angered by the loss of the Christmas Tree Ship. In their grief they did not weep; they protested. The fact that this anger was not reported widely may have had something to do with the obvious spin that the newspapers were putting on the story. But, even in the papers, there were strong hints. On December 7, 1912, the Chicago *Inter Ocean,* a

The schooner *Rouse Simmons* in better days long before it was lost on Lake Michigan. (Historical Collections of the Great Lakes, Bowling Green State University, Bowling Green, Ohio.)

politically conservative paper generally esteemed for its lack of sensationalism, reported that union sailors were considering the creation of a "black list" on which would appear the names of vessels considered unseaworthy as was the *Rouse Simmons*. The secretary of the Lake Seamen's Union is quoted as saying, "There are a half a dozen craft as bad as the *Rouse Simmons* now docking regularly at Chicago. . . . For their own safety the men ought to shun these boats." Neither did the union members ignore the fact that the survivors were left in great need by the loss of their loved ones. They helped to raise money to support the families of the drowned men. They also volunteered to help to move trees brought to Chicago on railroad cars onto a substitute schooner (the *Oneida*). By so doing, they helped to salvage some of the business and income for the family of Captain Schuenemann.

Another small window into the harsher feelings that were circulating after the loss comes from a couple of mentions of the Bausewein family's reaction to the death of young Philip, who had shipped out with Captain Schuenemann. The quest of Philip's mother and fiancée for information about the fate of their beloved was reported by the *Chicago Daily Tribune*. If the newspaper is to be believed, the two women made concerted efforts to stir authorities to look further into the fate of the missing schooner. They are portrayed as approaching union officials, the harbormaster, the county commissioner, a city officer, and even the mayor (who refused to see them). They also made phone calls to lifesaving stations around the perimeter of the lake. All this, however, was to no avail. Their fruitless efforts must have raised some of the same resentments that Captain Charles Nelson's daughter expressed when she talked to the papers about how her father had retired from the lakes and returned to sailing on the *Rouse Simmons* one last time as a personal favor to Captain Schuenemann. It is evident that the pain and protests of these and other survivors were being expressed long after the loss. It was only such vehement feelings that got the government to make a second search of Lake Michigan with a second revenue cutter, the *Mackinac*.[9]

Twenty-first-century Americans take for granted that after a disaster such as this there would be an investigation into the causes, litigation would be pursued by the aggrieved, and blame would be assigned. Even though no such thing happened after this tragedy, it should not be assumed that there were not deep feelings of anger and strong impulses toward faultfinding in the community. In that era investigations either did not occur or they were done superficially and no one was ultimately held accountable. Even in such a dramatic case as the *Eastland* disaster, which occurred in Chicago three years later and still ranks as the second most deadly maritime disaster in the history of the United States, the investigation led to no charges or indictments in spite of the fact that there were obvious signs of culpability. The owners of the *Eastland* never paid a dime in compensation for the hundreds of lives lost. This "hear no evil, see no evil" attitude was the standard of the day. It is as though the authorities were saying, "I don't want to hear what happened. I just want you to make the problem go away so that we can maintain our illusion that bad things don't happen here."[10]

There is a natural human tendency to try to bring something positive out of such an otherwise sad story, and indeed there are many positive things to say. The Schuenemanns were an American success story. The family made a great contribution to the lives of countless citizens of Chicago by their years of bringing Christmas trees to the city. Herman had mastered the business of harvesting, shipping, and marketing huge quantities of trees. The Christmas tree business was carried on with courage and spirit by Herman Schuenemann's wife and three daughters. But to focus on these things and gloss over the fact that as many as seventeen men lost their lives sailing on a vessel that had no business being out on Lake Michigan in a winter storm is to deny reality and distort history and carry forward the "hear no evil, see no evil" attitude.[11] To truly understand the significance of the loss of the *Rouse Simmons* the tragic nature of this event and the magnitude of the tragedy cannot be pushed to the side. In the year 1912 there were thirty-five deaths among sailors on the Great Lakes. One third to one-half of them came in one event, the sinking of the *Rouse Simmons*.

Chicagoans of a century ago were much more accepting of human death and misery than they are today. Life itself dictated a different set of expectations for them. Accidental deaths were normal events. Laborers who died in digging Chicago's freshwater intakes under Lake Michigan, employees who died in factory accidents and fires, and ordinary citizens who died at grade crossings of the many railroads that passed through the city were lamented, but they were considered acceptable sacrifices to progress. Technology had not advanced to the point that workplaces or neighborhoods where there were environmental dangers could be made safe. There was a prevailing fatalism that said that bad things were bound to happen and the best one could do was to try to avoid them.

Even so, it is hard to understand from a modern perspective how men and women could take the kind of risks that Great Lakes sailors took, especially in the weather conditions so frequently met in November and December. The condition of the *Rouse Simmons* was apparent before the schooner left Chicago. Indeed, the danger to sailors who served on vessels such as the *Simmons* was widely recognized and, in fact, was a target for reform by the Seamen's Union and progressive politicians such as Wisconsin's senator Robert LaFollette.[12]

It is even harder to understand how either Captain Herman Schuenemann or Captain Charles Nelson, ostensibly knowledgeable about the job to be done and the risks involved, could expose other people to the life threatening circumstances encountered by the schooner *Rouse Simmons* on November 23, 1912. When liability so clearly lies with employers to protect their employees from undue risks, it is easy to forget that a hundred years ago risk was taken as an inherent part of a job and the worker had to bear fully and alone the personal consequences when something went wrong. There were voices, to be sure, crying out to change the mentality of the day, but they had not won a very big following.

In his commencement address at the University of Illinois in 1893 Governor John Peter Altgeld, appalled by the price in human lives that was being paid for the building of an urban and industrial society, spoke passionately to his audience. "The fact that you met with an accident or got your legs broken, your neck twisted and your head smashed," said Altgeld, "is not equal [in importance] to a delivery of the goods."[13] In the minds of how many Chicagoans did it matter that the "goods" delivered were Christmas trees? How many would have blithely excused the drowning of seventeen souls for a cargo of evergreens that might just as easily have been shipped by railroad? How many would have made a distinction between this loss of life and the number of people who were killed by diphtheria, or maimed in factories, or crushed by poverty? The answer is that most Chicagoans accepted these prices paid because they were considered normal; people could not imagine an alternative. Only a few visionary reformers thought it possible to reverse the tide. Ironically, at the same time that Chicagoans were hearing the news about the loss of the Christmas Tree Ship, hearings were being held in Washington, D.C., on Senator LaFollette's bill to protect sailors from some of the most blatant dangers of their job.[14] The bill was opposed by the owners of lake vessels but was passed in February 1915.

This is the world that the Schuenemanns lived in. Sailors took risks. Injury, even death, was part of the cost of doing business. The Schuenemanns grew up hearing about accidents that deprived whole families of their sustenance, fires that decimated entire areas and left hundreds of families destitute, rivers that were receptacles for all forms of human waste and the breeding grounds of infection, and diseases that mysteriously ravaged whole communities. They, like everyone else, knew that tragedy was always close at hand. Working under the tutelage of older sailors who regularly risked their own safety and that of their men, the Schuenemann brothers were inured to the dangers of their own undertakings. Their hearts were not hardened to tragedy and loss. Rather, they, like their fellow citizens, accepted tragedy and loss as normal and inevitable parts of their workaday world.

Case after case of similar behavior by other captains can be cited. In 1880 the schooner *Mary Nau* was on the lake in December going from Pentwater, Michigan, to Chicago. It was missing for almost two weeks before appearing off Two Rivers caught in the ice. The *Inter Ocean* described the hardship of the crew: "She got into the ice, was all iced up herself, and remained fast for ten days. The crew suffered terribly from the cold, and worse than all, the store of provisions gave out, and for five days and nights the poor fellows were without anything to eat." Two years later the scow-schooner *Coaster* was out in December, and the captain and crew members suffered terrible frostbite from the face to the toes. In 1901 the three men on board the schooner *Caledonia* almost died of hypothermia bringing Christmas trees to southern Wisconsin. Stories of these events and others like them circulated freely about the docks and within the group of men who sailed the lakes. They may have warned some off, and made others cautious, but there were always those willing to take the gamble that it would not happen to them.[15]

There were, after all, other vessels out on Lake Michigan on November 22 and 23. Other lives were lost in the same storm. Some vessels of the same general size and age as the *Rouse Simmons* were also out in the storm of December 5 and 6. One was the schooner *J. V. Taylor*. Its captain, A. J. Anderson, provided a vivid report to the newspaper reporters when it finally reached Chicago from Alpena, Michigan, after almost two weeks and four layovers in search of shelter. During the trip the vessel's foreboom had been broken and needed to be patched together; its bow and deck load were encased in a very thick and very heavy coating of ice; it had expended all the salt and cinders that it had on board trying to cope with the icy conditions on deck and about the rigging; and its galley ran so low on provisions that the crew had to restock at out-of-the-way Bailey's Harbor, Wisconsin. When the experience of Captain Anderson and his crew on the *J. V. Taylor* is laid beside the story of the *Rouse Simmons,* some might conclude that similar decisions were made on both vessels. But in one respect there was a drastic difference. The *Taylor* sought shelter when the storm became too intense. The *Rouse Simmons* did not.

Why in the world did the *Rouse Simmons* not seek shelter once the danger was realized? It had passed the islands at the mouth of Green Bay, the entrance to the Sturgeon Bay Lake Michigan Ship Canal, and several ports that would have served as some protection. Captains Schuenemann and Nelson had sailed this coast many times before. They knew very well where the more sheltered anchorages were, and neither of them had been loath to seek shelter in the past. Yet they stayed out on the lake. Perhaps the answer lies in an equipment failure. The running rigging could have frozen in place. The bilge pumps might have been inoperable. The seams may have been opening. The centerboard winches (there were two of them on the *Simmons*) could have been frozen or broken. Or, more than likely, a combination of these and other problems could have occurred. And, complicating any attempts to remedy these or other problems, the schooner was packed with bundled pine trees, and those that were on deck were covered with ice.

Then there was the possibility of hypothermia, a stealthy killer that disables cognitive functioning at the same time that it is disabling the body. People can become hypothermic and not even be aware of how impaired they are. Judgment goes awry, and part of that poverty of judgment can be the failure to recognize how much danger one is in. In 1912 people did not know that alcohol increases the risk of hypothermia. On the contrary, having a drink was thought to warm a person up. (Hence, the Saint Bernard rescue dogs that were sent out with a keg of liquor around their necks.) But alcohol dilates blood vessels and capillaries, carrying more blood to the outer layers of the body, where it is chilled by the cold air combined with the water that soaks into clothing. "Equipment failure" might not be restricted to the vessel; perhaps the "equipment" of the sailors' bodies rendered them ineffective due to hypothermia.

Even though error in human judgment seems to be the root cause of the disappearance of the *Rouse Simmons,* we do not have to classify it as crazy, criminal, or amoral behavior. If it was, it would be necessary to describe the actions of thousands of people in 1912 as crazy, criminal, or amoral. It was bad judgment, terribly bad judgment, but no different than what the Schuenemanns and thousands of other sailors had been doing on Lake Michigan for the previous forty years. It was a refusal to accept the threat of disaster, based on many experiences of having averted disaster before. It was, at heart, a gamble. To lose would be incredibly costly. But Herman Schuenemann likely was focused much more on what could be won than on what could be lost.

These ideas, however, start the slide down the slippery slope of speculation. Once again, it should be said that the precise reason why the *Rouse Simmons* was lost that day will never be known. But let these speculations serve as a reminder that one need not resort to some terrible motive on the part of captain or crew, or to some unique fault in the vessel, or even to some particularly cruel act of nature to explain the tragedy. It was an event fully consistent with the time in which it occurred—a time when the relationship between work and human life was viewed differently than it is now. The drowning of those men in the cold and roiling waters of Lake Michigan, the loss of a venerable old vessel, the grievous disappointment of many citizens of Chicago, and the end of a beloved Christmas tradition were an outcome of a way of life practiced by independent and hardy risk-taking sailors from a hundred ports around the Great Lakes, a way of life that afforded no harbors of refuge from danger and death, a way of life that was doomed.

SIXTEEN

A STORY TO
PASS ON

However festive or sad the occasion, however gay or
gloomy the streets may be, whatever our surroundings,
the Christmas spirit is there. No one may say just wherein
it lies. It is like an unseen halo that glorifies and makes
holy every good thought and impulse, while it reveals in
darker relief whatever is tragic, unworthy or vicious. A
great disaster on Christmas Eve or Day shocks us as it does
[at] no other season; a great joy comes in that sweet rai-
ment of gladness that only Christmas brings.

—*Detroit Free Press,* December 13, 1903

In the hearts and minds of many Chicagoans and of many people
with an interest in maritime affairs all up and down the lakes, the
Rouse Simmons was not, and is not, forgotten. Tragic romance and
drama were associated with the loss from the first days that it was
reported. At the *Chicago Daily News* Charles V. E. Starrett penned a
poem entitled "The Ballad of the Rouse Simmons," while at the
Daily Journal Ben Hecht wrote "The Tale of the Christmas Tree."
For Starrett the theme was "man against nature" while for Hecht it
was "hope springs eternal." Starrett's poem focused on heroism.
Hecht's poem was about redeeming a tragic loss.[1]

In Starrett's ballad the brave captain of the Santa Claus ship pays no heed to his frightened crew and will not allow the threat of a storm and a watery grave deter him from delivering his cargo of trees. ("'We sail,' he said, 'for the children wait for our freight of Christmas trees.'") The poem reaches its climax when the ship is overcome by the waves and the crew is overcome by terror, but the captain accepts his fate with neither fear nor regret. ("'Captain,' they cry, 'the seams are rent, and the sea pours in below. And the schooner's pumps are old and worn.' And he answered, 'Be it so!'") In the denouement "death bellows afar," the captain's wife "watches and weeps" on a distant shore, and "the children wait in vain," for tragically, "the waves have claimed the Christmas ship and the children's Christmas trees." The reader is left only with the solace of knowing that captain and crew died sacrificially in an attempt to complete a noble task.

Ben Hecht would not leave his readers so bereft. His poem is not about the ship and its captain and crew at all but rather about a single Christmas tree, which becomes the key to happiness for some children. His tale begins when the Christmas ship is already "beneath the fathoms blue" and rising up from the "Christmas grave" comes a single Christmas tree. "Leaving behind the sunken dead" and reaching the "leeward shore," the little tree lies on the sand "bright with the drying foam" until it is found by a fisherman who takes it home to his children. There it fulfills its destiny. "Lighted with candles and laden with toys / Gaily and proudly it stands / On Christmas eve, and the fisherman's boys / Are clapping their little hands. / And this is the tale of the Christmas tree / That came from a grave in an inland sea." Hecht neatly ignores the tragedy and goes right on to offer consolation for a loss that is unnamed.

These two responses to the loss of the *Rouse Simmons,* the Christmas Tree Ship, have been repeated over and over again for almost a century now.

Initially, the story of the tragic loss was kept before the public by the simple fact that the Schuenemann family remained in the Christmas tree business for over two decades after Herman died. Then, with the loss of the family business, it began to fade into obscurity, until it was reawakened by the discovery of the remains of the *Rouse Simmons* on the bottom of Lake Michigan by a diver from Milwaukee, Kent Bell-richard.[2]

Just as Herman carried on without breaking stride when his brother died, so also his family—Barbara and their three daughters, Elsie, Hazel, and Pearl—went on after his death. Even in 1912 they salvaged something by taking the trees that Herman had shipped by rail to the river to be placed on an old schooner, the *Oneida,* which had been donated by its owner for the purpose. In subsequent years other schooners were used as a stage to sell trees from, but eventually, that too had to be renounced and the Schuenemann trees were sold from a storefront.

Barbara, it seems, was the driving force. (Soon after she died the family business ended, and the three daughters went on to pursue the careers and family lives that they had begun in the meantime.) Theodore Charrney wrote that Barbara would go personally to Manistique, Michigan, to supervise the harvesting and shipping of trees by railroad but that she was not received well by the local people because her personality lacked the warmth and enthusiasm that were so much a part of her husband.[3] The implication is that the business began to wane almost immediately.

The Christmas tree business had always been a family affair. Long before Herman's death, his wife and daughters had played a part in marketing the trees, making wreaths, organizing other laborers, and welcoming customers. So it is not surprising that they would continue using marketing techniques that they may very well have had a hand in devising. In 1912, in the thick of the tragedy, the elder daughter, Elsie, came forward as the public face of the business.[4] She was frequently quoted, although it is certain that much of what was reported about her in the newspapers was pure fiction. At first, Elsie was the voice of optimism, saying that she was sure that her father's schooner was merely detained by the weather and that it would soon arrive. But, as the loss became more and more apparent, Elsie became the voice of an indomitable spirit. The news stories quoted her as saying that she herself would sail a vessel up to Manistique and bring back another load of trees in time for Christmas. (This vow was ostensibly made when Christmas was just two weeks away.) The ambition was, of course, too fantastic to be given any credibility, but

A publicity shot of Elsie Schuenemann at the wheel of a docked schooner. She is actually facing the stern of the boat. (*Chicago Daily News* negatives collection, Chicago History Museum, DN-0065543.)

the remarkable "pluck" of this young woman helped to make her a new symbol that, at least in part, would fill the gap left by her father's death.

What the stories of the brave and impetuous young Elsie do not reveal is any sense that loss or grief over her father's death could interrupt the family business. She appears to be totally consumed with the thought that the show must go on. In the more sensationalist papers no signs of suffering or brokenness are reported. Not even a pause or a skipping of a beat because of her father's death. This may have been what the public wanted to believe, or an image that the surviving Schuenemann women felt compelled to project, but it does not mean that their loss was not felt keenly. Notably, Barbara, Herman's wife, is missing from the majority of the newspaper stories. The most obvious explanation is that she was lost in her grief and that Elsie was acting as a foil to shield her mother from the predatory press.

The *Inter Ocean,* which served as the counterpoint to the sensationalist reporting of other papers, provided a very different picture. In it Elsie makes no wild promises, but still she is unvanquished.[5] The article begins: "In a dingy little room at South Water and Clark Streets, where a lone window overlooks the Chicago river, yesterday there sat a beautiful, golden haired, and sad eyed girl. She was weaving Christmas garlands." Elsie was that golden haired girl who carried on while her mother, prostrate and hysterical with grief, was at home. She sits alone, but she is no less resolute in her determination to carry on. "Keeping everything from mother makes it hard to bear. But our friends have been so good to us. I don't know what we would have done without them. Everything we had was tied up in the schooner. And with father gone, not only our store but the source of providing more was taken away. One never knows what they can do until they have to. I am going to make an attempt to carry on father's Christmas tree business." She goes on to say that she will never go out on the lake to bring back trees in a vessel but with the help of friends will bring trees by railroad cars and sell them at the foot of Clark Street.

For years after, Elsie continued to promote the family business with carefully staged photographs of herself posed with a Christmas tree or standing at the wheel of a schooner. Hazel and Pearl, the twins, helped out too, and Barbara remained in the business right up until the Christmas before her own death.

In 1934 the Schuenemann daughters were still in the business and keeping alive the legend of the Christmas Tree Ship. While the three women worked at making wreaths and garlands at the shop at 1641 North LaSalle Street, "Big Bill" Sullivan, an alleged member of Captain Herman Schuenemann's crew of sailors and tree cutters, was selling trees and telling the story of his hunch that the *Rouse Simmons* was doomed. That hunch, he said, saved his life because he returned to

A scene from a Bailiwick Theater (Chicago) production of the musical *The Christmas Schooner* by John Reeger and Julie Shannon. (Photo by David Zak. Courtesy of the Bailiwick Theater, Chicago, Illinois.)

Chicago by railroad in 1912 instead of by the lake. "Big Bill's" story, as quoted by the Chicago *Tribune,* is not congruent with the actual course of events.[6] By then, however, it was the legend, not the facts, that people wanted to hear, and no doubt it was the legend that Big Bill wanted to emphasize because it sold Christmas trees, a luxury for many in the Great Depression.

The story of Chicago's Christmas Tree Ship has survived for almost one hundred years. It received a big boost when Kent Bellrichard found the wreck of the *Rouse Simmons* right where it should be between Kewaunee and Two Rivers, Wisconsin. The vessel lay there with its masts still in place, still laden with Christmas trees, and bearing much of the equipment and provisions that it went to the bottom with. Since then divers have carried away many of the artifacts, and these items have been dispersed between several known collections and, perhaps, private collections that are not known. But Bell-richard's discovery helped to spark a revival of interest in the legend, and, in turn, many others have picked up the story and produced their own renderings of it, from the wildly naive to the relatively historic, in poetry, song, adult and children's fiction, nonfiction, documentary, drama, and graphic art. Most eloquent are the paintings of maritime artist Charles Vickery, the musical by John Reeger and Julie Shannon entitled *The Christmas Schooner,* and the annual Christmas Tree Concert performed by singer and balladeer Lee Murdock.[7] In these wonderful works the parts of the story that are most noble, touching, and beautiful are brought into the present, where they help to inspire good deeds. Each December beginning in 2000 a United States Coast Guard vessel has brought Christmas trees from northern Michigan to Chicago for distribution to needy families.

Gone are the stories of the other Christmas tree captains like John McDonald, William McDonald, William Armstrong, William Henry, Charles Nelson, Arthur Dow, Johnny Doak, John Patrick Clark, Billy Dingman, and who knows how many others. They were men who populated the class of short-haul sailors on Lake Michigan, the waterborne equivalent of the hardscrabble farmers and the pioneering merchants who gave birth to many communities around Lake Michigan. In life there were few, if any, harbors of refuge for them, but in the legend launched by the Schuenemann family, there is now a place for their memory to be preserved and passed on.

Vessels That Engaged in the Christmas Tree Trade on Lake Michigan, 1876–1920

Type	Name	Official Number	Place Built
Schooner	*Actor*	106752	Manitowoc, WI
Schooner	*Arendal*	105281	Sheboygan, WI
Scow	*Augustus*	29961	Spoonville, MI
Scow	*Augustus*	29961	Spoonville, MI
Scow	*Augustus*	29961	Spoonville, MI
Tug	*Beaver*	unknown	unknown
Schooner	*Bertha Barnes*	2935	Sheboygan, WI
Schooner	*Caledonia*	4384	Saugeon, MI
Schooner	*Charley J. Smith*	125749	South Haven, MI
Scow	*Coaster*	4374	Geneva, OH
Scow	*Coaster*	4374	Geneva, OH
Scow	*Coaster*	4374	Geneva, OH
Schooner	*Conquest*	4582	Olcott, NY
Schooner	*Conquest*	4582	Olcott, NY
Steamer	*Corona*	125091	Manitowoc, WI
Schooner	*Dan Newhall*	6135	Milwaukee, WI
Schooner	*D'Artagnan*	unknown	unknown
Scow	*Emily & Eliza*	36582	Oak Harbor, OH
Scow	*Emily & Eliza*	36582	Oak Harbor, OH
Steamer	*Eugene Hart*	unknown	unknown
Schooner	*Experiment*	7523	St. Joseph, MI
Steamer	*Georgia*	unknown	Manitowoc, WI
Schooner	*George L. Wrenn*	10816	Fort Howard, WI
Schooner	*George L. Wrenn*	10816	Fort Howard, WI
Schooner	*George L. Wrenn*	10816	Fort Howard, WI
Schooner	*George L. Wrenn*	10816	Fort Howard, WI
Schooner	*George L. Wrenn*	10816	Fort Howard, WI
Schooner	*George L. Wrenn*	10816	Fort Howard, WI
Schooner	*George L. Wrenn*	10816	Fort Howard, WI
Schooner	*H. C. Winslow*	11200	Black River, OH
Schooner	*Ida*	1214	Milwaukee, WI
Schooner	*Industry*	unknown	unknown

Built	Tonnage	Used	Master
1890	13.64	1896	Arthur E. Dow
1873	gr. 207	1914	unknown
1885	gr. 64	1902	unknown
1885	gr. 64	1905	Captain Reese
1885	gr. 64	1909	Arthur E. Dow
unknown	unknown	1920	unknown
1872	330	1909	Herman Schuenemann
1861	54.17	1901	Hans Peterson
1879	gr. 42	1903	William Armstrong
1867	gr. 50.3	1879	unknown
1867	gr. 50.3	1881	unknown
1869	gr. 50.3	1883	Captain Jacobson
1853	gr. 150.79	1886	William H. McDonald
1853	gr. 150.79	1887	William H. McDonald
1870	gr. 470.23	1885	unknown
1852	gr. 129.47	1878	unknown
unknown	unknown	1913	G. W. Leaf
1874	gr. 63.6	1897	Martin Coyne
1874	gr. 63.6	1898	Martin Coyne
unknown	unknown	1896	unknown
ca. 1854	gr. 49.91	1897	August Schuenemann
1881	gr. 950	1901	unknown
1868	gr. 214	1903	Matthew Shomer
1868	gr. 214	1904	Herman Schuenemann
1868	gr. 214	1905	Matthew Shomer
1868	gr. 214	1906	Herman Schuenemann
1868	gr. 214	1907	William J. O'Brien
1868	gr. 214	1908	William J. O'Brien
1868	gr. 214	1909	Herman Schuenemann
1853	gr. 252.02	1896	John P. Clark
1876	gr. 169.56	1900	Charles Nelson
unknown	unknown	1890	James Flynn

Vessels That Engaged in the Christmas Tree Trade on
Lake Michigan, 1876–1920 (continued)

Type	Name	Official Number	Place Built
Scow	*Iris*	12096	Port Huron, MI
Schooner	*J. V. Taylor*	13874	Winneconne, WI
Schooner	*J. W. Wright*	76208	Oshkosh, WI
Schooner	*J. W. Wright*	76208	Oshkosh, WI
Schooner	*J. W. Wright*	76208	Oshkosh, WI
Schooner	*Joses*	13015	Holland, MI
Schooner	*Kate Hinchman*	14036	Detroit, MI
Schooner	*Kate Hinchman*	14036	Detroit, MI
Scow	*Lady Ellen*	140208	Algoma, WI
Scow	*Lady Ellen*	140208	Algoma, WI
Scow	*Lady Ellen*	140208	Algoma, WI
Schooner	*Lady Washington*	140241	Grand Haven, MI
Schooner	*Larabida*	75850	Sheboygan, WI
Gas	*Lillian*	unknown	unknown
Schooner	*Little Georgy*	15806	Sheboygan, WI
Schooner	*Little Georgy*	15806	Sheboygan, WI
Schooner	*M. Capron*	90772	Conneaut, OH
Schooner	*Margaret Dall*	17746	Michigan City, MI
Schooner	*Margaret Dall*	17746	Michigan City, MI
Schooner	*Mary L. Collins*	16614	Toledo, OH
Schooner	*Mary L. Collins*	16614	Toledo, OH
Schooner	*Mary L. Collins*	16614	Toledo, OH
Schooner	*Mary L. Collins*	16614	Toledo, OH
Schooner	*Mary Ludwig*	90601	South Haven, MI
Schooner	*Mary E. Packard*	90751	South Haven, MI
Schooner	*Melitta*	91309	Manitowoc, WI
Schooner	*Melitta*	91309	Manitowoc, WI
Schooner	*Minnie Mueller*	17574	Fort Howard, WI
Scow	*Monitor*	50397	unknown
Scow	*Mystic*	91169	Grand Haven, MI
Scow	*Mystic*	91169	Grand Haven, MI
Schooner	*Nancy Dell*	130147	Port Sheldon, OH

Built	Tonnage	Used	Master
1866	gr. 62.14	1882	unknown
1867	gr. 199.94	1913	unknown
1869	gr. 26.24	1889	William Armstrong
1869	gr. 26.24	1891	William Armstrong
1869	gr. 26.24	1892	William Armstrong
1866	gr. 120.57	1900	unknown
1862	gr. 236.42	1896	John P. Clark
1862	gr. 236.42	1897	unknown
1875	38.25	1876	John McDonald
1875	38.25	1877	John McDonald
1875	38.25	1891	William Henry Jr.
1877	76.32	1877	unknown
1876	gr. 52	1906	Arthur E. Dow
unknown	unknown	1922	unknown
1870	gr. 52.35	1897	Arthur E. Dow
1870	gr. 52.35	1898	unknown
1875	gr. 169.66	1895	Herman Schuenemann
1867	176.32	1896	Charles Nelson
1867	176.32	1904	E. F. Ellifson
1854	gr. 231	1897	Herman Schuenemann
1854	gr. 231	1898	Herman Schuenemann
1854	gr. 231	1899	Herman Schuenemann
1854	gr. 231	1900	Herman Schuenemann
1874	gr. 68.84	1892	William Armstrong
1875	gr. 101.46	unknown	Charles Nelson
1881	gr. 68.76	1906	Martin Coyne
1881	gr. 68.76	1909	Martin Coyne
1868	gr. 199	1917	unknown
unknown	83.87	1898	Herman Olson
1879	gr. 38.09	1894	unknown
1879	gr. 38.09	1895	unknown
1879	gr. 106.54	1901	August Brann

Vessels That Engaged in the Christmas Tree Trade on
Lake Michigan, 1876–1920 (continued)

Type	Name	Official Number	Place Built
Schooner	*Nellie Church*	18099	Fort Howard, WI
Schooner	*O. Shaw*	19332	South Haven, MI
Scow	*Ole Oleson*	155060	Oshkosh, WI
Scow	*Ole Oleson*	155060	Oshkosh, WI
Schooner	*Oneida*	18920	Ashtabula, OH
Scow	*Reindeer*	unknown	unknown
Schooner	*Robbie Knapp*	21947	Bailey's Harbor
Schooner	*Rouse Simmons*	110024	Milwaukee, WI
Schooner	*Rouse Simmons*	110024	Milwaukee, WI
Schooner	*Rouse Simmons*	110024	Milwaukee, WI
Schooner	*S. Thal*	115781	Oshkosh, WI
Schooner	*Sea Gem*	22582	Manitowoc, WI
Schooner	*Seaman*	23466	Cleveland, OH
Schooner	*Seaman*	23466	Cleveland, OH
Scow	*Sea Star*	22356	Irving, NY
Scow	*Sea Star*	22356	Irving, NY
Scow	*Supply*	23497	Black River, OH
Schooner	*Surprise*	22581	unknown
Schooner	*Thomas C. Wilson*	24579	Black River, OH
Schooner	*Thomas C. Wilson*	24579	Black River, OH
Schooner	*Truman Moss*	24454	Sandusky, OH
Scow	*Vermont*	25568	Huron, OH
Steamer	*Vesty V.*	161563	Muskegon, MI
Tug	*Watkins*	unknown	unknown
Schooner	*W. H. Hinsdale*	26360	Michigan City, IN
Diesel	*White Swan*	20226	Manitowoc, WI
Gas	*Wisconsin*	unknown	unknown

Note: The abbreviation "gr." in the Tonnage Column denotes gross tons.

Built	Tonnage	Used	Master
1867	gr. 123.23	1896	Arthur E. Dow
1870	gr. 40.66	1902	August Strecklow
1865	gr. 62	1885	unknown
1865	gr. 62	1886	August Schuenemann
1857	201	1912	unknown
unknown	unknown	1876	unknown
1872	gr. 15.25	1883	William Dingman
1868	gr. 205	1910	Herman Schuenemann
1868	gr. 205	1911	Charles Nelson
1868	gr. 205	1912	Charles Nelson
1867	gr. 55	1898	August Schuenemann
1863	gr. 103.21	1896	unknown
1848	gr. 181.99	1895	August Schuenemann
1848	gr. 181.99	1896	unknown
1855	gr. 95.48	1883	August Schuenemann
1855	gr. 95.48	1884	unknown
1861	gr. 89	1887	August Schuenemann
unknown	222.86	1889	William H. McDonald
1868	gr. 30.87	1893	August Schuenemann
1868	gr. 30.87	1894	August Schuenemann
1867	219.13	1902	Herman Schuenemann
1853	gr. 81	1900	Hans Hansen
1887	95.12	1888	William H. McDonald
unknown	unknown	1910	unknown
1850	61.5	1876	unknown
1904	7	1922	William Williamson
unknown	unknown	1919	unknown

Captains Who Engaged in the Christmas Tree Trade on Lake Michigan

Name	Number of Tree Voyages Known
William Armstrong	**5***
August Brann	1
John P. Clark	2
Martin Coyne	4
William Dingman	**1**
Arthur E. Dow	5
E. F. Ellifson	1
James Flynn	**1**
Hans Hansen	1
William Henry Jr.	**1**
[unknown] Jacobson	1
G. W. Leaf	1
John McDonald	**2**
William H. McDonald	**4**
Charles Nelson	5
William J. O'Brien	2
Herman Olson	1
Hans Peterson	1
[unknown] Reese	1
August Schuenemann	**8**
Herman Schuenemann	**11****
Matthew Shomer	2
August Strecklow	1
William Williamson	1

---

*Names in bold are captains who lived in Ahnapee. In addition, Captain Charles Nelson may have lived in Ahnapee, but the evidence is not conclusive.

**There were a number of voyages for which Herman Schuenemann chartered the vessel but was not in command as the master of the vessel. If these voyages are added in, the total number of Christmas tree voyages for Herman Schuenemann would be eighteen. The voyages on which another captain was master were those of the *Mystic* in 1895, the *George L. Wrenn* in 1903, 1905, 1907, and 1908, and the *Rouse Simmons* in 1911 and 1912.

Newspaper Reports of Vessels
Used by or on Behalf of
August or Herman Schuenemann

1875 November—Albert Sibilsky and Aug. Schoeneman [*sic*] had purchased the schooner *William H. Hinsdale* from Capt. John Doak. Shortly afterward the *Hinsdale* lost its anchor and had a close call at the harbor entrance. *Ahnapee Record,* November 11, 1875; November 18, 1875.

November—The *Hinsdale*'s steering mechanism failed while the schooner was entering the harbor at Ahnapee, but the vessel made it to safety by skillful use of the sails. *Ahnapee Record,* December 2, 1875.

December—The *Hinsdale* and crew were almost lost off Two Rivers Point in a gale. With a lot of pumping the vessel made Sheboygan and was later towed to Milwaukee for repair. *Ahnapee Record,* December 16, 1875.

1876 December—The schooner *William H. Hinsdale* left Ahnapee with a load of Christmas trees that went to Racine or Chicago. This may have been August Schuenemann's first trip with trees. *Ahnapee Record,* December 2, 1875.

1877 September—August bought a one-half interest in the schooner *William H. Hinsdale. Ahnapee Record,* September 13, 1877.

October 11—The *William H. Hinsdale* struck the pier at St. Joseph in a storm and was damaged. *Ahnapee Record,* October, 11, 1877.

October 19—The *William H. Hinsdale* collided with piling while entering the harbor at Chicago due to equipment failure. It was towed to safety by a tug. *Ahnapee Record,* October 20, 1877.

October—August Schuenemann was officially recorded as the

master of the schooner *William H. Hinsdale* on October 25. *Inter Ocean,* October 26, 1877.

November—The *William H. Hinsdale* struck the pier at South Haven, and it was feared that it would be a total loss. The three crew members on board had to be rescued from the rigging. *Ahnapee Record,* November 11, 1877.

1880 July—August Schuenemann was given command of the scow-schooner *Sea Star* by Charles L. Fellows with an Ahnapee crew. Fellows was an early settler at Ahnapee who captained his own vessel. He became a businessman and entrepreneur. *Ahnapee Record,* July 22, 1880.

1886 August commanded the schooner *Ole Oleson* during the summer. It was reported in his former hometown the next year. *Ahnapee Record,* September 29, 1887.

1886 November—The schooner *Ole Oleson* took a cargo of Christmas trees from Ahnapee to Chicago. The captain's name is not reported, but it may have been August Schuenemann who was in command of the vessel for at least a portion of that season. *Ahnapee Record,* September 23, 1886; November 4, 1886.

The *Ole Oleson* had also made year-end voyages with Christmas trees from Ahnapee in 1885. Unfortunately, the name of the captain is not given. *Ahnapee Record,* November 12, 1885.

1887 September—The loss of the schooner *Ole Oleson* in a gale between Muskegon and Milwaukee was reported. It was noted that Capt. August Schuenemann was in command of the *Oleson* "last summer" and the vessel was "well known" at Ahnapee. *Ahnapee Record,* September 29, 1887.

November—The scow-schooner *Supply* took a cargo of Christmas trees from Ahnapee to Chicago, but the captain is not named. *Ahnapee Record,* November 10, 1887. Forty-seven years later it was reported that "Capt. [Herman] Schuenemann, with his brother, August, gave Chicago its first boatload of Christmas trees in 1887." *Chicago Daily Tribune,* December 13, 1934.

1889   April 13—August sold the scow-schooner *Supply* at Chicago
for $650 to Anderson and Oleson. *Ahnapee Record,* April 25,
1889.

1889   May—August recently bought the schooner *Josephine Dresden*
from Racine parties for $1,400 and was reported taking ties
and posts to Chicago for Samuel Perry, an Ahnapee merchant. *Ahnapee Record,* May 16, 1889.

1894   October—The schooner *Thomas C. Wilson,* with Captain
Schennmann [*sic*], took a cargo of Christmas trees from
Sturgeon,Bay. The newspaper report noted that the deck of
the vessel had been housed over. *Sturgeon Bay Advocate,*
October 13, 1894; November 17, 1894.

1895   June—Rose Schuenemann sold the schooner *Thomas C. Wil-
son* for $600 to Heron F. Newton.
September 4—The schooner *Seaman,* Captain August L.
Schuenemann, was dismasted in Traverse Bay. It was
bound from Cleveland to Traverse City, light, to load a
cargo of lumber. *Inter Ocean,* September 5, 1895.
October—The schooner *Seaman* was used by August Schuen-
emann to take Christmas trees from Sturgeon Bay. *Sturgeon
Bay Advocate,* October 26, 1895; November 23, 1895.
October—The schooner *Mystic* was wrecked while en route to
Little Bay de Noquette for a cargo of Christmas trees for Herman Schuenemann. Herman had chartered the vessel and was
not on board when it went ashore. He was involved, however, in the attempt to salvage equipment from the *Mystic.*
Sturgeon Bay Advocate, November 2, 1895; November 9, 1895.
November—The deck staysail schooner *M. Capron* was chartered by Herman Schuenemann to take Christmas trees
from Sturgeon Bay to compensate for the loss of the
schooner *Mystic. Sturgeon Bay Advocate,* November 2, 1895.

1896   The schooner *Seaman* was owned by August Schuenemann
but captained by Charles Johnson while making a voyage to
Thompson['s Pier] in Northern Michigan. *Sturgeon Bay
Advocate,* June 6, 1896.

September 30—The schooner *Seaman* broke from its moorings in a storm at Chicago and damaged its rigging. *Inter Ocean,* October 1, 1896.

October—The schooner *Seaman* was used to take Christmas trees from Sturgeon Bay to Chicago by August Schuenemann. *Sturgeon Bay Advocate,* October 31, 1896.

1897 October—August Schuenemann arrived at Sturgeon Bay seeking a load of Christmas trees. He later chartered the schooner *Experiment* to carry Christmas trees. The article reports that the captain of the vessel was not August Schuenemann but rather Captain John Watt. *Sturgeon Bay Advocate,* October 16, 1897; October 30, 1897; November 13, 1897.

The schooner *Mollie* [*sic*] *Collins* arrived in Chicago with a cargo of Christmas trees under the command of Captain Oscar Armstrong but in the employment of Ed Shenniman [*sic*]. *Chicago Daily News,* December 8, 1897.

1898 September—August Schuenemann bought the schooner *S. Thal* after it had been sold by the U.S. marshal for a bad debt in Milwaukee. Captain Schuenemann planned to load the *S. Thal* with Christmas trees. *Sturgeon Bay Advocate,* October 1, 1898.

November 9—The schooner *S. Thal* was caught in a gale off Glencoe, Illinois, and was found broken up on the beach on the next day with no survivors. *Chicago Daily Tribune,* November 11, 1898.

November—Captain Herman Schuenemann arrived in Chicago on the schooner *Mary Collins* with a cargo of Christmas trees. *Chicago Daily News,* December 6, 1898.

1899 December—Herman Schuenemann arrived in Chicago with Christmas trees from the Upper Peninsula bought from the Chippewa in the schooner *Mary Collins. Chicago Daily News,* November 28, 1899; *Sturgeon Bay Advocate,* December 2, 1899.

1900 October—The schooner *Mary Collins* went ashore at Little Harbor, six miles south of Manistique, apparently with

Herman Schuenemann in command and on its way to load Christmas trees. The schooner *Ida,* Captain Charles Nelson, replaced the *Mary Collins* to bring Christmas trees from Manistique to Chicago for Herman Schuenemann. When the *Ida* arrived in Chicago it had on board some of the gear taken from the abandoned *Mary Collins. Chicago Evening Post,* November 26, 1900.

1902 November—Herman Schuenemann (misidentified as Capt. Henry Schoenemann) used the schooner *Truman Moss* to buy Christmas trees from Native Americans at the foot of Lake Superior. *Sturgeon Bay Advocate,* November 22, 1902.

1903 November—The schooner *George L. Wrenn* took a cargo of Christmas trees from Thompson, Michigan. The "Schuermann brothers" are mistakenly given as the owners of the cargo. No mention is made of the captain of the vessel. *Sturgeon Bay Advocate,* November 21, 1903.

1904 November—The schooner *George L. Wrenn* took 5,000 Christmas trees to Chicago from an unnamed point. *Sturgeon Bay Advocate,* December 3, 1904. The vessel had been found leaking dangerously twice earlier in the year. *Sturgeon Bay Advocate,* May 28, 1904; July 16, 1904.

1905 December—The schooner *George L. Wrenn* was the first schooner carrying Christmas trees to arrive in Chicago, where it docked at the familiar location beside the Clark Street bridge. *Chicago Daily News,* December 4, 1905.

1906 November—The *George L. Wrenn* was in Manistique to load with Christmas trees when floating debris from a severe storm blocked it in at the slip where it was docked. The news story described the *Wrenn* as barely seaworthy. *Ludington (MI) Chronicle,* November 28, 1906.

1908 October—The schooner *George L. Wrenn* made its only voyage for the year, leaving Chicago to go north for a cargo of Christmas trees. On its way it stopped at Sturgeon Bay to be recaulked. The captain was William O'Brien. *Sturgeon Bay Advocate,* October 15, 1908.

November—The schooner *George L. Wrenn* again stopped at Sturgeon Bay. This time it was on its way back to Chicago with its load of evergreens. The name of the captain was once again reported as William O'Brien. *Sturgeon Bay Advocate,* November 26, 1908.

1909 Herman Schuenemann chartered the schooner *Bertha Barnes* to bring a cargo of Christmas trees to Chicago. *Inter Ocean,* December 7, 1909.

1910 October—The schooner *Rouse Simmons,* Captain Herman Schuenemann, dropped off a dead sailor at Sturgeon Bay while en route to Manistique for a cargo of Christmas trees. *Sturgeon Bay Advocate,* October 6, 1910.

November—The *Rouse Simmons* arrived back in Chicago, and trees were being sold from a location near the Clark Street bridge. *Sturgeon Bay Advocate,* December 1, 1910.

1911 October—Herman Schuenemann and Charles Nelson stopped at Sturgeon Bay with the schooner *Rouse Simmons* to have it recaulked while going north to Manistique for Christmas trees. They had been caught in a gale off Two Rivers just prior to this stop. *Sturgeon Bay Advocate,* October 12, 1911.

November—The schooner *Rouse Simmons* returned to Chicago with its cargo of evergreens. *Sturgeon Bay Advocate,* November 30, 1911.

1912 October 3—The schooner *Rouse Simmons* left on its voyage north for Christmas trees.

November 22—The *Rouse Simmons* left Thompson's Pier near Manistique for Chicago with a load of Christmas trees. On November 23 the *Rouse Simmons* foundered in a storm between Kewaunee and Two Rivers, Wisconsin.

Notes

PREFACE

1. Bruce Catton, *Waiting for the Morning Train: An American Boyhood* (Garden City, NY: Doubleday, 1972; reprint, Detroit: Wayne State University Press, 1987), 230 (page citations are to the reprint edition).

2. The oft repeated and totally believable rationale for changing the town's name was that it was not very pretty sounding and did not evoke a pleasant image for those who had not been there. (The *A* in Ahnapee is short, as in *Anna,* and the accent is on the last syllable of the word, hence *Anna-PEE.*)

3. Catton, *Waiting for the Morning Train,* 232.

CHAPTER ONE

Epigraph from Ivan H. Walton, *Windjammers: Songs of the Great Lakes Sailors,* ed. Joe Grimm (Detroit: Wayne State University Press, 2002), 204.

1. Much has been written about the loss of the schooner *Rouse Simmons.* Most of it is based on the newspaper reporting of the time, which contains numerous mistakes and blatant misrepresentations of the facts. Much writing is also fanciful, and authors have not always been clear about how critical they have been with source material, further clouding the reality of what occurred. Some sources that have made an effort to present a more historical point of view are the following: Theodore S. Charrney, "The Christmas Tree Ship," 2 vols. (typescript, Newberry Library, Chicago, 1971); Frederick Stonehouse, *Went Missing, II* (Au Train, MI: Frederick Stonehouse and Avery Color Studios, 1984; reprint, Au Train, MI: Avery Color Studios, 1989), 163–72; Rochelle Pennington, *The Historic Christmas Tree Ship: A Story of Faith, Hope and Love* (published by the author, 2004); Fred Neuschel, "November 23, 1912: The Rest of the Story," *Anchor News* 21, nos. 1 and 3 (January–February and May–June 1990): 4–11, 44–52; Fred Neuschel, "Bringing Christmas to the City," *Chicago History* 21, no. 3 (December 1992): 44–55. Differences will still be noted among these authors, most of which are the product of different appraisals of the credibility of the source material being used. Finally, much of what is relayed about the Christmas Tree Ship comes from artistic representations that were never intended by their authors to be historically accurate.

2. For good portrayals of the waterfront in Chicago during the days of sail see A. A. Dornfield, "Chicago's Age of Sail," *Chicago History* 11, no. 3 (Spring–Summer 1973): 156–65; Theodore S. Charrney, "The Great Lakes:

Chicago Harbor a Century Ago," *Sea History* 47 (Summer 1988): 12; Theodore J. Karamanski, *Schooner Passage: Sailing Ships and the Lake Michigan Frontier* (Detroit: Wayne State University Press, 2000), 127–72; David M. Young, *Chicago Maritime: An Illustrated History* (DeKalb: Northern Illinois University Press, 2001).

3. Karal Ann Marling, *Merry Christmas: Celebrating America's Greatest Holiday* (Cambridge, MA: Harvard University Press, 2000), 160–96.

4. Robert Brenner, *Christmas Past* (Atglen, PA: Schiffer Publishing, 1996), chap. 12 passim.

5. Photos from the *Chicago Daily News* on the Internet.

6. Jim Benes, *Chicago Christmas: One Hundred Years of Christmas Memories* (Chicago: Cornerstone Press, 2000), 28–30.

7. *Chicago Daily News,* December 5, 1912.

8. *Chicago Daily Tribune,* December 5, 1912; *Chicago Daily News,* December 5, 1912.

9. It is generally agreed by students of the events that no definitive list of crew or passengers on the *Rouse Simmons* could be made. No official record was kept. The newspaper reports of the time, if taken together, do establish by consensus that some of the sailors can be identified by name, but they also agree that others were unattached individuals who will forever remain anonymous. Theodore Charrney, whose research included contact with relatives of Herman Schuenemann and family of at least one other crew member, offers his crew list in his unpublished work; Charrney, "The Christmas Tree Ship," 2:225–26.

10. The information about Herman's financial situation, including a list of people to whom he was indebted at the time of his death, is found in his "Last Will and Testament," Probate Court Records, Cook County, IL.

11. Herman Schuenemann's "Last Will and Testament" also contains direct evidence of the business, Northern Michigan Evergreen Company, and of his ownership of land in the vicinity of Manistique, Michigan.

12. How crucial timing was is illustrated over and over again by contemporary reports of the activities of the various Christmas tree merchants. *Door County Advocate,* November 2, 1889.

13. *Chicago Inter Ocean,* December 5, 1912; *Chicago American,* December 5, 1912.

14. It was not at all unusual for sailing vessels to go out on the lakes overloaded. In both the United States and Canada legislative hearings were conducted into safety on the lake. See U.S. Congress, Senate Committee on Education and Labor, *Report of the Committee of the Senate upon the Relations between Labor and Capital, and Testimony taken by the Committee,* vol. 1 (Washington, DC: Government Printing Office, 1885), passim.

15. The estimate of thirty thousand comes from a newspaper report and should not be taken with full confidence. See *Milwaukee Daily News,* December 6, 1912. Reports in 1898, 1899, and 1910, all years when ships of comparable size to the *Rouse Simmons* were used, give the number as ten thousand. *Chicago*

Daily News, December 6, 1898; November 28, 1899; *Chicago Inter Ocean,* November 30, 1910.

16. *Chicago Inter Ocean,* December 5, 1912.

17. For the *George Wrenn*'s condition see *Ludington Chronicle,* November 28, 1906. For the loss of the *Mary Collins* see *Manistique Pioneer-Tribune,* October 10, 1900; *Sturgeon Bay Advocate,* October 13, 1900; October 20, 1900; *Chicago Evening Post,* November 26, 1900. The *Advocate*'s report on October 20, 1900, that the schooner had been rescued was premature and erroneous.

18. *Racine Daily Times,* November 21, 1912.

19. *Milwaukee Sentinel,* November 21, 1912.

20. *Menominee Herald-Leader,* November 23, 1912; November 25, 1912; *Sault Ste. Marie Evening News,* November 25, 1912; *Sheboygan Press,* November 25, 1912.

21. *Muskegon Times,* November 27, 1912.

22. *Sheboygan Press,* November 23, 1912.

23. *Sturgeon Bay Advocate,* November 28, 1912.

24. *Annual Report of the U.S. Life Saving Service for the Fiscal Year Ended June 30, 1913* (Washington, DC: Government Printing Office, 1914), 61–62.

25. The sources for the loss of the schooner *Three Sisters* are *Menominee Herald-Leader,* November 25, 1912; November 27, 1912; *Sturgeon Bay Advocate,* November 28, 1912; December 5, 1912; *Kewaunee Enterprise,* November 29, 1912. An interesting addendum is that three men received the Carnegie Hero Medal for their efforts to rescue the crew. Cf. *Algoma Record-Herald,* February 19, 1970.

26. *Chicago American,* December 10, 1912; *Sturgeon Bay Advocate,* January 23, 1913.

27. Logbook of the Kewaunee, Wisconsin, Life Saving Station, entry for November 23, 1912, Records of the U.S. Coast Guard and Life Saving Service, Record Group 26, National Archives and Records Administration, Great Lakes Regional Branch, Chicago, Box 267.

28. Logbook of the Two Rivers, Wisconsin, Life Saving Station, entries for November 23 and 24, 1912, Records of the U.S. Coast Guard and Life Saving Service, Record Group 26, National Archives and Records Administration, Great Lakes Regional Branch, Chicago, Box 737.

29. There is no reliable source for the exact number of people on board the *Rouse Simmons* when it was lost. See chapter 15, "Unseaworthy," for a discussion of the number and composition of the crew.

CHAPTER TWO

Epigraph from Soren Kristiansen, *The Diary of Soren Kristiansen: Lake Michigan Schooner Captain, 1891–1893* (Iron Mountain, MI: Mid-Peninsula Library Cooperative, 1981), 40.

1. For the history of the community of Algoma cf. Liz Howell, *Land of the Great Gray Wolf* (Sister Bay, WI: Dragonsbreath Press, 1988); and Virginia Feld Johnson, *An-An-api-sebe: "Where Is the River?"* (Sturgeon Bay, WI: Silverdale Press, 2000).

2. The loss of the *Rouse Simmons* caused some in Algoma to recall that their city had once been home to the Schuenemann family, and long after the tragedy the connection was maintained. Cf. *Algoma Record,* December 6, 1912; December 13, 1912; January 21, 1916. Also see *Algoma Record-Herald,* January 9, 1925.

3. Captain Arthur E. Dow, Manitowoc, WI, to Rose Schuenemann, Chicago, autograph letter signed "*Rouse Simmons*" file, Herman Runge Collection, Milwaukee Public Library, Milwaukee, WI.

4. *Sturgeon Bay Advocate,* December 6, 1906; *Manistique Pioneer-Tribune,* December 7, 1906. A lengthy and detailed newspaper article with no date or source attribution is found in the Captain Arthur Dow file, Wisconsin Maritime Museum, Manitowoc, WI.

5. *Sturgeon Bay Advocate,* November 4, 1909.

6. The common terminology distinguishing between "deep-water" and "coastwise" sailors and vessels can be found frequently. See Jay Martin, "Sailing the Fresh Water Seas: A Social History of Life aboard the Sailing Vessels of the United States and Canada on the Great Lakes, 1815 to 1930" (Ph.D. diss., Bowling Green State University, Bowling Green, OH, 1995). On the Great Lakes, however, *all* sailing was coastwise in the nineteenth century inasmuch as sailors primarily navigated by dead reckoning (meaning that they relied on visual sighting of landmarks to verify their location). The category "short-haul sailor" is meant to differentiate between those on the Great Lakes who made long voyages (say, Chicago to Buffalo or Duluth to Cleveland or Detroit to Kingston) and those who stayed much closer to home. Another way to make this distinction is to speak of "intra-lake sailors" as opposed to "inter-lake sailors."

7. There is confusion about the name of the schooner *Mishicott.* The published version of Kristiansen's diary (Soren Kristiansen, *The Diary of Soren Kristiansen: Lake Michigan Schooner Captain, 1891–1893* [Iron Mountain, MI: Mid-Peninsula Library Cooperative, 1981]) spells the name *Mishicoff,* but this is clearly a mistake (probably attributable to the editor). Government enrollments (forms filed with the Federal Bureau of Navigation giving the specific identifiers of a vessel [size, tonnage, etc.], ownership, and home port) are definitive in identifying the vessel as the *Mishicott.*

8. Kristiansen, *Diary, passim.*

9. While the tree trade was very active on Lake Michigan, it seems that there was no such phenomenon on any of the other Great Lakes. On the East Coast, however, schooners were used to bring trees from the pineries of Maine to the urban areas of the northeast, and a modern rendition of the same trade is

found in the shipping of evergreens to the Hawaiian Islands for Christmas. A complete list of Lake Michigan Christmas tree ships known to date appears at the back of this book.

10. A list of captains known to have made Christmas tree ship voyages appears at the back of this book.

11. Marling, *Merry Christmas!* 160–96; Brenner, *Christmas Past,* 80–105.

12. Benes, *Chicago Christmas,* 7–24.

13. *Die Illinois Staats-Zeitung,* December 14, 1912.

14. *Die Illinois Staats-Zeitung,* December 19, 1912.

15. *Door County Advocate,* November 2, 1889.

16. *Milwaukee Sentinel,* December 15, 1888.

17. *Ahnapee Record,* December 7, 1876.

18. *Ahnapee Record,* December 18, 1876.

19. *Chicago Inter Ocean,* December 21, 1877.

20. *Sturgeon Bay Advocate,* October 19, 1895.

21. *Sturgeon Bay Advocate,* October 31, 1896; November 14, 1896.

22. *Sturgeon Bay Advocate,* November 15, 1902; November 22, 1902.

23. *Door County Advocate,* November 8, 1883.

24. *Ahnapee Record,* April 17, 1879.

25. *Ahnapee Record,* June 29, 1882.

CHAPTER THREE

1. Fred Neuschel, "The Everlasting Ella," *Anchor News* 22, nos. 1 and 2 (January–February and March–April 1991): 4–5, 32–36.

2. *Racine Weekly Journal,* December 20, 1871; *Milwaukee Sentinel,* September 6, 1872; *Kewaunee Enterprise,* November 5, 1872; November 19, 1872; *Door County Advocate,* November 21, 1872; *Ahnapee Record,* October 16, 1873; November 20, 1873.

3. *Sheboygan Times,* November 28, 1874.

4. *Ahnapee Record,* August 12, 1875.

5. The *Milwaukee News* is quoted in the *Ahnapee Record,* October 16, 1873.

6. *Ahnapee Record,* November 26, 1874.

7. *Ahnapee Record,* December 16, 1875.

8. For the story of the Peshtigo fire cf. Denise Gess and William Lutz, *Firestorm at Peshtigo: A Town, Its People, and the Deadliest Fire in American History* (New York: Henry Holt, 2003). Also see Rev. Peter Pernin, "The Great Peshtigo Fire," *Wisconsin Magazine of History* 54 (Summer 1971): 246–72; Robert Wells, *Fire at Peshtigo* (Madison, WI: Northword, 1983).

9. This stirring account by George W. Wing was published in the *Ahnapee Record-Herald,* the successor of the paper he founded, on the occasion of the centennial of the fire, October 6, 1971.

10. The story of how Ahnapee was spared is found in the *Algoma Record,* October 27, 1911.

11. *Racine County Argus,* December 28, 1871.

12. *Racine Advocate,* January 13, 1872.

13. *Milwaukee Sentinel,* December 13, 1871; December 14, 1871; December 18, 1871.

14. *Racine Advocate,* January 13, 1872.

15. *Racine Weekly Journal,* February 7, 1872.

16. William Callaway, "A Sailor's Narrative," in *Early Milwaukee,* ed. Roger Hunt (Madison, WI, 1977), 86.

17. Callaway, "Sailor's Narrative," 86–87.

18. *Kewaunee Enterprise,* January 10, 1872; *Milwaukee Sentinel,* February 16, 1872.

19. In recent years the lettering on the limestone obelisk in the Woodlawn Cemetery has become so worn that the names and dates are no longer legible, but the documents of the cemetery still tell the story as do newspaper reports from the time. The fire is extensively covered in the *DePere (WI) News,* October 14, 1871, and the *Door County Advocate,* October 12, 1871. It is possible that the dates on the monument are not the dates of death but the dates when the remains were located. The Williamson family home and sawmill, as well as the surrounding area, were totally destroyed by the fire, and, as was the case with many bodies found afterward, there may have been little left but a pile of ashes, making it very difficult to identify the bodies.

20. The obituary of Eliza Doak, wife of John Doak Sr., gives the history of their move from Canada to Green Bay. See *DePere (WI) News,* April 19, 1886. The obituary of John Jr. provides further details of the family history. Cf. *Ahnapee Record,* February 26, 1885.

21. Karamanski, *Schooner Passage,* 211–21. *History of the Great Lakes,* vol. 2, ed. J. B. Mansfield (Chicago: J. H. Beers, 1899), contains the biographies of many men whose careers as lake sailors were notorious enough to belong in a · "Who's Who" type listing. A high percentage of these men went through a formal process of on-the-job-training before they attained the rank of captain. Many had begun their career on sailing vessels, but the vast majority had moved to steam vessels, and many had become owners. But Mansfield's collection of noteworthies should not be taken as representative of all lake captains and certainly not of the independent short-haul sailors discussed in these pages.

22. Charles Mears to E. H. Denison, autograph letter signed, September 19, 1867; November 6, 1867; December 11, 1867; December 12, 1867; December 13, 1867; December 19, 1867; December 22, 1867; February 5, 1868; Charles Mears Papers, Chicago History Museum Library and Archives, Chicago, IL.

23. Isaac Stephenson, *Recollections of a Long Life, 1829–1915* (Chicago: published by the author, 1915), 99.

24. An example of the role of the vessel owner in selecting the master for

the vessel is found in the first appointment of August Schuenemann to a position of command. Cf. *Ahnapee Record,* July 24, 1879. At the time August was twenty-six years old, and his experience as a mariner had been confined to working on vessels that he owned a part interest in or that were owned by Captain Johnny Doak. In other words, August had no training outside of informal mentoring to qualify him as a vessel master.

25. *Ahnapee Record,* October 20, 1881.

26. In his discussion of the settlements of Foscoro and Silver Creek, Oscar Berg provides the history of one of those still smaller lakeshore communities that Ahnapee "parented." Cf. Oscar Berg, "Histories of Foscoro (Stoney Creek) and Silver Creek" (typescript, Kewaunee Public Library, Kewaunee, WI, n.d.).

CHAPTER FOUR

Epigraph from John Haeger, *Men and Money: The Urban Frontier at Green Bay 1815–1840* (Mt. Pleasant: Central Michigan University, n.d.), 5–6.

1. George W. Wing, "Early History of Kewaunee County," ed. Harold Heidmann (typescript, Algoma Public Library, Algoma, WI, 1936), 40–41.

2. *Kewaunee Enterprise,* August 28, 1867.

3. *Ahnapee Record,* June 20, 1889.

4. William Fagg, "The Diary of William Fagg" (autograph manuscript, microfilm edition, State Historical Society of Wisconsin, Madison). Unfortunately, large portions of the diary are too faded to be legible. It is especially lamentable that his entries around the time of the great fire of 1871 are indecipherable. In contrast, his entries written while serving in the Union army during the Civil War are not only readable, they comprise the most descriptive and lengthy passages.

5. The war was not embraced by many of the immigrant families in northeastern Wisconsin. Evasion of the draft was frequent, and there were even some furtive attempts to organize resistance. As was true all over the country, some of the more established settlers and businessmen who had accumulated sufficient wealth touted their support for the war but purchased substitutes to serve for them when they were drafted. In contrast, however, there were also many men who went uncomplaining into the army, suffered tremendous hardships, fought valiantly, and witnessed unspeakable horrors. William Fagg has already been mentioned. Others of this group also are mentioned in this book. The sources for this history are manifold. Among the newspaper stories, the retrospective writings of George Wing, published in the Ahnapee *Record* and Kewaunee *Enterprise,* are the best. Many of them were gathered together in an unpublished typescript by Algoman Harold Heidmann and can be found in the Algoma Public Library. General descriptions of the service of some of the individual army units can be found on the Internet. And, of course, the military records of

the individual men who served from Kewaunee County are preserved in the National Archives and Records Administration. A truly excellent published work by Kerry A. Trask focuses on the wartime years in Manitowoc County, Wisconsin, and provides a vivid picture of the kind of resistance among immigrants that was also seen in Kewaunee County, Wisconsin: Kerry A. Trask, *Fire Within: A Civil War Narrative from Wisconsin* (Kent, OH: Kent State University Press, 1995). Another source that does not shy away from the immigrants' resistance to serving in the Union army is John Henry Mertens, *The Second Battle: A Story of Our Belgian Ancestors in the American Civil War, 1861–1865* (published by the author, 1987).

6. Wisconsin Department of Veterans' Affairs, "History/Civil War Regimental Histories: 11th Wisconsin Infantry Regiment," available at http://museum.dva.state.wi.us/His_regiments.asp (accessed July 10, 2006).

7. Documentation of Frederick's service in Company E of the Wisconsin Eleventh Brigade is found in his pension papers, which are part of the military records preserved by the National Archives and Records Administration in Washington. His file contains letters attesting to his condition by Ahnapee physician Dr. Parsons and indicate that the government had to be petitioned repeatedly before Frederick was granted the pension that he merited as a disabled veteran.

8. *Ahnapee Record,* April 15, 1875.

9. *Ahnapee Record,* February 25, 1875; June 17, 1875. In the latter article Frederick is erroneously identified as August.

10. "Pension Records of Frederick Schuenemann, Company E, Wisconsin 11th Brigade" (Washington, DC: National Archives and Records Administration, Military Service Branch, n.d.).

11. The federal census for Ahnapee, Wisconsin, 1870, suggests that August's work life began at an early age. He is listed in that census, which gives his age as seventeen years old, as a farm laborer. The same census record shows that Herman was born in Wisconsin in 1865, the third of six children. Their father, Frederick, is listed as a wagonmaker—no longer a farmer. According to that census enumeration the family's neighbors were primarily tradesmen—a photographer, bookkeeper, tanner, laborer, shoemaker, carpenter, cabinetmaker, brickmaker, and blacksmith (there was also a Lutheran minister)—indicative of a move off the farm. Cf. U.S. Manuscript census schedules, Ahnapee Township, WI, 1870.

12. For Major William I. Henry cf. *Ahnapee Record,* January 17, 1889; *Algoma Record-Herald,* December 16, 1927; March 24, 1949. For Henry Harkins cf. *Algoma Record,* April 28, 1905; *Algoma Record-Herald,* August 22, 1968. For Charles Ross cf. *Commemorative Biographical Record of the Counties of Brown, Kewaunee and Door* (Chicago: J. H. Beers, 1895), 502; *Algoma Record-Herald,* May 4, 1923. For John McDonald cf. *Ahnapee Record,* July 30, 1885; *Algoma Record-Herald,* April 20, 1923; May 4, 1923.

13. *Kewaunee Enterprise,* February 27, 1867.

14. Wing, "Early History of Kewaunee County," 112.

15. *Door County Advocate,* July 11, 1867; *Chicago Times,* September 2, 1867.

16. *Kewaunee Enterprise,* June 5, 1867; *Ahnapee Record,* October 2, 1873.

17. Even more convincing evidence of this specialization of occupations is found in studying the federal census records for Ahnapee, where the number and variety of occupations increase as years go by. Cf. U.S. Manuscript census schedules, Ahnapee Township, WI, 1860, 1870, 1880.

18. *Ahnapee Record,* November 4, 1875.

19. *Ahnapee Record,* September 30, 1875; October 14, 1875; October 21, 1875; November 11, 1875.

20. *Ahnapee Record,* September 9, 1875; October 14, 1875.

21. *Ahnapee Record,* September 9, 1875.

CHAPTER FIVE

First epigraph from Harriet Martineau, *Society in America.* Second epigraph by William Graham Sumner quoted in Louis M. Hacker, *The World of Andrew Carnegie, 1865–1901* (Philadelphia: J. B. Lippincott, 1968), xxiii.

1. See Howell, *Land of the Great Gray Wolf,* 53–70; Johnson, *An-An-apisebe,* 21–41; *Commemorative Biographical Record of the Counties of Brown, Kewaunee and Door,* 501; and *Algoma Record,* December 10, 1915; February 9, 1923; March 30, 1923; April 20, 1923; August 5, 1927.

2. *Commemorative Biographical Record of the Counties of Brown, Kewaunee and Door,* 501; *Algoma Record,* December 10, 1915. The federal census of 1860 places the Perry brothers' property in the same district in which Joseph McCormick lived. Joseph's son, Marcus, also lived there and apparently lent his name to the postal office district of Marcus. See U.S. Manuscript census schedule, Forestville Township, WI, 1860.

3. François-Alexandre-Frédéric duc de La Rochefoucauld-Liancourt, *Travels through the United States of North America* (London: R. Phillips, 1799), 104.

4. Other potentially apocryphal stories include McCormick's presence at the critical battles of Tippecanoe, Queenston Heights, and Lundy's Lane in the War of 1812. It was also reported that he had fought in the Black Hawk War. Sources for McCormick's life include *Ahnapee Record,* September 2, 1875; *A Biographical Directory of the Indiana General Assembly,* vol. 1, 1816–99 (Indianapolis: Select Committee on the Centennial History of the Indiana General Assembly in cooperation with the Indiana Historical Bureau, 1980–84), 248.

5. An adulation of McCormick that refers to him as "a venerable man" and a "[King] Nestor in age and eloquence" appeared in the *Milwaukee Sentinel* for May 5, 1871. (Nestor was a hero of the Trojan War who advised the Greek chiefs in battle and was praised by Homer.) The reporter had been entertained by McCormick's stories of personal acquaintance with both Andrew Jackson and William Henry Harrison.

6. Sources for the lives of the Perry brothers are primarily the historical reminiscences published in the Ahnapee/Algoma newspaper. *Algoma Record,* December 10, 1915; April 24, 1969.

7. *Algoma Record-Herald,* April 27, 1923; March 26, 1970.

8. Matthias Simon to Edward Decker, autograph letter signed, January 26, 1884, Edward Decker Papers, State Historical· Society of Wisconsin, Area Research Center, University of Wisconsin at Green Bay, Green Bay, WI.

9. Judge Parish, "A Paper Read by Judge Parish at Norwalk [Ohio], June 8th," *Norwalk [Ohio] Reflector,* June 28, 1881; *Commemorative and Biographical Record of the Counties of Sandusky and Ottawa, Ohio* (Chicago: J. H. Beers, 1896), 55–60; Lewis Cass Aldrich, ed., *History of Erie County, Ohio* (Syracuse, NY: D. Mason, 1889), 302–3, 332–33, 423–24; Helen M. Hansen, *At Home in Early Sandusky* (Sandusky, OH: Sandusky Register, 1975), 9–12, 25–26, 56–58; J. Wilbur Jacoby, ed., *History of Marion County, Ohio* (Marion County Historical Society, 1976), 181–82; John A. Strutton, *The Old Homes of Norwalk (from written memoirs of Mrs. Charlotte Wooster Boalt)* (Norwalk, OH: private printing, 1938), 11.

10. Boalt Hall, which houses the law school at the University of California, Berkley, is named after Charles Griswold Boalt's brother, John Henry Boalt. John Henry was originally trained as a mining engineer but changed his focus to law after moving to the West Coast. He was very successful and represented many large business interests. Oscar T. Shuck, *Bench and Bar in California: History, Anecdotes, Reminiscences* (San Francisco: Occidental Printing House, 1889), 533–37.

11. Henry R. Timman, Norwalk, OH, to Fred Neuschel, October 31, 1993, typewritten letter signed, in the author's private collection.

12. "Ahnapee Piers" Folder, Edward Decker Papers.

13. [Charles] Henry [Justin] Edwards, Casco, WI, to his mother, Casco, ME, December 7, 1872, autograph letter signed, personal collection of Carolyn F. Edwards, Casco, ME.

14. For Edward Decker Jr. cf. *Kewaunee Enterprise,* November 4, 1904; November 11, 1904; *Algoma Record,* May 7, 1905; February 16, 1923. For the career of Edward Decker Sr. cf. Fred Neuschel, "The Clique vs. the Croakers: Class and Conflict in Small-Town Wisconsin," *Wisconsin Magazine of History* 81, no. 2 (Winter 1997–98): 83–108. For Decker's banking business cf. Bill Meindl, *Bank of Sturgeon Bay: The First Century, 1889–1989* (Sturgeon Bay, WI: Bank of Sturgeon Bay, 1989), 17–19.

15. *Ahnepee* was an early spelling of the name of the city. Why the spelling changed is unknown, but the fact that the vast majority of printed references to the town use the latter spelling makes it clearly dominant.

16. For the Ahnepee Pier Company's construction of the pier and legal battle with Judge C. G. Boalt cf. Folder "Pier Matters," envelope marked "county

judge had not jurisdiction," Edward Decker Papers; also "Charles G. Boalt vs. Ahnepee Farmers' Pier Company, January 31, 1867, Case No. 62," Kewaunee County [WI] Circuit Court.

17. For the clique takeover of the Farmers' Pier cf. Folder "Pier Matters," documents labeled "Ahnepee Pier Property," and "Boalt & Youngs Pine Land from State and Pier Matters"; C. G. Boalt to Edward Decker, October 30, 1868; C. G. Boalt to Edward Decker, November 9, 1868; Edward Decker to C. G. Boalt, November 13, 1868; December 10, 1868, all in Edward Decker Papers.

18. *Chicago Tribune,* August 24, 1868; and an undated George Wing newspaper article from the collection of Harold Heidmann.

19. William F. Whyte, "The Bennett Law Campaign," *Wisconsin Magazine of History* 10, no. 4 (June 1927): 373.

20. Herman Deutsch, "Yankee-Teuton Rivalry in Wisconsin Politics of the Seventies," *Wisconsin Magazine of History* (March 1931): 262–82; Herman Deutsch, "Yankee-Teuton Rivalry in Wisconsin Politics of the Seventies: Section II," *Wisconsin Magazine of History* (June 1931): 403–18.

21. Boalt's speech was printed in the newspaper. *Ahnapee Record,* July 17, 1880. Charles Griswold's lawyer brother, John Henry, was well known in California for his stance against Chinese immigration. In 1877 he read a paper to the Berkley Club in which he argued that "the Caucasian and Mongolian races . . . cannot live together harmoniously on the same soil unless one be in a state of servitude to the other." Shuck, *Bench and Bar in California,* 534.

CHAPTER SIX

1. *Kewaunee Enterprise,* February 23, 1870.

2. Fagg, "The Diary of William Fagg," August 6, 1870.

3. State of Wisconsin, "Chapter 430, An Act to Authorize the Town of Ahnepee in the County of Kewaunee to Issue the Bonds in Said Town to Aid in the Construction of a Harbor at the Mouth of the Ahnepee River," *Private and Local Laws Passed by the Legislature of Wisconsin in the Year 1870* (Madison, 1870): 1050–54.

4. The law authorizing the bond issue was repealed by the legislature in 1873.

5. Because the "outer harbor" came and went quickly, it is rarely mentioned in documents. A very informative and important article that catches the harbor development at this precise stage appears in the *Green Bay Advocate,* August 22, 1872. Diagrams accompanying the article show the proposed break wall that would enclose the outer harbor. This is also the only known diagram that shows both the old Ahnepee Farmers' Pier and the Boalt and Stebbins Pier in place. The Farmers' Pier fell into disrepair and was abandoned fairly quickly

after the clique took control of its management. Cf. *Ahnapee Record,* March 30, 1876.

6. U.S. Corps of Engineers, *Survey of Ahnapee Harbor, Wisconsin,* House Executive Document 172 (Washington, DC: Government Printing Office, 1897), 1–7.

7. *Ahnapee Record,* February 5, 1874; February 12, 1874; February 26, 1874; March 5, 1874; March 12, 1874; April 23, 1874.

8. *Ahnapee Record,* October 8, 1874; October 15, 1874.

9. *Ahnapee Record,* September 2, 1875; October 7, 1875; October 14, 1875; October 21, 1875; November 11, 1875; December 9, 1875.

10. *Ahnapee Record,* December 23, 1875. This pier is shown in maps of the harbor drawn by the U.S. Corps of Engineers surveyors.

11. D. W. McLeod to Edward Decker, autograph letter signed, June 10, 1876, Edward Decker Papers.

12. D. W. Stebbins to Edward Decker, August 26, 1876, Edward Decker Papers.

13. State of Wisconsin, *Revised Statutes of the State of Wisconsin* (St. Louis, MO, 1871), 115, 510–11, 749–50, 1698. The Ahnapee River (referred to as the Wolf River, its original name) is specifically identified as a navigable stream in the state of Wisconsin; *Revised Statutes of the State of Wisconsin* (St. Louis, MO, 1878), 477–81. Cf. also Ralph G. Plumb, "Harbor Administration: Harbors of Wisconsin" (bachelor's thesis, University of Wisconsin, 1901), 17–22, 41–43, for the history of riparian rights.

14. U.S. Corps of Engineers, "Survey of Ahnapee Harbor, Wisconsin," 1–7.

15. *Ahnapee Record,* September 19, 1878.

16. *Ahnapee Record,* January 2, 1879; May 1, 1879; June 5, 1879; June 19, 1879.

17. *Ahnapee Record,* May 15, 1879. In the same issue a brief but telling report shows that there was definitely an attempt by the clique to prevent expansion of the channel upstream and that there was a corresponding anti-clique bias among those who had an interest in harbor property: "The two harbor lots were sold to Sam Perry last Saturday for $300. D. W. Stebbins offered $400 for them on the condition that the money be expended below the bridge."

18. *Ahnapee Record,* June 30, 1881.

19. Neuschel, "The Clique vs. the Croakers," 99–100.

20. *Ahnapee Record,* July 17, 1873.

21. *Ahnapee Record,* July 17, 1873; November 27, 1873.

22. This story has appeared several times in Kewaunee County newspapers. See *Algoma Record-Herald,* January 5, 1934; *Kewaunee County Chronicle,* December 26, 1993.

CHAPTER SEVEN

1. The *Ahnapee Record* of September 4, 1873, contained the following words to the wise. "The policy of depending exclusively for trade and business on ties, posts, cord wood, bark, telegraph poles and lumber, is the height of folly, since, however immense our trade in this produce now, it is being rapidly reduced daily, and the time is not many years distant when the trade of the farming region must be an important proportion to the business of our towns, or that business must be materially reduced in volume."

Two years later the *Ahnapee Record* of July 29, 1875, cataloged the following manufacturing enterprises in the town: "three tanneries, two furniture and sash, door and blind factories, a grist mill, Stansky's brewery, three wagon and carriage factories, and other enterprises which contribute, in a greater or lesser degree, to the productiveness of this region."

A federal government report entitled *Report upon Forestry* presented to Congress graphically illustrates the decline in forestry products coming out of Ahnapee. In 1875 the town shipped out 2,333M board feet of lumber and 7,523M shingles. In 1876 it was only 115M board feet of lumber and 100M shingles. In 1877 lumber fell to 40M board feet, while shingles rebounded slightly to 485M. Franklin B. Hough, *Report upon Forestry,* 46th Cong., 2nd sess., House Executive Document 37 (Washington, DC: Government Printing Office, 1880), 50.

2. The *Ahnapee Record* of September 9, 1875, speaks to the contrast between the local and national economies: "An exchange intimates that the cry of hard times, like the smallpox, is catching. If it begins in the East to-day, it will reach the West to-morrow. . . . Merchants, however, have done well on the average. Mechanics have had steady work and at comparatively good wages. The farmers have sown their broad acres, and are now in the midst of a bountiful harvest. . . . There is no cause to grumble in a land where if you 'scratch the earth with a hoe, it will smile with a harvest.' This year will return its reward to the laborer, and there will be plenty, even if a few acres of wheat have been invaded by the bug."

3. *Ahnapee Record,* April 10, 1879.

4. *Ahnapee Record,* December 2, 1875.

5. Richard F. Palmer, ed., "Great Lakes Driftwood: Schooner-Scows," *Inland Seas* 42, no. 2 (Summer 1986): 78–83.

6. Jay C. Martin, "Not for Shallow Water Only: Scow Construction along the Maumee River, 1825–1859," *Marine History Lines* 10, no. 1 (Winter 1990–91): 2–6.

7. Lorne Joyce, "Stonehooking and Fishing Trade," in *At the Mouth of the Credit,* ed. Betty Clarkson (Erin, Ontario: Boston Mills Press, 1977), 37–38.

8. *Ahnapee Record,* June 3, 1875.

9. *Ahnapee Record,* June 2, 1875.

10. Townsend, *Tales from the Great Lakes,* 26.

11. Joyce, "Stonehooking and Fishing Trade," 37–38. In early Canada a *toise* was 6 feet, 4 3/4 inches, or 1.95 meters. A cubic *toise* was a standard measurement of stone used by masons. Peter Moogk, *Building a House in New France* (Markham, ONT: Fitzhenry and Whiteside, 2002), 132.

12. *Ahnapee Record,* December 2, 1875; December 16, 1875. Both of these accounts indicate that the *Hinsdale* was sailing without as basic a piece of equipment as an anchor.

13. *Ahnapee Record,* September 13, 1877.

14. *Ahnapee Record,* November 4, 1875; November 25, 1875. An indication of the animosity between Fellows and Boalt/Decker is found in a letter that Boalt wrote to Decker on December 10, 1868, about a prospective newspaper at Ahnapee. Boalt has a candidate for editor in mind who, he says, "wont [*sic*] be controlled by Chas. Fellows or any one else." The letter is in the Edward Decker Papers.

15. *Ahnapee Record,* October 21, 1875.

16. *Door County Advocate,* April 13, 1871.

17. *Kewaunee Enterprise,* July 5, 1871.

18. In 1879 the *Ahnapee Record* was very thorough in recording arrivals and clearances in the harbor. This is a clear indication of how important maritime commerce had become to the town and region. All of the facts cited here about the comings and goings in the harbor are from that source.

19. *Ahnapee Record,* April 3, 1879; April 10, 1879.

20. *Ahnapee Record,* April 17, 1879.

21. Photographs of the waterfront at Ahnapee during this period are very rare and often of poor quality. One was located by Algoma resident Harold Heidmann that is especially valuable because it shows the extensive field of wood stacked on the shore of the ice covered river awaiting shipment. In the river there are two small schooners stripped for winter layup. One can be positively identified as the *Lady Ellen;* the other is possibly the *Whiskey Pete.* This photo can be seen on the cover of the *Wisconsin Magazine of History* 81, no. 2 (Winter 1997–98).

22. *Ahnapee Record,* April 10, 1879; June 5, 1879.

CHAPTER EIGHT

Epigraph from "Safe in the Harbor" by Eric Bogle from the CD *Safe in the Harbor,* recorded by Lee Murdock, Depot Recordings DEP-013.

1. *Door County Advocate,* January 20, 1881.

2. *Ahnapee Record,* February 2, 1882.

3. A brief synopsis of the harbor development at Kewaunee is found in the *Kewaunee Enterprise,* July 4, 1913.

4. *Ahnapee Record,* January 9, 1879; February 13, 1879.

5. The story of Captain McDonald and the charlatan Chadwick is found in *Algoma Record-Herald* of September 14, 1967, and should probably be attributed to the paper's first editor, and the county's first historian, George W. Wing.

6. In one race, reported February 24, 1884, in the *Ahnapee Record,* Gold Dust Dick came in second on the ice of Sturgeon Bay. All proceeds, after the purse, were donated to the Red Cross to help flood victims in the Ohio Valley.

7. *Ahnapee Record,* September 23, 1886; November 4, 1886; May 26, 1887; July 28, 1887; *Milwaukee Sentinel,* February 21, 1888; *Ahnapee Record,* May 10, 1888.

8. *Ahnapee Record,* September 23, 1886.

9. *Milwaukee Sentinel,* February 21, 1888; *Milwaukee Sentinel,* July 18, 1888.

10. *Ahnapee Record,* August 4, 1884.

11. *Ahnapee Record,* November 3, 1887; November 17, 1887; December 15, 1887.

12. Enrollment 141, April 21, 1888, at the port of Milwaukee. Previous enrollment was surrendered due to sale of the vessel to Thomas Kearns of Milwaukee County.

13. *Ahnapee Record,* November 29, 1888; December 13, 1888.

14. *Ahnapee Record,* November 14, 1889.

15. *Ahnapee Record,* April 10, 1890.

16. *Ahnapee Record,* May 28, 1891.

17. *Ahnapee Record,* October 12, 1893.

CHAPTER NINE

Epigraph from Ivan H. Walton, *Songquest: The Journals of a Great Lakes Folklorist,* ed. Joe Grimm (Detroit: Wayne State University Press, 2005), 168.

1. *Ahnapee Record,* September 24, 1878; September 25, 1878; September 26, 1878.

2. *Sturgeon Bay Advocate,* November 21, 1902.

3. Carl Raymond Christianson, *Ship Building and Boat Building in Sturgeon Bay, Wisconsin: From the Beginning to 1985* (Sturgeon Bay, WI: published by the author, 1989), 66–91. See also William Lafferty, "Technological Innovation in Great Lakes Shipping: Leathem D. Smith and the Rise of the Self-Unloader," in *"A Fully Accredited Ocean": Essays on the Great Lakes,* ed. Victoria Brehm (Ann Arbor: University of Michigan Press, 1998), 155–98.

4. *Door County Advocate,* April 7, 1881; May 12, 1881; May 26, 1881.

5. *Door County Advocate,* November 10, 1881; November 24, 1881.

6. In 1885 the president of the Lake Seamen's Union testified to a Senate committee about the dangers that sailors faced. One of them was the undermanning of vessels, which was dictated not by the captains but by the owners. The

union president remarked that in some cases vessel captains knew they were undermanned but were afraid of losing their own heads if they spoke out. See U.S. Congress, Senate Committee on Education and Labor, *Report of the Committee of the Senate upon the Relations between Labor and Capital, and Testimony taken by the Committee* (Washington, DC: Government Printing Office, 1885), 1:426–35. ·

7. *Door County Advocate,* December 8, 1881.

8. James Glasgow, "Muskegon, Michigan: The Evolution of a Lake Port" (Ph.D. diss., University of Chicago, Chicago, IL, 1939), 30.

9. The Charles Mears Papers provide several insights into the captain's role on a schooner turned barge. The following excerpt is from a contract between the captain of the vessel, Thomas Clark, and its owner, Charles Mears, dated February 1872. Note that the Mears vessel mentioned, like the *Peoria,* worked sometimes as a scow-schooner and sometimes as a barge.

It is also understood by the Party of the First part [Captain Clark] that the Party of the Second part [Charles Mears] may at any time change said sailing vessel into a Barge to be towed by his Steam Barge, and if she is so changed the said Party of the First part is to furnish and pay crew, provisions, oil, and fuel[;] said crew to consist of one man besides himself and a cook, and that himself and crew are to help load said Barge and keep all property belonging to her in good order and condition. In consideration of the faithful performance of the above by the Party of the First part the said Charles Mears party of the Second part hereby agrees to pay the said Thomas Clark party of the First part as follows:

As Master of the Scow Black Hawk as a sailing vessel Seventy (70) dollars per month.

As Master of the Barge Black Hawk to be towed by Steam One Hundred and Sixty (160) dollars per month he to pay the above before described expenses out of said Amount.

Another contract between Mears and the owners of the Peshtigo Company, dated April 14, 1870, states explicitly that the captain of the barge is subservient to the captain of the steamer: "The Master of the Barge is to act under the control and direction of the captain of the Tug."

10. U.S. Congress, *Report of the Committee of the Senate upon the Relations between Labor and Capital,* 1:426–35.

11. *Ahnapee Record,* November 19, 1885; *Door County Advocate,* November 26, 1885; December 3, 1885.

12. *Sturgeon Bay Advocate,* October 21, 1886; November 4, 1886; Logbook of the Sturgeon Bay, Wisconsin, Life Saving Station, entry for October 10, 1886, Records of the U.S. Coast Guard and Life Saving Service, Record Group 26, National Archives and Records Administration, Great Lakes Regional Branch, Chicago, IL, Box 704.

13. In 1878 the Seamen's Mutual Benefit Society, which had been founded

in Chicago in 1860, became the Chicago Seamen's Mutual Benefit Union. While it was initially successful in organizing sailors to improve wages and working conditions, it eventually lost the upper hand to the Lake Carriers' Association, which represented vessel owners. Karamanski, *Schooner Passage,* 109–11.

For news reports of the early meetings of the Chicago Seamen's Union (which were held in secret) cf. *Chicago Inter Ocean* for March through May 1878, especially March 27, 1878; March 29, 1878; April 3, 1878; April 4, 1878; April 20, 1878.

14. Charles Mears Papers, contract between the captain of the vessel, Thomas Clark, and its owner, Charles Mears, dated February 1872.

15. *Door County Advocate,* April 29, 1886.

16. *Ahnapee Record,* April 23, 1874.

17. *Door County Advocate,* April 27, 1886.

18. *Door County Advocate,* June 21, 1883.

19. *Door County Advocate,* August 21, 1883.

20. *Door County Advocate,* July 10, 1884.

21. *Ahnapee Record,* July 28, 1887; August 4, 1887.

22. The schooner *Peoria* grew old fairly gracefully. Its last years were spent in sailing for a Beaver Island owner, Mannes Bonner, the same man who last owned the *Rouse Simmons,* and the schooner was not finally put out of action until 1901 at the ripe old age of forty-six.

23. *Ahnapee Record,* May 2, 1889; *Door County Advocate,* May 4, 1889.

24. *Ahnapee Record,* April 13, 1882.

25. For Christmas tree cargoes cf. *Door County Advocate,* November 3, 1889; *Ahnapee Record,* November 5, 1891; November 3, 1892. Other mentions of the *Wright* and its cargo are peppered throughout the pages of the *Record* for this period.

26. *Door County Advocate,* November 2, 1889.

27. *Sturgeon Bay Advocate,* November 21, 1902.

CHAPTER TEN

Epigraph from Bruce Catton, *Waiting for the Morning Train* (Garden City, NY: Doubleday, 1972; reprint, Detroit: Wayne State University Press, 1987), 232 (page citations are to the reprint edition).

1. Those with knowledge of steamboats on Lake Michigan will doubtless want to remind the author that steamboats were regular visitors to the pier at Ahnapee from the earliest days and continued to play a vital role on into the twentieth century. Most notable is the service provided by the Goodrich Company, which provided passenger and package freight service from the earliest days, when the town was still called Wolf River. So, a word of explanation is

due regarding the end of the maritime community at Ahnapee. Equating the end of the maritime community with the end of the use of schooners and scow-schooners is not intended to dismiss the contribution of steamboats. Rather it is a recognition that while steamboats carried passengers and package freight, sailing vessels carried the vast majority of commercial cargoes in and out of the harbor. So, when trade via sailing vessels dwindled to a mere trickle by the end of the nineteenth century, one might accurately say that Ahnapee (now Algoma) was no longer a maritime-dependent community.

2. Not to be confused with its contemporary the *Emma Taylor*.

3. The *Ahnapee Record* provides frequent brief reports of the activity in the harbor for 1893.

4. A list of references for all these events in the life of the *Lady Ellen* would obviously be very lengthy. Suffice it to say that all of them are documented in the *Ahnapee Record* and/or the *Door County Advocate*.

5. The data in the text regarding arrivals, clearances, boat types, and cargoes was gathered by an issue-by-issue reading of the *Ahnapee Record* for the years of 1879 and 1893. The tonnage of the vessels can easily be found with the online database maintained by the Wisconsin Marine History Society. It is necessary to exempt the Goodrich steamers from this data because their arrivals and departures were not recorded in the newspaper consistently and, in spite of the fact that they had a schedule, they did not always keep to the schedule. Additionally, there is no record of the kind or amount of freight that the Goodrich boats carried other than the generic term *package freight*.

6. A few of those 261 visits were by vessels whose business was really at the smaller pier communities near Ahnapee, such as Foscoro and Horn's Pier, that did not have moorings protected from storms. They stopped at Ahnapee on the way to and/or from those points to await a safe and propitious time to conduct their trade at the piers where they were exposed to the full force of whatever wind or wave pattern prevailed on the lake.

7. The few mentions of the routine visits by the Goodrich line steamers suggest that quite a bit of the freight formerly carried by sailing vessels had been consigned to steam, but there are no hard figures to confirm this.

8. Palmer, "Great Lakes Driftwood"; Martin, "Not for Shallow Water Only."

9. The Charles Robert Starkweather Papers, Chicago History Museum Library and Archives, contain a port list for the 1838 season at Chicago.

10. Henry N. Barkhausen, "William Wallace Bates: Part I," *Anchor News* 19, no. 3 (May–June 1988): 44.

11. Jefferson Davis, *Report of the Secretary of War in Compliance with a Resolution of the Senate of the 29th ultimo Calling for Copies of Survey of Lieutenant Colonel Graham of Harbors, &c., in Wisconsin and Michigan,* Senate Executive Document

77, 34th Cong., 1st and 2nd sess. (Washington, DC: 1856), 1–296.

12. Stan Mailer, *Green Bay & Western: First 111 Years* (Edmunds, WA: Hundman Publishing, 1989).

13. Ray Specht and Ellen Specht, *History of the Green Bay and Western* (Boston: Railway and Locomotive Historical Society, 1966), 51.

14. *Ahnapee Record,* July 16, 1891.

15. Specht and Specht, *History of the Green Bay and Western,* 51–53.

CHAPTER ELEVEN

1. Ivan H. Walton, *Songquest: The Journals of a Great Lakes Folklorist,* ed. Joe Grimm (Detroit: Wayne State University Press, 2005).

2. For Seavey's life cf. Lewis C. Reimann, *Between the Iron and the Pine: A Biography of a Pioneer Family and a Pioneer Town* (published by the author, 1951), 179–80; William J. Duchaine, "Swashbuckling 'Pirate' Is Lake Legend," *Milwaukee Journal,* February 17, 1963; William J. Duchaine, "Yo, Ho, Ho, How the Swabs Made Way for Roaring Dan," *Chicago Tribune,* April 22, 1962; William D. Ellis, "Captain Daniel Seavey," *Inland Seas* (Winter 1988): 253–57.

3. Even small communities were visited by such boats, which sometimes were called "bum boats." An example was written up in the *Sturgeon Bay Advocate* on October 7, 1894. The scow-schooner *Oak Orchard* had been anchoring offshore, where Captain Nightingale was running his racket. The captain was hauled before a county judge who levied the minimum fine with the understanding that the *Oak Orchard* would find some other neighborhood to do business in. Captain Nightingale announced before he left that he planned to make Ahnapee his next stop.

4. Duchaine, "Yo, Ho, Ho, How the Swabs Made Way for Roaring Dan"; Duchaine, "Swashbuckling 'Pirate' Is Lake Legend."

5. Logbook of the U.S. Revenue Cutter Tuscarora, entries for June 22–28, 1908, Records of the U.S. Coast Guard and Life Saving Service, Revenue Cutter Service, Record Group 26, National Archives and Records Administration, Main Building, Washington, DC, Box 2506.

6. *Milwaukee Sentinel,* September 30, 1872; October 15, 1872; *Chicago Times,* September 30, 1872.

7. *Sturgeon Bay Advocate,* October 27, 1900.

8. *Door County Advocate,* July 5, 1877; *Ahnapee Record,* June 27, 1878.

9. *Ahnapee Record,* April 10, 1884; *Door County Advocate,* June 26, 1884.

10. *Ahnapee Record,* June 18, 1885.

11. *Ahnapee Record,* July 18, 1889; November 27, 1890.

12. U.S. Coast Guard and Life Saving Service, Logbook of the Sturgeon Bay, Wisconsin, Life Saving Station, entries for October 15–16, 1909; *Sturgeon Bay Advocate,* October 21, 1909.

CHAPTER TWELVE

1. There are numerous excellent works on Chicago during this period. Several that illustrate well the points made in this chapter are Robin F. Bachin, *Building the South Side: Urban Space and Civic Culture in Chicago, 1890–1919* (Chicago: University of Chicago Press, 2004); William Cronan, *Nature's Metropolis: Chicago and the Great West* (New York: W. W. Norton, 1991); Ray Ginger, *Altgeld's America: Chicago from 1892–1905* (New York: Marcus Wiener Publishing, 1958); Donald L. Miller, *City of the Century: The Epic of Chicago and the Making of America* (New York: Simon & Schuster, 1996); Ross Miller, *American Apocalypse: The Great Fire and the Myth of Chicago* (Chicago: University of Chicago Press, 1990).

2. Henry N. Fuller, *With the Procession* (New York: Harper & Brothers, 1895; pbk. ed., Chicago: University of Chicago Press, 1965), 72–73. Page numbers are from the paperback edition.

3. Fuller, *With the Procession,* 73.

4. Miller, *City of the Century,* 470.

5. Rudolf A. Hofmeister, *The Germans of Chicago* (Champaign, IL: Stipes Publishing, 1976), 10–11.

6. Next to his name in the *Lakeside Directory* of 1884 appeared the title "capt."

7. *Ahnapee Record,* November 20, 1884. The newspaper report states that the *Sea Star* was carrying a cargo of lumber and shingles for its owner, Charles L. Fellows, and that the ship was "completing her cargo with Christmas trees." This leaves open the possibility that August, not C. L. Fellows, was the prime mover behind this Christmas tree venture. It was not at all uncommon for a captain to invest his own money in some portion of the cargo his vessel carried.

8. Leon Raether, *The History of St. Paul's Evangelical Lutheran Church, Algoma, Wisconsin, 1862–1992* (n.d.), 9.

9. *Ahnapee Record,* April 5, 1883. Frederick came in third in the race, receiving just nine out of sixty votes cast.

10. *Ahnapee Record,* April 15, 1875.

11. The pension record for Frederick Schuenemann is in the National Archives, Washington, DC.

12. *Ahnapee Record,* February 25, 1875; June 17, 1875.

13. *Ahnapee Record,* April 11, 1876; May 25, 1876; *Door County Advocate,* September 1, 1881.

14. *The Lakeside Directory of the City of Chicago* lists August Schuenemann as a resident of the city in 1884–85 and 1888–98; Herman is listed every year from 1892 to 1912. Absence from the directory does not necessarily mean that one or the other was not living in Chicago, however, as the preparers of the directory did not actively seek out residents as a census taker would.

Theodore Charrney states: "During the winter months Herman and Barbara made the cabin of the Josephine Dresden their home, while at the same time the ship was thus under surveillance from the marauding bands of river pirates. . . . When the sailing season began anew in the spring, Barbara would go ashore to live, usually with her employer, for she worked as a house-maid. Then Captain Herman would prepare the Josephine Dresden for her sailing season. Most of his lumber trips were in the Green Bay area but he also traveled to Ludington or Muskegon, on Michigan's west shore, occasionally." Charrney, "The Christmas Tree Ship," 2:42–43. Unfortunately, he does not provide the source for this information, and other sources call this into question. Herman and Barbara's marriage certificate gives their address in 1891 as 170 LaSalle Street. The *Lakeside Directory* lists Herman and his wife as living at 170 LaSalle Street in 1892, 1893, and 1894. Thus only the winter of 1890–91 is left open to the possibility of living on board ship, and Herman had not yet been married at that time.

15. The schooner *Dresden* was in the family from 1889 to 1893 (per the *Ahnapee Record* of May 16, 1889; *Beeson's Marine Directory* for 1890–93, and enrollment records for 1889–93).

16. John J. Flinn, *Chicago, the Marvelous City of the West. A History, an Encyclopedia and a Guide* (Chicago: Flinn & Sheppard, 1891), 505.

17. *Lakeside Annual Directory of the City of Chicago,* 1895.

18. Miller, *City of the Century,* 446–48, quotation at 446; Hartmut Keil and John B. Jentz, eds., *German Workers in Industrial Chicago 1850–1910: A Comparative Perspective* (DeKalb: Northern Illinois University Press, 1983), 139–42.

19. Charrney, "The Christmas Tree Ship," 2:111–12, 127–28.

20. Amanda Seligman, "Near North Side," *Encyclopedia of Chicago,* http://www.encyclopedia.chicagohistory.org/pages/876.html (accessed January 11, 2007).

21. *Sturgeon Bay Advocate,* November 30, 1889. The descriptor *flat-bottom* suggests that the *S. Thal* may have been a scow, but the term *scow* has not been found associated with it. Jay Martin has pointed out that "scows" did not always have a squared off bow, and for that reason did not always appear above the waterline as scows, and he states that the flat bottom below the waterline is a more reliable trait of the breed (Martin, "Not for Shallow Water Only").

22. The Sturgeon Bay newspaper reported that Captain Schuenemann had to invest in new rigging and painting before he could put the vessel to use. *Sturgeon Bay Advocate,* October 1, 1898.

23. Initially, the *Thal* was left out of reports of this storm because its loss was overshadowed by another wreck right at Chicago's doorstep. Cf. *Chicago Daily News,* November 10, 1898. News of the wreck of the *Thal* came a day later. Cf. *Chicago Daily News,* November 11, 1898; *Chicago Daily Tribune,* November 11, 1898.

CHAPTER THIRTEEN

Epigraph from "The Christmas Tree Ship," music and lyrics by Lee Murdock, BMI, 1989.

1. Marling, *Merry Christmas*, 43–120.

2. Hofmeister, *The Germans of Chicago*, 11.

3. A chronology of the vessels owned or used by August and Herman Schuenemann appears at the back of this book.

4. Charrney, "The Christmas Tree Ship," 2:41.

5. Charrney, "The Christmas Tree Ship," 2:39–40.

6. *Chicago Daily News,* December 6, 1898.

7. *Chicago Daily News,* December 8, 1897.

8. Marling, *Merry Christmas*, 197–242.

9. For example, cf. *Chicago Inter Ocean,* November 30, 1910.

10. *Chicago Inter Ocean,* November 30, 1910.

11. *Chicago Inter Ocean,* November 30, 1910.

12. *Chicago Daily News,* December 8, 1897.

13. *Chicago Daily News,* November 28, 1899.

14. Quoted in Charrney, "The Christmas Tree Ship," 2:159.

15. *Chicago Inter Ocean,* December 7, 1909.

16. *Chicago Inter Ocean,* December 7, 1909.

17. Newspaper reports on the wreck of the *Mary Collins* are conflicting and full of inaccuracies. Apparently, there was hope early on that the vessel was not badly damaged and could be salvaged, but it was not to be. Theodore Charrney did the grunt work of tracing the career of the *Collins,* including the ultimate surrender of its enrollment by Herman Schuenemann twenty months after the grounding when attempts to get the schooner back afloat were finally abandoned. Cf. Charrney, "The Christmas Tree Ship," 1:57–67, 109. Also see note 17 to chapter 1.

18. Charrney, "The Christmas Tree Ship," 1:94; *Chicago Evening Post,* November 26, 1900.

19. Charrney, "The Christmas Tree Ship," 1:119–24.

20. *Sturgeon Bay Advocate,* May 28, 1904; July 16, 1904; *Ludington Chronicle,* November 28, 1906; *Sturgeon Bay Advocate,* October 15, 1908.

21. *Ludington Chronicle,* November 28, 1906.

22. *Chicago Inter Ocean,* December 7, 1909.

23. *Sturgeon Bay Advocate,* November 7, 1903; May 28, 1904. Cf. also Charrney, "The Christmas Tree Ship," 1:430. Charrney characterizes the *Simmons* as a "tramp ship" after the Hackley & Hume Company sold it to an individual, John Leonard, in 1898. The term *tramp ship* means that the vessel no longer had a consistent and long-term mission. Instead, it went from odd job to odd job as opportunity allowed.

24. *Sturgeon Bay Advocate,* October 5, 1911.

CHAPTER FOURTEEN

1. *Chicago Daily News,* December 4, 1912; *Chicago American,* December 4, 1912.

2. *Muskegon News Chronicle,* December 6, 1912; December 7, 1912.

3. *Chicago Daily News,* December 6, 1912; December 7, 1912; *Chicago American,* December 6, 1912; December 7, 1912; *Muskegon News Chronicle,* December 6, 1912.

4. Logbook of the U.S. Revenue Cutter Tuscarora, 1909–1912, entries for December 4–6, 1912.

5. *Milwaukee Daily News,* December 2, 1912.

6. *Chicago Daily News,* December 5, 1912.

7. Logbook of the U.S. Revenue Cutter Tuscarora, 1909–1912, entries for December 4–6, 1912.

8. *Chicago American,* December 5, 1912.

9. *Chicago Daily News,* December 6, 1912.

10. *Chicago Inter Ocean,* December 12, 1912.

11. *Sturgeon Bay Advocate,* December 12, 1912.

12. Logbook of the Two Rivers, Wisconsin, Life Saving Station, entries for December 6, 1912.

13. *Chicago Daily News,* December 6, 1912; *Chicago American,* December 6, 1912.

14. *Chicago Daily News,* December 7, 1912; *Chicago Inter Ocean,* December 9, 1912.

15. *Chicago American,* December 10, 1912.

16. *Sturgeon Bay Advocate,* January 23, 1913.

17. *Chicago Daily News,* December 13, 1912.

18. *Sturgeon Bay Advocate,* December 12, 1912.

19. *Sturgeon Bay Advocate,* December 26, 1912.

20. *Manitowoc Daily Herald,* December 14, 1912; *Sturgeon Bay Advocate,* December 19, 1912; *Sheboygan Press,* December 13, 1912; December 20, 1912.

21. *Chicago American,* December 13, 1912; *Chicago Daily News,* December 13, 1912.

22. *Chicago American,* December 13, 1912.

23. *Milwaukee Sentinel,* December 6, 1912.

24. *Milwaukee Daily News,* December 12, 1912; *Chicago Inter Ocean,* December 14, 1912; December 15, 1912; *Sault Ste. Marie Evening News,* December 14, 1912.

25. U.S. Department of Treasury, *Annual Report of the Revenue Cutter Service* (Washington, DC: Government Printing Office, 1914), 126–28.

26. *Milwaukee Daily News,* December 14, 1912; Logbook of the U.S. Revenue Cutter Mackinac, 1907–1912, entries for December 14–16, 1912, Records of the U.S. Coast Guard and Life Saving Service, Revenue Cutter Service,

Record Group 26, National Archives and Records Administration, Main Building, Washington, DC, Box 1371.

27. *Sault Ste. Marie Evening News,* December 17, 1912.

28. *Sturgeon Bay Advocate,* October 12, 1911; *Grand Haven Daily Tribune,* December 3, 1912; *Sturgeon Bay Advocate,* November 7, 1903.

29. "The Tale of the 'Christmas Tree' Ship," *Columns,* November–December 2006, 8–9. (*Columns* is a bimonthly newsletter published by the Wisconsin Historical Society.)

CHAPTER FIFTEEN

Epigraph from Ivan H. Walton, *Songquest: The Journals of a Great Lakes Folklorist,* ed. Joe Grimm (Detroit: Wayne State University Press, 2005), 131.

1. Charrney, "The Christmas Tree Ship," 2:225–26.

2. *Chicago Daily News,* December 5, 1912; *Chicago Daily Tribune,* December 5, 1912. The Bausewein family took an active part in trying to determine the fate of the *Rouse Simmons.* Mrs. Bausewein was reported to have been behind the effort to verify the existence of the note in the bottle. Cf. *Sheboygan Press,* December 20, 1912.

3. *Chicago Daily Tribune,* December 13, 1934.

4. *Chicago American,* December 5, 1912.

5. *Chicago Inter Ocean,* December 5, 1912.

6. *Sturgeon Bay Advocate,* October 12, 1911; November 30, 1911.

7. *Chicago American,* December 5, 1912.

8. Charrney, "The Christmas Tree Ship," 2:192–93, 195–97.

9. *Chicago Daily Tribune,* December 5, 1912; *Chicago Daily News,* December 5, 1912; *Sheboygan Press,* December 20, 1912.

10. Jay Bonansinga, *The Sinking of the Eastland: America's Forgotten Tragedy* (New York: Kensington, 2004), 210–19.

11. Initial newspaper reports state that seventeen died. As has been seen, no source can identify that many victims. Nonetheless, the number seventeen has not been totally disregarded, because it is very possible that unnamed passengers or crew were on board.

12. Victor Olander Papers, Folders October–November 1913 and December 1913, Chicago Historical Society Archives, Box 83.

13. Ginger, *Altgeld's America,* 1.

14. *Chicago Daily News,* December 13, 1912.

15. *Door County Advocate,* December 14, 1882; *Kenosha Evening News,* November 29, 1901.

CHAPTER SIXTEEN

1. *Chicago Daily News,* December 7, 1912; *Chicago Daily Journal,* December 6, 1912.

2. Charrney, "The Christmas Tree Ship," 2:319, 325.

3. Charnney, "The Christmas Tree Ship," 2:295.

4. *Chicago Daily Journal,* December 9, 1912; December 13, 1912; *Chicago American,* December 10, 1912; December 12, 1912; *Inter Ocean,* December 10, 1912; December 11, 1912; December 12, 1912; December 13, 1912; *Chicago Daily Tribune,* December 11, 1912; December 2, 1915; December 13, 1934.

5. *Inter Ocean,* December 10, 1912.

6. *Chicago Daily Tribune,* December 13, 1934.

7. Charles Vickery prints can be seen at the Clipper Ship Gallery in LaGrange, Illinois, and at www.CharlesVickery.com. Productions of *The Christmas Schooner* are licensed by Music Theater International, 421 West 54th St., New York, NY 10019 (www.MTIshows.com). Lee Murdock is represented by Artists of Note, P.O. Box 11, Kaneville, IL 60144–0011, and is on the Web at www.leemurdock.com.

Sources

NEWSPAPERS

Algoma, Wisconsin
  Ahnapee Record
  Algoma Record-Herald
Chicago, Illinois
  Chicago American
  Daily Journal
  Daily News
  Evening Post
  Die Illinois Staats-Zeitung
  Record-Herald
  Tribune
  Inter Ocean
DePere, Wisconsin
  News
Detroit, Michigan
  Free Press
Grand Haven, Michigan
  Daily Tribune
Green Bay, Wisconsin
  Advocate
Kenosha, Wisconsin
  Evening News
Kewaunee, Wisconsin
  Enterprise
Ludington, Michigan
  Chronicle
Manistique, Michigan
  Pioneer Tribune
Menominee, Michigan
  Herald-Leader
Milwaukee, Wisconsin
  Daily News
  Journal
  Sentinel
Muskegon, Michigan
  Times

Racine, Wisconsin
Daily Times
Sheboygan, Wisconsin
Press
Sturgeon Bay, Wisconsin
Advocate

PRIMARY SOURCES

Fagg, William. "The Diary of William Fagg." Autograph manuscript. Madison, WI: State Historical Society of Wisconsin, microfilm edition.

Decker, Edward. Edward Decker Papers. Green Bay, WI: State Historical Society of Wisconsin, Area Research Center, University of Wisconsin, Green Bay, WI.

"Last Will and Testament of Herman Schuenemann." Cook County, IL: Probate Court Records.

Logbook of the Kewaunee, Wisconsin, Life Saving Station. Records of the U.S. Coast Guard and Life Saving Service, Record Group 26. Chicago: National Archives and Records Administration, Great Lakes Regional Branch, Box 267.

Logbook of the U.S. Revenue Cutter Mackinac, 1907–1912. Records of the U.S. Coast Guard and Life Saving Service, Revenue Cutter Service, Record Group 26. Washington, DC: National Archives and Records Administration, Main Building, Box 1371.

Logbook of the U.S. Revenue Cutter Tuscarora. Records of the U.S. Coast Guard and Life Saving Service, Revenue Cutter Service, Record Group 26. Washington, DC: National Archives and Records Administration, Main Building, Box 2506.

Logbook of the Sturgeon Bay, Wisconsin, Life Saving Station. Records of the U.S. Coast Guard and Life Saving Service, Record Group 26. Chicago: National Archives and Records Administration, Great Lakes Regional Branch, Box 704.

Logbook of the Two Rivers, Wisconsin, Life Saving Station. Records of the U.S. Coast Guard and Life Saving Service, Record Group 26. Chicago: National Archives and Records Administration, Great Lakes Regional Branch, Box 737.

Charles Mears Papers. Chicago History Museum Library and Archives.

Charles Mears Papers. Pentwater (MI) Historical Society.

Victor Olander Papers. Chicago History Museum Library and Archives.

Charles Robert Starkweather Papers. Chicago History Museum Library and Archives.

UNPUBLISHED SECONDARY SOURCES

Berg, Oscar. "Histories of Foscoro (Stoney Creek) and Silver Creek." Typescript. Kewaunee Public Library, Kewaunee, WI, n.d.

Charrney, Theodore S. "The Christmas Tree Ship." 2 vols. Typescript. Newberry Library, Chicago, IL, 1971.

Empey, Laura Ann. "A Brief History of Algoma, Wisconsin." Bachelor's thesis, Mount Mary College, Milwaukee, WI, 1960.

Glasgow, James. "Muskegon, Michigan: The Evolution of a Lake Port." Ph.D. diss., University of Chicago, Chicago, IL, 1939.

Linak, Jim. "Early History of Kewaunee County." Typescript. Kewaunee Public Library, Kewaunee, WI, 1989.

Martin, Jay. "Sailing the Fresh Water Seas: A Social History of Life aboard the Sailing Vessels of the United States and Canada on the Great Lakes, 1815 to 1930." Ph.D. diss., Bowling Green State University, Bowling Green, OH, 1995.

Plumb, Ralph G. "Harbor Administration: Harbors of Wisconsin." Bachelor of letters thesis, University of Wisconsin, Madison, WI, 1901.

Wing, George W. "Early History of Kewaunee County." Typescript. Edited by Harold Heidmann. Algoma Public Library, Algoma, WI, 1936.

ARTICLES

Barker, Stan. "Paradise Lost." *Chicago History* 22, no. 1 (March 1993): 26–49.

Barkhausen, Henry N. "William Wallace Bates: Part I." *Anchor News* 19, no. 3 (May–June 1988): 44–48.

Barkhausen, Henry N. "William Wallace Bates: Part II." *Anchor News* 19, no. 4 (July–August 1988): 64–67.

Callaway, William. "A Sailor's Narrative." In *Early Milwaukee,* edited by Roger Hunt, 70–87. Madison, WI, 1977.

Charrney, Theodore S. *Commemorating the Fiftieth Anniversary of the Loss of the Schooner Rouse Simmons.* Chicago: privately printed, 1962.

Charrney, Theodore S. "The Great Lakes: Chicago Harbor a Century Ago." *Sea History* 47 (Summer 1988): 12–15.

Charrney, Theodore S. "Potato Ships Brought Cargo to Chicago River." *Waterways Journal* (April 1988): 47–49.

Charrney, Theodore S. "The Rouse Simmons and the Port of Chicago." *Inland Seas* (Winter 1987): 242–46.

Deutsch, Herman. "Yankee-Teuton Rivalry in Wisconsin Politics of the Seventies." *Wisconsin Magazine of History* (March 1931): 262–82.

Deutsch, Herman. "Yankee-Teuton Rivalry in Wisconsin Politics of the Seventies: Section II." *Wisconsin Magazine of History* (June 1931): 403–18.

Dornfeld, A. A. "Chicago's Age of Sail." *Chicago History* 11, no. 3 (Spring–Summer 1973): 156–65.

Dow, Arthur Jr. "Story of the Schooner LA RABIDA." *Anchor News* (November–December 1984): 129–31.

Duchaine, William J. "Swashbuckling 'Pirate' Is Lake Legend." *Milwaukee Journal,* February 17, 1963.

Duchaine, William J. "Yo, Ho, Ho, How the Swabs Made Way for Roaring Dan." *Chicago Tribune,* April 22, 1962.

Ellis, William D. "Captain Daniel Seavey." *Inland Seas* (Winter 1988): 253–57.

Joyce, Lorne. "Stonehooking and Fishing Trade." In *At the Mouth of the Credit,* edited by Betty Clarkson, 37–43. Erin, Ontario: Boston Mills Press, 1977.

Keil, Hartmut, ed. "A German Farmer Views Wisconsin, 1851–1863." *Wisconsin Magazine of History* 62, no. 2 (Winter 1978–79): 128–43.

Kelley, Harry. "Captain Timothy J. Kelley." *Anchor News* 12, no. 4 (July–August 1981): 84.

Lafferty, William. "Technological Innovation in Great Lakes Shipping: Leathem D. Smith and the Rise of the Self-Unloader." In *"A Fully Accredited Ocean": Essays on the Great Lakes,* edited by Victoria Brehm, 155–98. Ann Arbor: University of Michigan Press, 1998.

Martin, Jay C. "Not for Shallow Water Only: Scow Construction along the Maumee River, 1825–1859." *Marine History Lines* 10, no. 1 (Winter 1990–91): 2–6.

Neuschel, Fred. "Bringing Christmas to the City." *Chicago History* 21, no. 3 (December 1992): 44–55.

Neuschel, Fred. "The Clique vs. the Croakers: Class and Conflict in Small-Town Wisconsin." *Wisconsin Magazine of History* 81, no. 2 (Winter 1997–98): 83–108.

Neuschel, Fred. "The Everlasting Ella." *Anchor News* 22, nos. 1 and 2 (January–February and March–April 1991): 4–5, 32–36.

Neuschel, Fred. "Life on the Ahnapee River." *Anchor News* 23, no. 5 (October–November–December 1992): 92–100.

Neuschel, Fred. "November 23, 1912: The Rest of the Story." *Anchor News* 21, nos. 1 and 3 (January–February and May–June 1990): 4–11, 44–52.

Palmer, Richard F., ed. "Great Lakes Driftwood: Schooner-Scows." *Inland Seas* 42, no. 2 (Summer 1986): 78–83.

Parish. "A Paper Read by Judge Parish at Norwalk [Ohio], June 8th." *Norwalk [OH] Reflector,* June 28, 1881.

Pernin, Rev. Peter. "The Great Peshtigo Fire." *Wisconsin Magazine of History* 54 (Summer 1971): 246–72.

Seligman, Amanda. "Near North Side." *Encyclopedia of Chicago.* http://www

.encyclopedia.chicagohistory.org/pages/876.html (accessed January 11, 2007).

Smith, Capt. Oscar B. "The Schooner LA PETITE." *Inland Seas* 26, nos. 2, 3, and 4 (Summer, Fall, and Winter 1970): 102–17, 198–228, 275–91.

State of Wisconsin, "Chapter 430, An Act to Authorize the Town of Ahnepee in the County of Kewaunee to Issue the Bonds in Said Town to Aid in the Construction of a Harbor at the Mouth of the Ahnepee River." *Private and Local Laws Passed by the Legislature of Wisconsin in the Year 1870,* 1050–54. Madison, 1870.

U.S. Congress. *Report upon Forestry,* by Franklin B. Hough. 46th Cong., 2nd sess., House Executive Document 37. Washington, DC: Government Printing Office, 1880.

U.S. Corps of Engineers. *Survey of Ahnapee Harbor, Wisconsin.* House Executive Document 172. Washington, DC: Government Printing Office, 1874.

Warner, Edward S., and Colleen Oihus Warner. "Lives and Times in the Great Lakes Commercial Trade under Sail." *Hayes Historical Review* 11, no. 1 (Fall 1991): 5–16.

Warner, Edward S. "Towing with Steam Tugs: An Aspect of the Great Lakes Commercial Trade under Sail." In *"A Fully Accredited Ocean": Essays on the Great Lakes,* edited by Victoria Brehm, 45–57. Ann Arbor: University of Michigan Press, 1998.

Whyte, William F. "The Bennett Law Campaign." *Wisconsin Magazine of History* 10, no. 4 (June 1927): 363–90.

PUBLISHED BOOK LENGTH SOURCES

Adams, Judith A. *The American Amusement Park Industry: A History of Technology and Thrills.* Boston: Twayne Publishers, 1991.

Aldrich, Lewis Cass, ed. *History of Erie County, Ohio.* Syracuse, NY: D. Mason, 1889.

Algoma Hardwoods. Centennial Album. Edited by Ray Birdsall. Algoma, WI, 1992.

Bachin, Robin F. *Building the South Side: Urban Space and Civic Culture in Chicago, 1890–1919.* Chicago: University of Chicago Press, 2004.

Behrend, Carl. *The Legend of the Christmas Ship.* Munising, MI: published by the author, 2005.

Benes, Jim. *Chicago Christmas: One Hundred Years of Christmas Memories.* Chicago: Cornerstone Press, 2000.

Bonansinga, Jay. *The Sinking of the Eastland: America's Forgotten Tragedy.* New York: Kensington Publishing, 2004.

Brehm, Victoria, editor. *"A Fully Accredited Ocean": Essays on the Great Lakes.* Ann Arbor: University of Michigan Press, 1998.

Brenner, Robert. *Christmas Past*. Atglen, PA: Schiffer Publishing, 1996.

Catton, Bruce. *Waiting for the Morning Train: An American Boyhood*. Garden City, NY: Doubleday, 1972. Reprint, Detroit: Wayne State University Press, 1987.

Christianson, Carl Raymond. *Ship Building and Boat Building in Sturgeon Bay, Wisconsin: From the Beginning to 1985*. Sturgeon Bay, WI: published by the author, 1989.

Commemorative Biographical Record of the Counties of Brown, Kewaunee and Door. Chicago: J. H. Beers, 1895.

Commemorative and Biographical Record of the Counties of Sandusky and Ottawa, Ohio. Chicago: J. H. Beers, 1896.

Creviere, Paul J. Jr. *Wild Gales and Tattered Sails*. Published by the author, 1997.

Cronon, William. *Nature's Metropolis: Chicago and the Great West*. New York: W. W. Norton, 1991.

Donahue, James L. *Steaming through Smoke and Fire, 1871: True Stories of Shipwreck and Disaster on the Great Lakes*. Holt, MI: Thunder Bay Press, 1990.

Flinn, John J. *Chicago, the Marvelous City of the West. A History, an Encyclopedia and a Guide*. Chicago: Flinn & Sheppard, 1891.

Fuller, Henry B. *With the Procession*. New York: Harper & Brothers, 1895. Pbk. ed., Chicago: University of Chicago Press, 1965.

Gess, Denise, and William Lutz. *Firestorm at Peshtigo: A Town, Its People, and the Deadliest Fire in American History*. New York: Henry Holt, 2003.

Ginger, Ray. *Altgeld's America: Chicago from 1892–1905*. New York: Marcus Wiener Publishing, 1958.

Hacker, Louis M. *The World of Andrew Carnegie, 1865–1901*. Philadelphia: J. B. Lippincott, 1968.

Hansen, Harry. *The Chicago*. New York: Farrar & Rinehart, 1942.

Hansen, Helen M. *At Home in Early Sandusky*, Sandusky, OH: Sandusky Register, 1975.

Hill, Libby. *The Chicago River: A Natural and Unnatural History*. Chicago: Lake Claremont Press, 2000.

Hilton, George W. *Eastland: Legacy of the Titanic*. Stanford: Stanford University Press, 1995.

Hirthe, Walter M., and Mary K. Hirthe. *Schooner Days in Door County*. Minneapolis: Voyageur Press, 1986.

History of Marion County, Ohio. Chicago: Leggett, Conway, 1883.

History of Seneca County, Ohio. Chicago: Warner, Beers, 1886.

Hofmeister, Rudolf A. *The Germans of Chicago*. Champaign, IL: Stipes Publishing, 1976.

Howell, Liz. *Land of the Great Gray Wolf*. Sister Bay, WI: Dragonsbreath Press, 1988.

Jacoby, J. Wilbur, ed. *History of Marion County, Ohio*. Marion County Historical Society, 1976.

Johnson, Virginia Feld. *An-An-api-sebe: "Where Is the River?"* Sturgeon Bay, WI: Silverdale Press, 2000.

Karamanski, Theodore J., and Deane Tank Sr. *Maritime Chicago.* Published by the authors, 2000.

Karamanski, Theodore J. *Schooner Passage: Sailing Ships and the Lake Michigan Frontier.* Detroit: Wayne State University Press, 2000.

Keating, Ann Durkin. *Chicagoland: City and Suburbs in the Railroad Age.* Chicago: University of Chicago Press, 2005.

Keil, Hartmut, and John B. Jentz, eds. *German Workers in Industrial Chicago 1850–1910: A Comparative Perspective.* DeKalb: Northern Illinois University Press, 1983.

Keil, Hartmut, and John B. Jentz, eds. *German Workers in Chicago: A Documentary History of Working-Class Culture from 1850 to World War I.* Urbana: University of Illinois Press, 1988.

Kristiansen, Soren. *The Diary of Soren Kristiansen: Lake Michigan Schooner Captain, 1891–1893.* Iron Mountain, MI: Mid-Peninsula Library Cooperative, 1981.

Mailer, Stan. *Green Bay & Western: First 111 Years.* Edmunds, WA: Hundman Publishing, 1989.

Mansfield, J. B., ed. *History of the Great Lakes.* 2 vols. Chicago: J. H. Beers, 1899.

Marling, Karal Ann. *Merry Christmas: Celebrating America's Greatest Holiday.* Cambridge, MA: Harvard University Press, 2000.

Meindl, Bill. *Bank of Sturgeon Bay: The First Century, 1889–1989.* Sturgeon Bay, WI: Bank of Sturgeon Bay, 1989.

Mertens, John Henry. *The Second Battle: A Story of Our Belgian Ancestors in the American Civil War, 1861–1865.* Published by the author, 1987.

Miller, Donald L. *City of the Century: The Epic of Chicago and the Making of America.* New York: Simon & Schuster, 1996.

Miller, Ross. *American Apocalypse: The Great Fire and the Myth of Chicago.* Chicago: University of Chicago Press, 1990.

Pennington, Rochelle. *The Historic Christmas Tree Ship: A True Story of Faith, Hope and Love.* Published by the author, 2004.

Raether, Leon M. *The History of St. Paul's Evangelical Lutheran Church, Algoma, Wisconsin, 1862–1992.* n.d.

Reimann, Lewis C. *Between the Iron and the Pine: A Biography of a Pioneer Family and a Pioneer Town.* Published by the author, 1951.

Sandusky, Mansfield & Newark Railroad. *Guide, Gazetteer and Directory of the Sandusky, Mansfield & Newark Railroad.* Sandusky, OH: A. Bailey, 1869.

Shuck, Oscar T. *Bench and Bar in California: History, Anecdotes, Reminiscences.* San Francisco: Occidental Printing House, 1889.

Specht, Ray, and Ellen Specht. *History of the Green Bay and Western.* Boston: Railway and Locomotive Historical Society, 1966.

Stephenson, Isaac. *Recollections of a Long Life, 1829–1915*. Chicago: published by the author, 1915.

Stonehouse, Frederick. *Great Lakes Crime: Murder, Mayhem, Booze & Broads*. Gwinn, MI: Avery Color Sudios, 2004.

Stonehouse, Frederick. *Went Missing, II*. Marquette, MI: Frederick Stonehouse and Avery Color Studios, 1984. Reprint, Au Train, MI: Avery Color Studios, 1989.

Strutton, John A. *The Old Homes of Norwalk (from written memoirs of Mrs. Charlotte Wooster Boalt)*. Norwalk, OH: private printing, 1938.

Townsend, Robert B. *Tales from the Great Lakes: Based on C. H. J. Snider's "Schooner Days."* Toronto: Dundurn Press, 1995.

Trask, Kerry A. *Fire Within: A Civil War Narrative from Wisconsin*. Kent, OH: Kent State University Press, 1995.

U.S. Congress, Senate Committee on Education and Labor. *Report of the Committee of the Senate upon the Relations between Labor and Capital, and Testimony taken by the Committee*, vol. 1. Washington, DC: Government Printing Office, 1885.

U.S. Department of Treasury. *Annual Report of the Revenue Cutter Service*. Washington, DC: Government Printing Office, 1914.

Walton, Ivan H. *Songquest: The Journals of a Great Lakes Folklorist*. Edited by Joe Grimm. Detroit: Wayne State University Press, 2005.

Walton, Ivan H. *Windjammers: Songs of the Great Lakes Sailors*. Detroit: Wayne State University Press, 2002.

Wells, Robert W. *Fire at Peshtigo*. Madison, WI: Northword, 1983.

Winters, Donna. *Great Lakes Christmas Classics*. Caledonia, MI: Bigwater Publishing, 1998.

Young, David M. *Chicago Maritime: An Illustrated History*. DeKalb: Northern Illinois University Press, 2001.

VIDEO/DVD/CD

Murdock, Lee. *Fertile Ground*. DEP009. Barrington, IL: Depot Records, 1989.

Songs from "The Christmas Schooner"—a Musical by John Reeger & Julie Shannon. Glenview, IL: Louisa May Alleycat Music (e-mail: LMAMusic@aol.com), 2000. Production of the musical is licensed by Music Theatre International, 421 West 54th St., New York, NY 10019 (www.MTIshows.com).

Southport Videos. *The Christmas Tree Ship*. Kenosha, WI: Southport Videos, 1992.

Acknowledgments

$\mathscr{S}$pecial thanks to the staff of the following libraries and institutions where research was done, as well as to the taxpayers, members, and donors who keep the doors open.

Algoma Public Library, Algoma, Wisconsin

Area Research Center of the State Historical Society of Wisconsin at the University of Wisconsin, Green Bay, Wisconsin

Chicago Museum of History Library and Archive, Chicago, Illinois

Harold Washington Public Library, Chicago, Illinois

Historical Collections of the Great Lakes, Bowling Green State University, Bowling Green, Ohio

Kewaunee County Historical Society, Kewaunee, Wisconsin

Michigan Historical Center, Lansing, Michigan

Milwaukee Public Library, Milwaukee, Wisconsin

National Archives and Records Administration, Great Lakes Regional Branch, Chicago, Illinois

National Archives and Records Administration, Main Branch, Washington, DC

Newberry Library, Chicago, Illinois

Rogers Street Fishing Village, Two Rivers, Wisconsin

State Historical Society of Wisconsin, Madison, Wisconsin

Wisconsin Marine Historical Society, Milwaukee, Wisconsin

Wisconsin Maritime Museum, Manitowoc, Wisconsin

In Algoma, Wisconsin, thanks to Jeanette Winkler, who took an interest in the research from the start and pointed me in the right direction to meet some fine friends and great helpers. First and foremost among them was Harold Heidmann, now deceased, who, along with his most gracious wife, Marie, shared his knowledge of local history, his home, his comradery, and lessons in the game of Sheep's Head. Harold's family goes a long way back in Kewaunee County and Algoma and have contributed to the region's welfare right up to the present in many and diverse ways. Also in and around Algoma: Liz Howell, Virginia Johnson, Judy Srnka, Ann Schmidt, George Miller, Leon Raether, Jerry Abzug, Jim Linak, Bill Meindl, the rector of St. Agnes Episcopal Church, and the indefatigable Jag Haegle.

Thank you also to individuals who read and critiqued early versions of the manuscript: Edward Warner, C. Patrick Labadie, Henry Barkhausen, and James Barry. They are truly experts in maritime history, and their advice was much appreciated.

Thank you to divers Chris Kohl and Keith Meverden, who shared firsthand knowledge of the remains of the schooner *Rouse Simmons.*

Thank you to individuals who contributed illustrative material: Brendon Baillod for use of a unique and extraordinary image from his private collection; Bert and Jay Jacobs of the Clipper Ship Gallery in LaGrange, Illinois, who are the authorized dealers for the artwork of Charles Vickery; Julie Shannon, who collaborated with John Reeger in the creation of the inspiring musical *The Christmas Schooner;* Janet Pearson, a descendant of Captain Henry Harkins, Ahnapee sailor and Civil War hero.

A special thank you to the editorial staff at the University of Michigan Press in Ann Arbor—Mary Erwin, Christina L. Milton, and Anna M. Szymanski. A book is not a book until the editor says it's a book. You spoke, and it was so. We won't say how much blood and sweat went into cleaning it up.

Finally, thank you to the readers for sharing the story.

Fred Neuschel
Crystal Lake, IL

Index

Vessel names and page numbers of illustrations are italicized. Vessels are alphabetized by the first letter of the first name or by first initial.